Janet Macdonald

has written over thirty books, including a number on cookery. Her parallel interests in food and naval history led her to undertake a Masters degree, and the resulting research into the victualling of the Nelsonic navy formed the starting point for this book. She was recently a featured historian on BBC Radio 4's Food at Sea programme.

FEEDING NELSON'S NAVY

The True Story of Food at Sea in the Georgian Era

JANET MACDONALD

CHATHAM PUBLISHING
LONDON

This paperback edition first published in Great Britain in 2006 by
Chatham Publishing
Lionel Leventhal Ltd,
Park House, 1 Russell Gardens,
London NW11 9NN

British Library Cataloguing-in Publication Data

Macdonald, Janet
Feeding Nelson's navy : the true story of food at sea in the Georgian era
1. Great Britain. Royal Navy – Provisioning – History – 18th century
2. Great Britain. Royal Navy – Provisioning – History – 19th century
3. Great Britain. Royal Navy – History – 18th century
4. Great Britain. Royal Navy – History – 19th century
5. Great Britain. Victualling Office – History
6. Cookery, Marine – History 7. Great Britain – History, Naval – 18th century
8. Great Britain – History, Naval – 19th century
I.Title
359.8'1'0941'09033

ISBN-10 1-86176-288-7
ISBN-13 978-1-86176-288-7

Designed and typeset by Roger Daniels

Printed and bound in Great Britain by
Creative Print and Design Group, Ebbw Vale, Wales

CONTENTS

ACKNOWLEDGEMENTS

This book represents the first stage of what I hope will be a very long journey – a journey which started with a food writer reading of some marvellous meals in a fictional series about a Napoleonic War naval captain and his friend, moved on to a general interest in the true history of what has come to be called 'Nelson's Navy' and from there to the world of academia, archives, and serious historical research. Much of the fine detail for the book came from the research for my MA dissertation 'Victualling the British Mediterranean Fleet, July 1803 – June 1804' (hence the predominance of references to that fleet, but other logs and documents strongly suggest that these reflect the general situation).

Along my journey I have received help and encouragement from many people, to all of whom I will be eternally grateful:

At the Greenwich Maritime Institute, my tutor Professor Roger Knight, the director Professor Sarah Palmer, Doctor Roger Morriss, who taught me how to use the various archives, and my fellow students who shared information with me, but especially Charles Consolvo and David Elvin.

At the archives, Jennie Wraight and Iain MacKenzie of the Admiralty Library; Jane Wickenden at the Institute of Naval Medicine; Andrew Helm at the Nelson Museum, Monmouth; Matthew Sheldon, Head of Research Collections and Richard Noyce, Curator of Artifacts at the Royal Naval Museum Portsmouth; Lt-Cdr. Nowoskielski, C.O. of HMS *Victory*; the staff at the British Library, the Caird Library at the National Maritime Museum at Greenwich, the Public Record Office, and the library of the Wellcome Trust.

Elsewhere, Professor Richard Harding of the University of Westminster for suggestions on logistics literature, John Harland for advice on stowage, Roel Mulder for information on Dutch naval food, Brian Vale for information on South America, Spain and Portugal, Andrew McCoig who checked my calorie and vitamin calculations and Clive Gardner who helped with Richard Ford.

Dave Balderstone, Compuserve History forum; Bryn Hughes, General Manager of HMS *Trincomalee*; Tyrone Martin of USS *Constitution*; Mark Nesbitt, Royal Botanic Gardens, Kew; Michael & Jane Phillips; Mr E J Revell; Bill Sargeant; Lord de Saumarez; Roderick Stewart of the *Unicorn* Preservation Society; Tim Voelcker; and all my e-friends at the Searoom forum who have shared information and ideas with me on this and many other topics.

And last but by no means least, my husband Ken Maxwell-Jones: assistant researcher, editor, proofreader, coffee maker and recipe sampler.

FOREWORD

THE FIRST THREE THINGS you encounter when you start to read about the Georgian navy are all horror stories: the work of the press gangs, flogging, and the appalling food. I have my doubts as to whether the first two are as bad as they are painted, and I find it impossible to believe in the third. A navy fed on rotten meat and weevilly biscuits? My experience of the British working man is that the men would not have tolerated this, nor, on such a diet, would they have been capable of the very hard physical work involved in sailing and fighting a ship, let alone doing it with the enthusiasm and success which they did.

So my basic disbelief set me off on the trail of research into exactly what Nelson's navy did eat, how they ate it, where it came from and how it got to them. In the process I discovered the fascinating edifices of the Victualling Board and its sister organisations the Navy Board, the Sick and Hurt Board and the Transport Board, and their numerous employees in London and at naval establishments all over the world. The other side of the story, which is equally fascinating, is how the food was cooked and eaten, and the fact that sharing meals is not only a major social occasion but one which is important for maintaining the cohesion of any group of people.

Mealtimes also served a simpler purpose; that of refuelling the fleshy machines that kept the navy sailing. There is a simple progression: continuous hard work (and both sailing the ship and handling the guns are very hard work indeed) requires fit and healthy men; men will only stay fit and healthy if they are well fed. It is the naval version of Napoleon's army marching on its stomach.

It is comparatively easy to feed a navy in peacetime, when numbers are low; it is also comparatively easy to feed a navy when it is operating in home waters and can return to port to replenish its stocks of food and drink. But when you are engaged in a major war, with over 1000 ships and 140,000 men (as was the case at the high point of the Napoleonic Wars in 1810) and when over half that force is operating in foreign waters, the logistics of keeping all those men fed would have been insurmountable without an efficient organisation to arrange things. Add to this the facts that for most of the period we are discussing, the only methods of preserving food were to dry it, salt it or pickle it, and the only practical bulk packaging materials were wooden casks and cloth bags, and you begin to see why the Admiralty elected to feed the navy on foodstuffs that owed more to durability than to what we would now think of as a balanced diet: salt meat, dried pease, oatmeal, hard tack and a little butter and cheese, with beer, wine or watered spirits to wash it down.

Once you know what they ate, questions come to you: was there no fresh meat, no vegetables or fruit? What about fish, or poultry? How was the food cooked and who cooked it? Where did it come from and how did it get from there onto the ships? Did the officers eat at the same time as the men? How many men ate at a time, and what about the men on urgent watch duties such as lookout or steering? Is it true about weevils and rats? Fortunately history has left us plenty of information about most, if not all, of these things, in the form of official correspondence between the Admiralty and the subsidiary departments involved in getting food to the men in both health and sickness. There are also some private letters and memoirs which brings the story beyond the official. Alas, most of these private papers were written by officers, and they tended to report their own experiences rather than those of the men; they also took a great deal for granted, so there are many areas where we have no evidence for the fine details. However, we can make some informed guesses while we wait for the hoped-for lost journals to emerge from an attic and fill the gaps; speculations on such details have been indicated as such.

INTRODUCTION

SO, HOW DO YOU FEED thousands of men when they are afloat in ships which may not touch land for months at a time, where cooking facilities are very basic, where there are no refrigeration systems and where food can be preserved only by salting, pickling or drying?

The answer, of course, is that you base the rations on foodstuffs which will tolerate those preservation methods and remain edible for many months: salted meat, salted or dried fish, dried pease or beans and items made from cereal grains. This is not just a nautical solution; until canning became generally accepted and affordable in the middle of the nineteenth century it was the principal solution to preserving food through the winter in northern lands, when plants stopped growing and when farming methods could not support large herds of livestock through the cold months. So at sea, they ate throughout the year what landsmen ate during the winter. By long tradition, the seaman's diet was based on salt meat, dried pease and hard-baked biscuit; on 31 December 1677, Samuel Pepys drew up a victualling contract which set the ration for each man at one pound of biscuit and one gallon of beer each day, with a weekly ration of eight pounds of beef, or four pounds of beef and two of bacon or pork with two pints of pease. The meat was served on Sunday, Monday, Tuesday and Thursday; on the other three days they had fish (either fresh cod, or wind-dried or salt cod or hake) with two ounces of butter and four ounces of Suffolk cheese (or two-thirds that amount of Cheddar).[1]

By 1733, when the British Admiralty published its first formal set of *Regulations and Instructions relating to His Majesty's Service at Sea*[2] (hereafter 'the *Regulations*'), the fish had disappeared to be replaced by oatmeal and sugar and the ration entitlement had evolved into the table below:

Table of '...daily Proportion of Provisions [to be] allowed to every Man serving in His Majesty's Ships'[3]

	Biscuit *(Pounds Avoirdupois)*	Beer *(Gallons Wine Measure)*	Beef *(Pounds Avoirdupois)*	Pork *(Pounds Avoirdupois)*	Pease *(Pint Winchester Measure)*	Oatmeal *(Pint Winchester Measure)*	Butter *(Ounces)*	Cheese *(Ounces)*
Sun	1	1		1	1 half			
Mon	1	1				1	2	4
Tues	1	1	2					
Wed	1	1			1 half	1	2	4
Thurs	1	1		1	1 half			
Fri	1	1			1 half	1	2	4
Sat	1	1	2					
Total	7	7	4	2	2	3	6	12

'Together with an allowance of vinegar, not exceeding half a pint to each man per week.'

This basic ration had not changed when Nelson joined the Royal Navy in 1770, did not change throughout his lifetime, and continued, more or less unchanged, until after 1847 when the Admiralty finally accepted the new technology of canning.[4] This is not to say that these listed items were the only things issued to the navy; for occasions when the basic items were not available, or when the men deemed the quality unacceptable and refused them, there were official substitutes (see Appendix 2). It should be noted, however, that the officially-listed substitutes were the only ones for which the Admiralty, through the Victualling Board, would pay. Woe betide the captain or purser who bought anything else without a written order from the commander-in-chief, unless stuck in a place where the official items were not available at all.

This standard ration gives an average daily intake of almost 5000 calories. (This figure is usually given as 4500, but having traced this oft-quoted figure back to its origin, it transpires that the calculation is seriously flawed in several respects. For details of a more accurate calculation, see Appendix 3.) Such an average daily calorie intake seems excessive by modern standards, when an active man is thought to need between 2500 and 3000 calories a day; even the crews of modern sailing ships, doing more or less the same work, need no more than 3200 calories daily, but modern crews do not have to haul three-ton guns around and they do not have to expend calories on keeping warm. Georgian sailors did not have reliably waterproof clothing or warm, dry sleeping quarters; for the below-decks men other than those in the sickbay, there was rarely any source of heat other than the galley fire, which was normally extinguished after dinner was served at midday. In really bad weather it was too dangerous to light that fire at all and they did not even have the comfort of a hot meal or drink.

It is interesting to compare this ration with that of contemporary soldiers: they had slightly more meat (one pound per day rather than six pounds per week), another pint of pease, only one-third of the amount of oatmeal, and either butter or cheese, not both. They received the same daily pound of bread or biscuit, or flour in lieu (which conjures up a picture of boy scouts cooking flour and water 'dampers' moulded round a stick over a camp fire). Alcohol seems to have been issued as and when it was available; in the West Indies and North America during the American War of Independence, what had started as an issue of rum as a reward for hard duties became a normal ration of one-third of a pint per day, justified as being necessary to purify the water.[5] In Wellington's Peninsula campaign, wine was drunk when available. Beer, unless found in towns *en route*, was not a practical drink for armies on the move; it would not tolerate long-distance land transportation over bad roads and armies rarely had the transport facilities to spare for bulky liquids. Unfortunately they also rarely had adequate transport facilities for the official food ration and in many campaigns the troops went short of food unless they could forage it along the way. This is one advantage of being a sailor: you may stand a risk of drowning but you do carry your provisions with you on the ship rather than having them trail far behind on an ox-cart or pack mule.

We should also consider the diet of the land-bound civilian worker in Georgian England. This is rather poorly documented, but social historians have tended to believe it was somewhat restricted, stating that 'the unskilled labourer in the towns and the agricultural labourer in the country lived chiefly on bread, cheese, small beer, with meat, perhaps, once a week'.[6] This statement should, however, be taken with some scepticism; such labourers, like seamen, expended a lot of physical effort in their work and needed calories to do it. Their intake may have been restricted in variety, but it could not have been skimpy. Nor does the fact that they earned low wages and lacked cooking facilities at home mean they did not eat meat. Meat comes in many cheaper forms than slabs of skeletal muscle: sausages made of blood and oatmeal (black pudding) or tripe and chitterlings (white pudding), cows' heels or pigs' feet, haslet or brawn, can all be eaten cold and are just as nutritious as a slice off the joint.

Before we look at the naval foodstuffs in detail, it is worth emphasising that what we are discussing here is the official diet of the Royal Navy, not that of merchant seamen. There is often some confusion among lay people about the status of what has come to be known as 'the merchant navy'; this term gives the impression that there is a separate merchant service run by some government organisation akin to the Admiralty, but this is not the case. No such organisation exists or has ever existed, which means that there was nothing to ensure that merchant seamen were properly fed or watered until 1844 when legislation on victuals began, firstly relating to drinking water, then to the provision of antiscorbutics, then, in 1867, making recommendations (not legal requirements) on the quality and quantity of food. But even then, without trade unions to help, there was little a merchant seaman could do, short of the impracticable method of taking the owners to court. Their employers were, for the most part, small shipowners operating on small budgets; some of these owners, or the masters they employed, chose to save money by skimping on the seamen's food. It was not universally bad: some seamen ate very well – one merchant master wrote to his owners about a seaman who was proving expensive to feed because he would eat several pounds of meat at a sitting, which implies that the meat was always there on the table to be eaten.[7] On the other hand there are many reports of small portions, the best cuts of meat going to the master and mates, casks full of rubbish and so on. It was probably the merchant service which produced most of the stories of bad food. Many of the others came from very long early voyages, such as that reported by Antonio Pigafetta who sailed round the world with Magellan in 1520, or from the fertile imaginations of novelists such as Smollett, which were then repeated by naïve writers such as John Masefield, who was in his early twenties when he wrote *Sea Life in Nelson's Time*. Many of the stories he repeats in this book smack of an ancient mariner getting more and more outrageous as the grog went down, and of course they nicely reinforced the late Victorian sense of superiority over their forebears.

Such stories may make good blood-curdling reading, but they are not a true representation of the facts. As we shall see later, by the mid-1790s, the Admiralty, through the Victualling Board, had systems in place to ensure that the food provided for naval seamen was both good and plentiful, and that it was issued with scrupulous fairness.

It is at this point that the Spithead Mutiny of 1797 is often advanced as evidence that the food was not good and plentiful. This idea comes from one of the subsidiary requests from the mutineers 'that our provisions be raised to the weight of sixteen ounces to the pound and of a better quality [and] there be a sufficient quantity of vegetables…'. Some writers suggest that the provisions were a major cause of the mutiny but this is not so; they were an additional thought on the lines of 'while we're about it, let's get all our other grievances sorted out'.[8] The real cause of the mutiny was the inadequacies of naval pay. This had not been increased since 1653 despite inflation and steady increases in the rates of pay for merchant seamen, and to further inflame the sailors' sense of injustice, the army had been given a pay rise. The mutineers' timing was immaculate: a high percentage of the Channel Fleet was at Spithead and joined the mutiny, this being at a time when fear of invasion from France was high. The mutiny continued for several weeks, after which the government was ready to accede to almost any demands to get the fleet back to sea; they increased the pay by some 23 per cent and instructed the pursers to issue the full amount of victuals. But as far as victuals were concerned, the only difference that can be directly attributed to the mutiny was the quantity issued. The Physician of the Fleet, Dr Thomas Trotter, had been campaigning for a general issue of vegetables for some time before the mutiny and they were already being sent out to the squadrons blockading Brest; indeed, they had also been provided for the fleets blockading Brest and Quiberon Bay between 1757 and 1762. As far as the quality was concerned, Charles Middleton (later Lord Barham), Comptroller of the Navy Board, had been working on improving the quality of victuals since 1781. He proposed that quality should be monitored by retaining random samples for inspection after twelve months. This not only put the onus on the contractors to provide good quality, but also freed those contractors of potential blame for deterioration due to poor storage or other problems caused after they had made their deliveries.[9]

The matter of provisions being 'raised to the weight of sixteen ounces to the pound' was due to the practice of pursers issuing rations at a rate of seven-eighths of the stated amounts, which gave rise to the expression 'a pursers' pound', meaning fourteen ounces. This is often presented as a deliberate bit of chicanery by crooked pursers seeking to line their pockets at the expense of the long-suffering sailors, but it was nothing of the sort. As the Victualling Board knew full well, dispensing food from bulk and the various accidents that could happen on board was bound to lead to some wastage; the purser's eighth was an officially-recognised buffer to allow him to balance his accounts. This is evidenced by their issuing a new set of weights two each purser, the old weights obviously having given short weight. As we shall see later when we look in depth at the pursers' business, when the ration was 'increased' after the mutiny, the Victualling Board found another way to compensate the pursers for their wastage losses. Did pursers in general take advantage of the seamen by keeping them short of food? Some might have done, but given the situation of a ship full of dark nooks where aggrieved seamen could lurk with a belaying pin, it is unlikely to have been a general practice. Even without resorting to this sort of thing, the seamen had a mechanism for complaining about food, as for other complaints, and could take these complaints as far as their commander-in-chief if necessary.

Groups of men with little else to do will often complain about the food; it is only when other things are wrong that they do more than complain. Unfairness over food was one of the grievances on *Bounty* in 1788 but it took a lot more before they were ready to rebel on the grand scale.[10] There has been a more recent case, known to the historians at the Admiralty Library as 'the great mashed potato mutiny'. At Singapore in 1945 the crew of the landing ship *Northway* were served badly-prepared reconstituted mashed potato after some had spent the morning peeling real potatoes (it transpired that the cooks had managed to burn these). This was the trigger to down tools and refuse orders to fall in, but again this single incident was not the sole cause, having been preceded by some weeks of complaints about the food in general. A court martial followed and various members of the crew were found guilty, the ringleader receiving five years penal servitude and the others minor punishments, mostly suspended detentions.[11]

There have been other minor mutinies related to bad beer, but in general they are very rare. This indicates pretty strongly that although the men might have enjoyed chilling the marrow of gullible civilians with stories of awful food, the reality was rather different.

Chapter 1

BASIC RATIONS

As we have seen, the navy had a laid-down scale of victualling, but that rather bald table does not tell even half the story. It is worth considering each item, or 'species' as they called it, to examine exactly what it was and where it came from. Things that could go wrong and how this was dealt with are discussed in Chapter 3, as are the logistics of loading, handling and stowing. The detail of issuing and cooking the food and how and when it was eaten are discussed in Chapters 4 and 5.

Bread and Biscuit

The staple item of the seaman's diet was a daily pound of bread or biscuit. To a certain extent the two words were used to mean the same thing; when they meant bread in loaf form, they called it 'soft bread'. For the general below-decks population, this was only available when in port, or (assuming there was someone on board capable of baking it) when they were in the sickbay. When *Gibraltar* was stationed in Naples harbour for long periods in 1803 and 1804, the master's log shows that she received a daily delivery of 600 'soft' loaves; when a delivery was missed (perhaps due to a Saint's day) they had a double delivery on the day before or after. Since there were about 600 men on board, this suggests that each loaf weighed one pound; there is no indication of whether this bread was white or wholemeal.[1]

In England, bread production was subject to legislation which covered the weight of loaves, the type of flour used and how loaves were to be marked. Those made of 'fine white' flour (actually a pale cream colour) was the most expensive, as this flour had to be 'bolted' (sieved) through fine cloth and thus was more time-consuming and difficult to produce; loaves made from this flour had to be marked with a 'W'. The next type was 'standard wheaten' bread, marked 'SW' which is more or less what we call wholemeal today, except that this meal could contain quite large pieces of grain. The cheapest and lowest quality bread, made with seconds flour, was called 'household' bread and was marked 'H'. The most popular was the white loaf; this popularity lead to unscrupulous bakers adding alum, which improved the texture of a loaf made from inferior flour as well as improving the colour. The naval surgeon turned novelist Tobias Smollett was quick to join other alarmists in stating that chalk or bonemeal was used, but this is unlikely as these additives would have spoiled the texture of the loaves and reduced their size.

Other unofficial additions were flour from cheaper grains such as barley or rye, or pea flour, but all of these were dark and thus could only be used with the brown flours. They would also, since they contain less gluten than wheat, make for a poorly textured loaf. However, when bad harvests caused steep price rises, these and other things were added to wheat flour. The Board of Agriculture did conduct experiments with buckwheat, maize, oats, chestnuts, turnips and potatoes. More specifically, between 1793 and 1800 and in 1809 the Victualling Board experimented with mixtures of wheat, molasses and potato, or wheat, molasses and barley; of the two, the captains whose crews had eaten them reported that the first type was preferred but that it looked and tasted rather like gingerbread.[2] The author has made the same experiments: buckwheat flour and cooked mashed potato do make quite good light bread if added to wheat flour in the proportion of three parts wheat to one part buckwheat/potato; the other items make a dense heavy bread which is tolerable when fresh but tends to go green and hairy after three or four days. Turnip or swede bread is acceptable on the day of baking but then takes on an unpleasant 'cabbage water' flavour. Bread made of good wheat flour alone will keep in a sealed container for up to ten days.

Given all of the above, it is not surprising that the Royal Navy preferred biscuit to bread. Biscuit would keep for many months, it came in handy pieces, and because it did not require any form of leaven it did not need any great skill to make and it could be made in large quantities more quickly than the equivalent weight of soft bread. And the ingredients were simplicity itself: flour, water, a minimal amount of salt. The method was equally simple: water was added to flour, it was mixed, kneaded until smooth, rolled, cut, stamped with the broad arrow (affectionately known as the 'crow's foot') which marked it as Crown property, baked, cooled and packed.[3] This process required no great degree of knowledge or careful temperature control, both of which were essential for the methods of bread-making used at the time. For bread the flour was put in a trough, a hollow was made in it, and leaven and some of the water was added. It then had to be left for an hour or more while it fermented, before the rest of the water was added and mixed in. It was then kneaded, left to rise for an hour or so, kneaded again, cut up and shaped, left to rise again and finally baked. This whole process meant more space, more time, and, because it was essential that the dough had to be in a certain condition at its various stages, it also required trained bakers who could recognise when the dough was ready to work with.

It should be explained that the forms of leaven available at that time were not as dependable as they are now. Some yeasts were available from the brewing industry but since, as we will see below, brewing was a seasonal activity, fresh yeast was not always on hand; dried forms of yeast were not developed until well into the nineteenth century.[4] The alternative was what we now know as 'sour-dough starters'; these are retained amounts of risen dough which are added to new flour and water and then work by feeding on the new flour. This process takes longer than using yeast, and requires an even more skilled eye than does yeast-raised dough.

Some of the biscuit was bought from outside contractors, some was made by the Victualling Board at its depots in Deptford, Portsmouth and Plymouth, and later in some of its victualling yards abroad.[5] They were made of wholemeal, some of the surviving specimens containing quite large pieces of recognisable wheat grains. The contracts for outside bakers stated that the biscuits should 'weigh not less than five to the pound' (*ie* at least 3.2 ounces or 91 grams each) and that they should be packed in bags of a hundredweight. The shape was not specified and they could be square, round or octagonal, usually pricked with holes and with the broad arrow and a letter designating the bakery stamped in the middle. This compressed the dough, making the middle even harder than the rest; eaters tended to leave this hard piece until last, designating them 'pursers' nuts'.

It was almost impossible to bite into these biscuits without first soaking them. The normal technique was to break bits off on the edge of the table, or to use a hard object to crush them, having first wrapped them in a piece of cloth to avoid explosive dispersal. These pieces could be sucked and chewed, or added to soup or gravy. Despite their hardness, these biscuits were tasty enough. It was when they became damp that the taste deteriorated and the livestock moved in. The secret of keeping the biscuit dry and sweet was to pack it in airtight boxes; the Dutch knew this as early as the seventeenth century. American sailors knew it too, but somehow the message did not get through to the British Admiralty until well into the nineteenth century. Captain Basil Hall, writing of his experiences during the War of 1812, remarked on this: American biscuit, he said, was tasty and good quality and he attributed this to their practice of keeping it sealed up until needed, whereas the British practice was to ventilate the bread room in fine weather with the aid of wind-sails which funnelled air down from above. Unfortunately in warm weather this air was warm and moist while the cellar-like bread room was cold; the biscuit absorbed this damp air and the process of deterioration started.[6]

When the bread ran short, or had deteriorated beyond the eatable stage, the standard substitute was rice, issued on an equal-weight basis: one pound of uncooked rice was considered by the Victualling Board to be equal to one pound of biscuit. Since it was only ever referred to as 'rice', we do not know whether this rice was brown or the polished white version.

Meat

The meat ration, as shown in the table on page 10, seems straightforward: beef twice a week and pork twice a week, but the true situation was rather more complex. Far from land, both the beef and the pork would be salted, and as long as there were adequate stocks of both, the ration would be one pound of salt pork on two days and, theoretically, two pounds of salt beef on two days. However, the *Regulations* state: 'For the better preservation of the health of the seamen, it is ordered, that one day in every week there shall be issued out to them a proportion of flour and suet in lieu of beef...' and it goes on to say that they were also to be supplied with canvas for pudding bags.[7] This seems to suggest that on one day a week dinner consisted of suet pudding and no meat, but this is unlikely. What probably happened was that half of each mess opted for flour and suet one day while the other half opted for beef, then the process was reversed on the other beef day, so each beef day consisted of one pound of beef with suet pudding for each man. The official substitution rate was four pounds of flour, or three pounds of flour and one pound of raisins, being equal to four pounds of beef, and half a pound of suet being equal to one pound of raisins. The normal ratio for suet puddings or dumplings is, to quote the pastry cook's mantra, 'half fat to flour'. Fat, for either puddings or dumplings, does not have to be suet; beef dripping or the beef fat that rises to the top of the liquid when the meat is boiled will do as well. So although the issue of three pounds of flour and a half-pound of suet would in theory leave a spare two pounds of flour, there was scope for obtaining other fat for puddings as well as using the flour in other ways.

Pork, as far as the crew were concerned, usually meant salt pork. Officers might, and often did, keep pigs on board and there was theoretically no reason why some of the men should not, with the captain's permission, have done the same, but the only record of this being allowed serves to demonstrate the problems attached. In 1780 Thomas Pasley in the *Sibyl* (28) was *en route* to the Cape of Good Hope to collect a convoy of Indiamen and he stopped at the Cape Verde islands for water. He found there was plenty of food to be bought and allowed his men to buy what they wanted; he remarked that few of the messes did not buy 'three or four pigs, as many goats and half a dozen fowls'. Then a couple of days later they sailed and he commented that the ship was absolutely full of hogs and goats and resolved that he would have to order the hogs to be killed first, as the goats made much less mess. A little reflection allows one to calculate that a 28-gun frigate would have somewhere in the region of 30 messes and thus over 100 pigs and the same number of goats on board.[8]

As the table shows, pork was issued with pease and as far as the Victualling Board was concerned, it always was; the substitution of fresh meat was on the basis of three pounds of fresh meat being equivalent to 'a two-pound piece of Salt Pork with Pease'.[9] Pork of any sort is an unfashionable meat now among the anti-fat brigade and even those who are not fanatical about avoiding fat often express distaste at the idea of salt pork. This is strange: what are ham, gammon and bacon if not salted pork meat? And what of the popular French dish *petit salé*? Beef might also be salted and here again some modern people do not like the idea, but it is, in many forms, a classic dish: British boiled beef and carrots, New England boiled dinner, Jewish hot salt beef sandwiches, pastrami, and corned beef (so-called because it was preserved with large grains or 'corns' of salt). These are the modern equivalents of what Georgian sailors were eating.

Salt meat, classed with butter as 'wet' provisions ('dry' being cereals and pease), came either ready-packed from contractors or arrived on the hoof at the British victualling yards, to be slaughtered and salted-down there. A very high proportion of the pre-packed meat came from Ireland and most of that from 'the ox-slaying city of Cork', the 'slaughter-house of Ireland'; the rest came from the adjacent cities of Limerick and Waterford. The wet provisioners of Cork were proud of their reputation for quality; in 1769 they had formed a committee and established a grading system to enable high standards to be set and maintained.[10] In both Ireland and England, the cattle travelled long distances to the great autumn cattle fairs, modern estimates suggesting that somewhere in the region of 80,000 cattle changed hands each year at the London fairs alone. Some of the cattle sold at Barnet Fair (north of London) had started their journey in Anglesey, swimming the Menai Straits and walking on shod hooves along the drove roads to their destinations.[11] You can still see evidence of these routes in parts of England, where the modern road has very wide grass verges.

The killing season began in the autumn and carried on through the winter, partly because meat killed and packed in cool weather keeps better than that prepared when it is warm and partly because the difficulty of feeding cattle through the winter months meant that farmers did not want to keep them. It was not until after the end of the Napoleonic Wars that the practice of growing turnips and other roots for winter feed was generally adopted. The temperature at killing time was even more critical for pigs, so that season started a good month later than for cattle. Pigs, like cattle, were driven to market but over much shorter distances; they lose weight quickly and, being rather more intelligent than cattle, are much more troublesome to control. Since pig-fattening was a more intensive activity than cattle-raising, some farmers tended to specialise on a large scale, especially those close to the big cities. These specialist pig-fatteners often fed the pigs on brewers' grains, the barley which had been used in the brewing and distilling process. It was not long before some laterally-thinking brewers and distillers realised that they could make more money by fattening pigs than by selling the exhausted grain, and they set up fattening sheds next to the breweries. In 1740 there was some discussion between the Victualling Board and the Admiralty about the relative merits of this 'town-fed' pork and whether it reduced in weight when cooked more than the 'country-fed' version, which finally concluded that there was no difference between the two types. They thought that the 'town-fed' version ought to be cheaper and was therefore preferable for that reason.[12]

The Victualling Board had issued instructions on the cutting and salting of meat as early as 1716, and despite a steady stream of people offering to sell their 'new, better and secret' methods of doing this, reissued the same instructions at regular intervals. There is no great secret to salting meat, for the procedure is simple. First you cut the meat into suitable pieces: for the navy this was four pounds for beef, two pounds for pork (or sometimes double that weight, these being referred to as 'double' pieces). This task was done by 'randers' and 'messers' in a sort of production line. Some historians have erroneously changed what they thought was a spelling error, calling the first worker a 'render', presumably on the basis that he 'rends' the meat, but a rander is one who cuts meat into strips and a messer one who cuts it into smaller pieces. At this point you might wonder how they achieved accuracy, but of course if they did the job continuously they soon acquired the ability to judge weight by hand and eye. No-one expected each piece to weigh exactly the stated weight: the instructions for checking the weight of the contents of a cask say:

> And to judge whether the flesh served to His Majesty's ships holds out in just weight, the following rule is to be observed, viz. Every twenty-eight pieces of beef cut for four pound pieces, taken out of the cask as they rise, and the salt shaken off, are to weigh one hundred pounds avoirdupois, and every fifty-six pieces of pork, cut for two pound pieces, and taken out and shaken in the like manner, are to weigh one hundred and four pounds; and therefore, if, according to this standard, upon the weighing a whole cask of beef or pork, in the presence of two or more of the warrant officers of the ship, there shall be found a deficiency of weight, the captain may order the purser to issue to the seamen so much more beef or pork as shall make up the deficiency;...[13]

There is another example of the scrupulous fairness of the Victualling Board: being perfectly aware that there are different qualities of meat on a carcass, their master butchers were instructed to cut the prime pieces slightly small and the other pieces slightly large, thus dividing it 'in the most equitable manner'.[14]

There must still have been some small pieces left over and one wonders what happened to them – perhaps they were packed into special casks and marked accordingly. Inevitably some of these small pieces went home in the workers' pockets, a practice which was known and accepted, as long as the pieces were not too large. Small scraps were probably sold to the same people who bought the offal and other by-products such as heads, feet and bones. The contracts for outside suppliers and the instructions for packing meat in the Victualling Board's own yards stipulated that these were not to be included, nor beef legs or shins. We will see what the Victualling Board did with the shin meat later on.

The meat having been cut up into appropriate pieces, the salting process could begin. Although they would not have been aware of it in these terms at that time, the salting process, having first drawn out much of the water in the meat, combines with the rest and makes it unavailable for bacteria to feed on. Saltpetre (potassium nitrate), which was used at the time, was thought to aid the penetration of the salt and co-incidentally give the meat a uniform pink colour. It also, unfortunately, tends to harden the meat over time; to counteract this, people salting meat for home use often added sugar. The first part of the process was to rub the pieces of meat with the dry salt and saltpetre mix, then lay them in a bin and cover them with more dry salt. As the salt drew out the water from the meat, the resultant brine was drawn off, poured back over the meat and more salt added, this being done twice a day for six days. Then the meat was packed into barrels with more dry salt between the layers and left to stand for several days. This extracted more liquid, so the cask was then turned on its side with the open bung-hole at the bottom and given twenty-four hours to drain, before the bung was replaced and the cask filled with strong brine. The simple test for brine strength was that the meat should float.[15]

Victualling agents and pursers were instructed to check all meat casks when they were received, to ensure that none of the brine had escaped, topping them up if necessary. Salt meat, when removed from its cask, was wet, which gives the lie to stories of its being hard and glistening with salt crystals. If the brine leaked out, the meat did not dry up, it rotted; there are many reports of meat being condemned as uneatable because the brine had leaked. Once sealed, each cask was marked with the contents and a unique number which enabled its source to be identified if it was sub-standard. Although in theory meat casks were meant to contain a standard number of pieces, entries in log-books made when the casks were opened show that many did not, some having more pieces than marked, some less.

Although the standard sizes of meat pieces may have been fixed to tally with the number of men in an average mess, they were also of a size which allowed the salt to penetrate right through the meat. With over-large pieces of meat, the salt will not penetrate and the meat will putrefy. This, combined with poor-quality salt and over-large barrels, caused a major fuss in 1804 over a consignment of meat from Russia intended for the navy in the Mediterranean and the army based at Malta. The story starts with St Vincent (now the First Lord of the Admiralty) agreeing with Nicholas Vansittart of the Treasury that it would be a good idea to obtain some provisions from 'the Russian provinces', thus helping to cement the relationship with Russia. An agent, one William Eton, was sent to the Black Sea port of Odessa to organise some supplies, including hemp and made-up cordage and sailcloth, and at the same time to make a bulk purchase of wheat, pease and meat. Nelson, who was commander-in-chief in the Mediterranean at this time, was informed and told to arrange for transports to collect the provisions and take them to Malta. For some reason which is not known, Nelson was violently opposed to the idea, or at any rate opposed to Eton, remarking in a letter to William Otway, the naval commissioner at Gibraltar, 'I never saw Mr Eaton [*sic*], but my opinion of him was formed some years ago; and from all I hear I have no reason to alter it. He is, as Burke said of a noble Marquis "a giant in promises, a pigmy in performance",' and later, 'I agree perfectly with you respecting Mr Eaton, and we must watch what comes from him; for first samples are, with knowing ones, always the best...'. Elsewhere, he referred to Eton rather rudely as 'this sort of gentry' and insisted that when the supplies finally arrived in Malta they should be inspected and tested before acceptance. However, Nelson did not pass up the opportunity to send a lieutenant with the transports to gather trade and military intelligence on the Russian provinces round the Black Sea.

In due course, the first shipload of provisions arrived in Malta, and were inspected and sampled by the masters of three naval ships; the pease and wheat were declared good but the pork, tongues and hogs' lard were not (there was no mention of beef). Nelson wrote to the Admiralty secretary on the lines of 'I told you so' and ordered the agent victualler at Malta to accept the wheat and pease and sell off the meat for whatever it would fetch. Eton, when he heard of this, wrote to excuse himself, explaining that the decision to send him had been delayed to the point where he arrived too late to buy the best of the animals on the hoof; the meat had already been packed, having been cut it into over-large pieces, using inadequate quantities of inferior dirty salt and put into over-large casks. When he had explained and demonstrated the proper way to do it, the local Russian general was, Eton said, so impressed by the results that he wanted Eton to stay and teach the local workers how to do it 'the English way'. As a result, the next batch would be much better, as long as his instructions to buy were not delayed again.

Eton was also corresponding with Sir John Borlase Warren, who was at that time the British ambassador to Russia at St Petersburg. Some of this correspondence consisted of intelligence reports but most of it concerned his purchases for the navy and his relationship with another agent, Henry Lavage Yeames, who had taken on some of the purchasing task. This relationship soon fell into disarray, each man accusing the other of incompetence, stupidity, cupidity, and generally erratic behaviour. Eton, apparently, made a practice of flying into a violent temper whenever crossed: '...his conduct,' said Yeames, 'has been uniformly as if he intended to destroy the British credit here'. Both agents sent detailed memoranda to Warren, pleading for his intervention, and in Eton's case, also pleading for those instructions to buy more supplies.

These were not forthcoming. Warren had resigned his post and gone home and the Victualling Board were not pleased with Eton. As well as buying the actual provisions themselves, he had also taken the unauthorised decision to buy 'the Great Baths at Caffa' to use as a storehouse; by the time he had had this building repaired, the cost had risen to over £1700. 'Except for the wheat and pease,' the Victualling Board wrote to the Admiralty, 'our judgement is that Mr Eton's mission to Russia has not been attached with any advantages to the service of this department.' Even then, the saga was not finished. Russia changed sides and embargoed all British property, including the bathhouse at Caffa and its contents. Then Russia changed sides again, and the Victualling Board, now trying to finalise Eton's accounts, reported to the Admiralty that the bathhouse had been demolished to make way for other buildings, and its contents had been sent for the use of the Russian navy at Sevastopol, so there seemed no point in keeping Mr Eton's account open any longer. They owed him £849.17.2¼, but suggested that before they paid him, perhaps they should make sure he did not owe money to any other of the naval departments, or any other government body. The Admiralty agreed, suggesting that since Eton had also purchased cordage and sailcloth, the Navy Board was the first place to check; it seems that Mr Eton's reputation had caught up with him and he had become generally unpopular everywhere.[16]

Salt meat was all very well, but fresh beef was thought to be better. It did not have to be steeped to get rid of the salt, and although the stories about aged salt beef being hard enough to carve into snuff boxes were probably exaggerated, there can be no denying that it does become tougher as it ages; this problem does not occur with fresh beef. But the real consideration at the time was that it was thought that salt food caused scurvy, this being one of the reasons for dropping salt fish from the naval ration. Finally, it had become traditional for vegetables to be served with fresh meat when in port, which was obviously popular with the men. Fresh beef was declared to be equal in weight to salt beef, and slightly less so than pork: the rule here was three pounds of fresh beef for two pounds of salt pork with pease. Judging by log reports of receipts of fresh beef when in port, it was served almost every day, at a rate of one pound per man. *Gibraltar*, with her 600-man complement, received daily deliveries of fresh meat averaging 590 pounds.[17] According to William Dillon, when his ship was at Spithead in 1794, it had to be collected from the slaughterhouse early in the morning (often as early as 2am) on a 'first come, first served' basis. It was cut into quarters – a piece which can be carried on the shoulder of a strong man – and as Dillon learned to his cost, it was necessary to keep a close eye on it all the time; on one occasion a whole quarter disappeared between the slaughterhouse and the boat.[18]

The other method of providing fresh beef was to carry live cattle on board ship and slaughter them as needed. This was a common practice and had the advantage of allowing salt provisions to be saved for times when no fresh was available. It may not always be possible to find a port with a supply of salt meat, but if you can get within boat-reach of land you can usually find a merchant or farmer to sell you some cattle (or sheep or pigs); even if you are nominally at war with the country, as long as there is no military presence and you have specie for payment, pragmatism tends to override patriotism. In 1805 Cornwallis' fleet blockading Brest found that the inhabitants of the islands off Brittany were perfectly happy to sell them live cattle and other fresh provisions.[19] Carrying live cattle was only practical on a short-term basis since cattle do not stand up well to long sea journeys, as was found during the American War of Independence when attempts were made to send live cattle across the Atlantic. Of one shipment of 290 cattle, only 105 were still alive on arrival, and the attempt was abandoned as being both impractical and expensive.[20]

By 1800, most commanders-in-chief were convinced that fresh meat was essential for maintaining the health of the seamen; Nelson was fanatical about it, being firmly convinced that excessive salt was one of the causes of scurvy. When he was in the Baltic in 1801, he had arranged for one of the senior pursers to obtain fresh meat and cattle for his squadron, and when he took over the Mediterranean command in 1803, he took great pains to obtain live beasts. His first attempts to do this by organising supplies himself or through his captains were not entirely successful. His method was to appeal to the consuls at Naples, Barcelona and the Maddalena Islands; although these gentlemen tried, most of these dealings came to nothing, partly due to difficulties of collection and unacceptable prices, partly due to poor communications. In one case, Captain Keats had been in contact with an ex-army officer called Archibald MacNeill in Naples, who offered to supply beasts on a monthly basis starting in September. This offer was accepted and Nelson ordered transports to collect the cattle, but when he heard no more, cancelled the transports. The following January he received a letter from MacNeill saying he had instructed his partner, Warrington, to organise the bullocks, but again there was no further contact until June when a letter arrived from Warrington saying 100 beasts were ready to collect. By this time Nelson had made other arrangements, so he agreed to collect this set of cattle but that was the end of the deal. While all this was going on, Nelson had been using the services of a senior purser to organise supplies of cattle, first from the Barcelona area and then, when the Spanish seemed ready to join Napoleon and declare war against Britain, from the Maddalena Islands at the north end of Sardinia.

These islands had good anchorages and were reasonably close to the main cruising grounds off Toulon. Apart from the times when several ships arrived together at the islands, the procedure was for one of the larger ships, usually a Third Rate, to go off and pick up a substantial number of beasts then distribute them among the squadron on her return.[21] When the individual ships only received a few cattle at a time, they seem to have slaughtered them soon after receipt: the log books show 'received x bullocks' on one day, and 'killed x bullocks, weight xxx pounds' either later on the same day or on the next. When they received larger numbers, they also recorded receipt of 'fodder' or 'hay', then recorded the numbers killed and their weight, a few at a time, over the next week or so. But sometimes they kept them longer, reporting large numbers taken on board over a couple of days, then batches of them being killed over several weeks.

These cattle, with a few exceptions, were bullocks and all were the animals we think of now as cattle (*ie*, the domestic 'cow', *Bos taurus*). Admiral Pellew, when commander-in-chief in the East Indies, insisted that neither live buffaloes (*Bubalus bubalis*, the Asian water buffalo) nor their meat were to be accepted; other commanders-in-chief and the Victualling Board itself stated that heifer beef was not acceptable. Even so, a few cows did sneak through the system, usually with a calf at foot. There are several log entries which show this, followed by a report of killing an animal which weighed so little it can only have been the calf; these may have gone to the sickbay. Perhaps the idea was to provide milk but it would have needed a crew member capable of persuading the cow to let down her milk – not always an easy task if she is not used to being milked.

What is noticeable when studying these log reports of killing cattle is the great disparity in weights, beasts producing anything between 140 and 675 pounds of meat. This was not a random thing, but more or less related to where they came from. The lightest mostly came from the Maddalena Islands and Sardinia itself, the heaviest from Italy, especially from Naples. (John James, one of the consuls who had offered to supply cattle from Naples remarked that the average weight of the Calabrian cattle he was offering would be 540 pounds.) Although the weight of a beast is influenced by its age, and what we now call 'management systems' (*ie* where it is kept and how it is fed), these different weight ranges when associated with locations indicate that we are considering different breeds of cattle. It has not been possible to find out exactly what breeds these cattle were but there are modern British equivalents: Herefords are quite large, Dexters are very small.

It is actually incorrect to refer to these Georgian-age cattle as 'breeds': strictly speaking, a breed is the product of selective reproduction in controlled conditions, with that breeding recorded in a herd book, something which was not done until later in the nineteenth century. The correct term is a 'landrace' (not to be confused with the modern pig breed of that name), a type of animal which has adapted over time to the local conditions. So, given that Sardinia is a mountainous country with sparse grazing, it is not surprising that its cattle would be small, and that countries with flatter areas of good grass, such as southern Italy, would have larger cattle. Another consideration is that goods tend to be moved around mountains by agile pack animals such as mules, and in flatter terrain on carts drawn by placid traction animals such as neutered cattle, which are also in demand for ploughing. These tasks require not only placidity but strength, which means they must be large and carry a lot of muscle. Examples of what are now known as 'traction cattle' include Charolais, Simmenthal and the enormous Italian Chianina. How these cattle, and the sheep which accompanied them, were kept on board, despatched and butchered, will be discussed in Chapter 3.

Although mutton was listed as a substitute meat (three pounds of mutton being equal to four pounds of salt beef or two pounds of pork with pease), no examples of it being received have been found by the author, other than in the form of live 'sheep for the sick'. We do not know exactly what was meant by the term 'sheep'. Although there was a type of mouflon in Sardinia and Corsica (*Ovis musimon*), these would not have been domesticated and the sheep bought by the navy would thus have been the local landrace of the domestic sheep (*Ovis aries*), and probably mature animals. The concept of a one-year-old lamb being raised for its meat is a modern one: sheep, then, were too valuable as producers of wool or milk and cheese to kill them at the 'young, tender and easily digested' stage. Milk-fed or sucking lambs were an Easter delicacy on the continent but these would mostly have been males of the milk breeds, which carry very little wool; milk-fed lamb was rarely eaten in England where the sheep were mostly wool breeds. So a sheep for meat would be a mature animal and its meat would be the gamey mutton, not the more easily-digested meat of a juvenile. Although mutton broth was thought to be a good restorative for the sick, it is hard to see how it would have been any better than beef broth.

Mutton was considered suitable for the sick at that time because it had properties which served to balance the 'humours', and it continued to be popular as food for the sick well into the nineteenth century. However, another possible explanation is that provisions for the sick had to be accounted for separately. It would have been easier to charge a single purchase of sheep to the sickbay than a series of small amounts of beef. Even more likely, though, is the comparative ease of keeping a small flock of live sheep on board against a number of bullocks, even allowing for the fact well-known to farmers that sheep only have one ambition in life, and that is to find a reasonable excuse to die! Even allowing for this propensity, live sheep meant an ongoing supply of fresh meat for the sick instead of the less desirable salt version.

Although lamb is sometimes salted in Norway, making a product called *fenalår*, this is exceptional; neither lamb nor mutton seem to be salted elsewhere, either for nautical or land-bound use. This may be related to the small size of the animal, but is more likely because sheep meat has a higher water and fat content than beef and thus penetration of the salt into the tissues could be slowed down to an extent which could allow the centre to rot before the salt reached it. To embark on a major operation such as salting-down large quantities of meat, you have to be sure it will work well.

Salting was not the only method of preserving meat. In the 1660s, Robert Boyle described his successful experiments in preserving cooked meat in butter. The meat was roasted, cut up and packed into a cask and melted butter was poured in to fill all the airspaces. He claimed that it kept well for over six months, even in the hot voyages to the East Indies. This is more or less the same method as used for making the French delicacy *confit de canard* (or *d'oie*), where the thighs of duck or geese are cooked and preserved in their own fat. The British version of this is 'potted' meat, which had become so popular in the eighteenth century that a subset of the pottery industry developed to supply the pots. However, those pots were quite small and not practicable for large-scale supplies, although no doubt many officers brought them to sea with their private stores. The principle of hermetic sealing with fat eventually developed into the method using glass jars which the British call bottling and Americans canning. Glass was not a practicality for general ships' victualling on a large scale, but the idea of canning eventually developed and transformed the whole business of victualling.

Poultry

Chickens were kept on most ships, where they supplied eggs for the officers and the sick until they went off lay and were eaten. Officers also brought cockerels, ducks and even geese to sea, but rarely turkeys, which are not the easiest of birds to keep alive in cold, damp conditions. The seamen were, however, not averse to eating any migrating birds which were rash enough to rest within grabbing distance; some of them would 'fish' for albatrosses or other sea birds with a baited hook on a fine line.

And sometimes, on special occasions, an indulgent captain might treat them to a feast. Basil Hall did this for Christmas in 1815, when he was fitting out the sloop *Lyra* at Deptford, buying one goose and one turkey for each mess at Leadenhall market. All went well until after dinner, when one of the crew could not resist showing off to the crew of an adjacent ship, asking them how many geese and turkeys they had eaten that day. 'None' said the others, and 'Look at that and weep, you hungry-faced rascals!' said the sailor, waving a drumstick in each hand. This was too much to bear; the drumsticks were pulled out of his hands and flung in his face and a general melee ensued.

The following year, the ship was in the Canton river alongside several Indiamen, and Hall's steward reported that the main topic of conversation below was Christmas dinner and the fact that there were plenty of chickens, ducks and geese in the nearby village. Hall felt that it would be unkind to deprive the men of such a treat and agreed that the poultry could be bought. He thought no more of it until dawn on Christmas morning when a tremendous racket broke out, bringing on deck not only Hall but the crews of all the Indiamen. Hall's crew had taken the poultry aloft during the night, tied their feet to the yards, cross-trees, gaff and jib-boom on six-feet long pieces of twine and then sat there with them, trying to keep them quiet (and getting scratched and bitten in the process). When the sun came up, the birds were dropped, setting up a screaming, quacking, cackling and flapping, accompanied by yells from the men, to draw the envious attention of all viewers. Hall does not report whether a general scrap resulted this time!

Butter and Cheese

Butter- and cheese-making were, like meat-packing, seasonal activities, the difference being that these were spring and summer tasks, when the new grass and the newly-calved cows produced the most milk. Yet, although they both started as milk, as far as the navy was concerned most of the butter came from Ireland while all of the cheese came from England. For many decades the cheese favoured by the Victualling Board was the hard Suffolk cheese, which, being made from skim milk, was cheaper than the full-fat versions from Cheshire or Cheddar. Suffolk cheese kept a long time but even at its best it was not popular – hard enough to start with, it became harder with keeping and there are stories of it being carved into buttons. Badly or hastily made, it became either too hard to eat or turned soft, went bad, stank, and became infested with long red worms (*Eisenia foetida*). During the Seven Years' War the urgent demand for naval provisions led the Suffolk cheese-makers to cut the necessary curing time and the complaints about this cheese became so common and so bitter that in 1758 the Victualling Board more or less abandoned Suffolk cheese and turned instead to Cheshire, Cheddar, Gloucester or Warwickshire cheese. Although more costly and not so long-keeping, these cheeses immediately reduced the level of complaints, although they were issued on the basis of two-thirds of a pound of Cheshire being equal to one pound of Suffolk. For shipboard purposes, these would be whole cheeses, wrapped in the tough muslin-like fabric called cheesecloth. Packed in barrels until needed, they were then kept in shaped racks in the steward's room. The individual cheeses weighed between twelve and thirty-seven pounds, depending on the place of manufacture, the smallest being from Gloucester and the largest from Cheshire. They were stored in casks until 1799, then kept in shaped racks in the bread room.[22]

Fully aware of the comparatively short 'shelf-life' of cheese and butter, the Victualling Board introduced two rules: one for the suppliers which said that if any of a batch of these products did not stay good for six months, they would not be paid for any of it and would have to remove the remainder from the stores at their own expense; and another to ships' pursers which required them to issue all their stocks within three months of receiving them, failing which they would receive no credit for the unused portion.[23]

Bad cheese rotted and stank, while bad butter became liquid and rancid. This was partly due to the difficulty of keeping it sufficiently cool, but mainly due to inadequate care in manufacture. To make butter, you start by leaving milk, which is an emulsion of fat and water, to stand so that the cream rises, then put the cream in a churn and agitate it so that the fat globules separate from the water and adhere to each other. In time, the fat becomes a solid mass separate from the watery liquid now called buttermilk. However, droplets of this buttermilk will be trapped within the mass of butter and these must be removed by a process of washing and working it with paddles. It is this watery buttermilk content which makes the butter rancid. It is impossible to get it all out and so all butter will go off eventually, but if too much buttermilk is left in or the butter is handled by dirty hands or paddles, it goes rancid even more quickly. Adding salt to butter helps retard the process; almost all butter made in England and Ireland was salted to help it keep. One process which does extend the keeping quality of butter is to heat it gently until the last of the buttermilk separates and sinks to the bottom. The fat can then be poured off and left to set; this is known as clarified butter or, in India, ghee. The East India Company's personnel must have been aware of this, but the concept does not seem to have worked its way back to Britain and the Victualling Board.

Unlike rotten cheese, which was good for nothing, there were uses for rancid butter. Whether or not it was still within the allowed date when found to be bad, if the boatswain did not want it for lubrication purposes, it was to be returned to the victualling stores and then sold. Although some of this was no doubt bought for land-bound lubrication tasks, some of it may have gone to butter 'cleaners' who washed it in fresh water to remove the salt and the smell, then washed it again with fresh milk and finally worked it back into a product which could be sold to the unsuspecting as 'fresh' butter. This practice was mostly carried out in London; in Ireland, where they took butter-making very seriously, the butter industry was subject to strict legislation, one section of which forbade mixing old butter with new.[24] Whether produced in England or Ireland, the standard practice was to pack butter in 56-pound firkins.

There were various official substitutes for butter and cheese. For one pound of cheese, these were one pound of rice, one pound of sugar, half a pint of oil, half a pound of cocoa, or a quarter of a pound of tea. For one pound of butter, the substitutes were one pound of sugar or one pint of oil. The type of oil is not specified, but at that time and given that ships going to the Mediterranean were not supplied with oil, the purser having to buy it there, it can have been none other than olive oil.

Butter and cheese were issued on the same day as oatmeal and sugar, on the three meatless or 'Banyan' days. There was, of course, the usual pound of biscuit, so if no meat had been saved, the cheese was probably eaten with the biscuit, as the butter might have been. On the other hand, the butter might, as with the sugar, been added to the cooked oatmeal, turning it into a dish of 'buttered groats'. Quite how the oil was eaten, we can only guess. Soft bread dipped in oil will absorb quite a lot and is a common snack in Mediterranean basin countries to this day, but biscuit will not absorb oil like this. Smollett's novel *Roderick Random* describes a dish of hot pease with oil and chopped onion mixed in; it could also have been used as a dressing for cold or raw vegetables. Oil might also have been added to soup, or, with the co-operation of the cook, used as a frying medium for fish, onions or pieces of meat.

Vinegar

Added as an afterthought to the official list, half a pint of vinegar was issued once a week, but whether it was wine or malt vinegar is not specified. As with the oil, it could be used as a condiment or even, when circumstances permitted, used to make simple pickles. On a large scale (not from the seamen's issue) it was used as a disinfectant about the ship; the seamen might have used some of theirs to deter vermin and sweeten their mess areas, just as before the introduction of modern cleansing agents housewives used it to wipe out fridges and cupboards.

Pease

Pease, meaning the hard dried pease which were one of the staple foods of the time on land as at sea, come in two forms. The oldest, the Carlin pea (*Pisum sativum* ssp *arvense*), is a small, dark brown pea which is still traditionally eaten during Lent in some north-eastern counties of England. Also known as grey peas, these are a sub-species of the green garden pea which we mostly buy in its frozen form today (*P. sativum* ssp *sativum*). By Georgian times, this earlier pea had been replaced for most purposes, including naval victualling, by the mature form of the garden pea. For those who wonder if the term 'pease' means the dried form while 'pea' means the soft fresh form of this vegetable, it should be explained that the modern spelling is just that: a modern way of spelling the old word; here we will continue to use the old form unless the fresh version is meant.

Dried pease are either whole, green and wrinkled (still in their skins), or yellow, 'split' (*ie* separated into their two halves), unwrinkled and skinless. The whole green variety take a lot longer to soften and cook; they really need overnight soaking as well as several hours of cooking. Yellow peas are more accommodating: they can be cooked in a pudding bag, in which case they will swell and form a mass which is soft enough to eat with a spoon when hot and sets into a solid cake when cold, which can then be sliced and eaten in the hand. If boiled loose in plenty of water, they will break down into an unctuous thick warming soup; this soup is traditionally enhanced by adding pieces of pork or ham.

There is some dispute about whether the pease used by the navy during Nelson's period were whole or split. An editorial note in James Anthony Gardner's recollections remarks that at that time pease were issued whole, and that split peas were not issued until 'about 1856'.[25] What they mean by 'about 1856' is that the Admiralty circular was issued in that year and said that once the existing stocks of whole peas were used, split pease would be supplied instead.[26] However, this is not to say that split pease were never used before that date; although the author has been unable to find any conclusive evidence either way, given the Victualling Board's propensity to choose the cheapest option every time, it is quite possible that split pease were used earlier than 1856.

Whether whole or split, these pease mostly came from East Anglia, either grown there or imported from the Baltic countries through the port of Yarmouth. Pease are a crop of northern climes; ships on stations further south substituted the local dried pulse. In the Mediterranean or the West Indies it was 'calavances', a type of haricot bean (*Phaseolus vulgaris*) also known as the French, canellini or navy bean; sometimes chick peas (*Cicer arietinum*) might have been substituted. In the East Indies the substitute was referred to as 'dholl', which equates to the modern spelling of dhal or dal; this could be anything from split chick peas to the larger forms of lentils (*Lens esculenta*), some of which are very much like the yellow pea. All these were issued weight for weight for pease. There is just one problem attached to these assorted pulses: they have an unfortunate effect on the intestinal system, which cannot have improved the atmosphere below decks. However, for those of a competitive nature and a robust sense of humour this probably had some entertainment value!

Oatmeal

This also came from East Anglia or the Baltic, and was a coarser version of the 'porridge' oats we use today. It was mainly used to make porridge or 'burgoo' and eaten for breakfast with some form of sweetening, either sugar or molasses. Nelson got into a terrible tizzy about this sweetening in the Mediterranean when *Victory*'s captain, Hardy, wrote him a formal letter in September 1804 stating that there had been no molasses in the ship since the previous June, and requesting that since there had not been an additional issue of oatmeal to make up for this, the men should be paid for the missing molasses as 'savings of provisions'. Nelson sent a copy of this letter to the Admiralty with his own covering letter, remarking that he thought the men should be paid for the daily allowance of oatmeal when there was no molasses to go with it, 'as it was found that generally a man could not get a pint of dry Oatmeal down his throat'. Could there not be a supply of cocoa or tea sent in lieu of molasses, as had been the case when he was in the West Indies, or at least sugar, he asked. These two letters were passed from the Admiralty to the Victualling Board, whose response was on the lines of 'What is he talking about?' They never had tea or cocoa as a substitute for molasses in the West Indies, and anyway, no-one was expected to eat dry oatmeal, since it was always made into porridge in a big batch by the ship's cook; furthermore, the issue of oatmeal was a pint every two days, not a pint a day.[27]

It would have been surprising if there had been any need to find substitutes for molasses in the West Indies, where it came from; unless this was a piece of heavy sarcasm, Nelson's memory was at fault here, as was his knowledge of breakfast below decks. He may have been confused by the situation of substitutes for the oatmeal: one pound of sugar for two quarts of oatmeal, or five and three-quarters pounds of molasses for one gallon of oatmeal. These substitutes may have been another situation like that of suet and flour as a substitute for beef, where a sweet-toothed mess could juggle the individuals' issues to benefit all. The other possible substitutes for oatmeal were wheat or 'pot' barley (a version of the grain which has some of its hull removed, but not as much as does modern 'pearl' barley); these were substituted on an equal weight basis and both were boiled and sweetened to make an acceptable substitute for oatmeal porridge, rather like the Medieval dish frumenty.

Oatmeal was never terribly popular with English sailors. Jeffrey de Raigersfeld reported that when operating in the Shetland Islands during an oatmeal shortage, his men were nothing loath to trade their oatmeal with the islanders for eggs and poultry.[28] Eventually the Victualling Board recognised this and the thrice-weekly issue of oatmeal was halved and two ounces of sugar issued instead.

Rice

Used as a substitute item (one pound of rice for one pound of bread or cheese, one pint of pease or a quart of oatmeal), rice was the standard breakfast dish for the men on the East Indies station, either boiled dry or served slightly wet and known as 'congee'. (The officers usually had theirs in the form of curry.) Elsewhere it was little known until 1795, when a series of particularly bad harvests led to a wheat famine and the East India Company brought several shiploads of rice back from India. Although in fashionable circles it became patriotic to eat rice, it was never very popular with sailors.[29]

Fruit

The only officially-listed fruit was the dried raisins issued as part of the substitute for salt beef. Raisins are, of course, dried black grapes, traditionally muscatel grapes from Malaga; they could themselves be substituted by half their weight of currants, another form of dried grape whose name is a corruption of 'raisins from Corinth'. On the East Indies station, the dried grape was called 'kismish', which is presumably the same thing as the modern kishmish sultana made from the green 'Thompson seedless' grape. There are, of course, many other forms of dried fruit which the men would have bought for themselves whenever opportunity allowed.

Nelson and other officers who accepted the idea that citrus fruit were good antiscorbutics would direct their pursers to buy lemons and oranges for the crews when the opportunity occurred. The logs of many of the ships on the Mediterranean station, under various commanders-in-chief including Nelson, show frequent purchases of lemons or oranges, either in small batches for their own ship or in larger quantities to share out among the rest of the fleet.

Vegetables

Like citrus fruit, vegetables were something which pursers bought for their ships when opportunity permitted; they could also obtain them from victualling yards. It had been traditional to do this long before the Spithead mutineers expressed their desire for vegetables in 1797; in the *Additional Regulations and Instructions* published with the 1790 edition of the *Regulations and Instructions* a clause remarked that it had long been the practice of pursers, when fresh meat was served, to include 'such a quantity of greens and roots to … give sufficient satisfaction to the men …'.[30]

Other than the numerous log entries which just say 'vegetables', the most commonly mentioned are cabbages and onions. Nelson in particular was convinced that onions were health-giving, remarking in a letter, 'I find onions are the best thing that can be given to seamen.'[31] Leeks are also frequently mentioned, these entries being late in the winter when onions would no longer be available. An interesting point about the onions is that these were, as often as not and even when bought in large quantities, described by number rather than weight or bagsful: *Gibraltar* received 300 onions every day while stationed in Naples harbour, and 6000 the day before she left; other ships received 2400 or 3000. Given the Victualling Board propensity for nit-picking over precise accounting, it is likely that these numbers were exact, not guesses, and indeed these sorts of numbers occur again and again, in different ships at different places. As one cannot see the lieutenants or masters who were responsible for these log entries actually counting loose onions, these consistent figures suggest that onions traditionally came in strings of a certain number: twenty-five or thirty perhaps. The cabbages also came by number, but a cabbage is much larger than an onion and smaller numbers were involved: *Gibraltar* at Naples received eighteen each day. Sometimes, rather than cabbages, the description 'greens' is used, either as a single description or sometimes 'x bunches of greens'. This probably meant kale (*Brassica oleracea convar. acephela*) or the type of loose-headed cabbage known in America as 'collard greens' ('collard' being a corruption of 'kale').

In the Mediterranean, another frequent purchase was pumpkins. The nomenclature of this class of the *cucurbita* family is complex and by no means clear-cut: the term 'pumpkin', depending on whether you are in Britain, America, the Caribbean or Australia, may mean either the big orange fruit with a light and watery flesh, or the orange, green, grey, cream, pinky-yellow or multi-coloured and denser fleshed, chestnutty-tasting, fruit that modern Americans and British call winter squash.[32] Short of finding a detailed journal of a contemporary Neapolitan market gardener, we may never know exactly which these were, but although the Royal Navy of the time would not have been aware of it, either version is a good source of several useful vitamins and trace elements. They also have seeds with a tasty 'nut' for those who have the inclination to nibble them open.

Carrots and turnips are sometimes mentioned, but until well into the nineteenth century, rarely potatoes, although during the 1795 wheat famine the Victualling Board were offered (and refused) a large quantity by a correspondent, and Dillon mentions eating what he called 'toast made from potatoes' on shore during that hard winter. The reason potatoes do not seem to have been bought often may relate to their propensity for turning green and poisonous if exposed to light or sprouting if exposed to warmth; but it is more likely to have been related to the fact that there was somewhat of a social stigma attached to them. Having been continually referred to by social reformers as an ideal food for the poor, the potato had come to be seen as something only to be eaten by the desperate, a label that would not have fitted the image sailors had of themselves.

It has not proved possible to find out with any precision exactly which varieties of vegetables were grown at this period but it is likely that many of them were like those shown in Vilmorin-Andrieux's late nineteenth century book *The Vegetable Garden*. Like animals, different varieties of vegetables and fruit developed in different parts of every country, adapting themselves to suit local conditions, with seeds being passed down through the generations. Currently known as 'heritage' plants, these old varieties are now being jealously preserved by various organisations anxious to protect genetic variation against the depredations of big seed companies and tidy-minded bureaucrats.

Fish

Because it has a nasty tendency to become damp and then putrid, and because of the 'salt causes scurvy' theory (see page 25), dried or salt fish had been dropped from the official naval diet. After centuries of conflict with France and Spain, there may also have been an adverse psychological connection with the fact that the dreaded and hated Catholics ate such fish on several days each week. Fresh fish was another matter, and all ships were supplied with fishing tackle which they were meant to use when opportunity permitted and when they were in 'a place where fish can be had'. The resultant catch was first to be offered to the sickbay and the remainder shared out among the crew, on a rota system if necessary. This fish was to be considered a free, extra item, not a substitute for anything else.[33] Perhaps for this reason, fishing is so rarely mentioned in log books that one might suppose it never happened.

Journals, memoirs and letters home tell a different story. Captain Duff, of the *Mars*, when on blockade outside Cadiz in the months before Trafalgar mentions in a letter that they had the trawl out and that his share of the catch was 'a very good turbot'.[34] William Mark, cruising off Havre le Grace in 1800 also mentions trawling, remarking that it served as a useful diversion for the men in a situation where there was little else to do.[35] The inshore waters of the Mediterranean, where the most fish are to be had, were not always the best place to make the attempt. Patrolling up and down off a port like Toulon may seem a likely place to try a trawl, but there was always the danger of an enemy frigate dashing out. The preferred method for obtaining fish in the Mediterranean was to get it from a local fishing boat. The Royal Navy tended to leave fishing boats alone, finding them useful sources of information as well as food, and some fishing boats took to carrying fruit and vegetables when they knew the Royal Navy was about. However, there were occasions when the French navy took to pressing fishermen to man warships and at these times fishing boats were seized and the crews taken prisoner.

In tropical waters there were the flying fish, or the 'dolphins' (actually bonito) which pursued them, or even porpoises. Basil Hall reports a porpoise being caught half an hour before the officers' dinner. He told his steward to cut and grill some steaks from it and pass the rest to the crew. Not having encountered the idea of eating porpoise before, the crew were dubious about eating it and a seaman was appointed to hover outside the cabin door. When the steward came out he was waylaid and questioned: 'Did they really eat it?' The steward showed the empty dish and the seaman scampered off to report to his mates. By the time the officers had finished dinner and the captain and surgeon went up to view the remains of the porpoise, there was nothing left to see.[36]

Sharks were also popular prey for seamen fishing in warm waters. Raigersfeld tells of their using pieces of salt pork to bait the shark hooks and thirteen-footers duly being hauled in and despatched with an axe. Then as many men as could sit astride the carcass did so, each hacking off a slice in front of him, having first warned the man behind to watch out what he was doing with his knife. The resultant slices were par-boiled, salted and peppered and grilled, the result reputedly tasting rather like cod.[37] Landsman Hay mentions shark being layered with slices of pork and then baked.[38]

Other things came out of the sea besides fish. Dillon tells of an alligator washed out to sea when he was on the Jamaica station; foolish enough to swim round the ship, it was soon caught and eaten. It looked and apparently tasted like veal, but Dillon, not fancying it, refused the piece he was offered. And anybody who had the opportunity caught turtles, keeping them alive on board by turning them upside-down to prevent escape and dousing them with sea water to keep them moist, or, according to Landsman Hay, keeping them in what he describes as 'our water tank'.[39] In 1813, when there was a shortage of beef on Bermuda (one of the victualling ports for the North American squadron), the Victualling Board agreed that one and a half pounds of turtle could be issued in lieu of one pound of beef.[40] Giant tortoises, too, although not sea-creatures, were to be had on islands in the Pacific and Indian Oceans. The American frigate captain David Porter raved about their 'luscious and delicate' taste, having acquired a number from some captured whalers. Having tasted them and found how good they were, the Americans remarked sadly about the numbers which had been thrown overboard by the whalers in their attempts to evade capture. Then, a few days later, sailing back over the same stretch of water, they found about fifty tortoises still alive, floating in a group, which they picked up and stowed away, no doubt drooling happily in the process!

Drinks

The official drink for seamen was not, as is popularly thought, grog, but beer – the daily allowance was one gallon. However, it should be explained that this was not what we now know as a British gallon, but 'wine' measure, which is five-sixths of that amount (a British gallon 'wine measure' is equivalent to the American gallon). To those accustomed to modern beers this sounds a lot, but the beer issued to seamen, like the normal table beer on land, was 'small' or weak beer of 2 to 3 per cent proof. (Modern British bitter beer is about 4 per cent, American Budweiser is 5 per cent, Guinness is 4.4 per cent and European lagers such as Heineken are 5 per cent.) The advantage of beer is that having been boiled in the manufacturing process it is reasonably free from bacteria; if it does not 'go off', beer will last in the cask for months whereas water, unless it starts off sterile and goes into a sterile container, becomes nastier and nastier over time.

Beer does go off quite easily in warm weather, which makes it cloudy, sour or vinegary; one brewer's response to complaints about a batch of beer was that it had been left out in the sun on the quayside. For this reason, brewing was essentially a cool season activity. But even in cold weather, using imperfectly cleaned casks could make the beer go sour and acidy in a few days. Although some beer was supplied by contractors, the Victualling Board also brewed its own, first at Tower Hill in London, then at Deptford, and eventually at Plymouth and Portsmouth. Apart from its keeping qualities, the main reason for making beer the official drink was that it attracted lower excise duty than wine or spirits. The government was concerned about theft and smuggling, and for this reason in the navy it was actually forbidden to open casks of wine or spirits within reach of the British coast for fear of the contents being diverted ashore.[41]

When the beer ran out, and on stations where it was not available, the official preference was for wine, although this was often fortified with brandy to improve its keeping qualities. One pint of wine was deemed equivalent to one gallon of beer (modern wine bottles hold 75 centilitres, or one and a third pints). We do not know the strength of wine at that time, but now most table wines are about 11 to 13 per cent proof and fortified wines are about 20 per cent. Table wine then probably was much the same strength as it is now. Wine was obtained from Italy and Sicily, and from France or Spain when Britain was not at war with them. Probably, via canny merchants and neutral vessels, it still originated in those countries when Anglo-French or Anglo-Spanish wars were in progress – two of the wine merchants in Barcelona supplying Nelson in the Mediterranean in 1804 as war with Spain loomed were confident that this would not stop supplies. One remarked that if necessary he would send it in neutral ships, the other hinted delicately that he knew whose palm to grease to ensure that stocks would not be confiscated.[42]

One might suppose that the wine supplied for seamen would be the sort of rough red favoured by working men in the Mediterranean basin countries today, but white wine from Portugal, Italy and Sicily was also bought by the Victualling Board and pursers on the spot. Like other forces stationed in the Mediterranean, Nelson's fleet bought locally and drank whichever colour was available. When wine and spirits were bought for naval stores in England, a special dispensation was obtained from the Treasury to exempt it from customs duty.

Most ships carried supplies of spirits as well as wine, the official issue being on the basis of a half-pint of spirit equalling a gallon of beer. There must have been some occasions when the captain deemed it appropriate to issue spirits instead of wine when wine was still available – in cold weather, perhaps, or when particularly arduous duties called for a quick booster or reward – but although this seems a reasonable supposition, the author has not yet found any reports of this practice. The type of spirit drunk depended on where they were and what was made locally. In the Mediterranean, it was brandy, on the East Indies station it was arrack and on the West Indies station it was rum. Later, at the instigation of the politically-strong West Indies merchants, rum became the standard spirit. Whichever it was, the rule was that it was to be diluted with water 'and none suffered to drink drams'.[43]

The strengths of the brandy and arrack are not known, nor with any accuracy is that of the rum of the day, but it is believed to have been at least four times as strong as the 'Navy' rum sold today; that official half-pint would have been the equivalent of two modern bottles. The requirement to dilute spirits is thought to have originated with Admiral Edward Vernon, in the West Indies in 1740. He ordered the rum ration to be diluted with a quart of water, this to be done on the open deck in a scuttle butt kept for that purpose, in the presence of the lieutenant of the watch, and of course any of the crew who cared to observe the process to make sure they were not given short-measure. Admiral Vernon was known as 'Old Grog' from his habit of wearing a cloak made of grosgrain (a heavy corded silk fabric) and his rum and water mixture came to be known by the same name.[44] Later, on the advice of Doctor Trotter, lemon or lime juice was added to the mixture as an antiscorbutic. Rum has come to be known as 'Nelson's blood', perhaps by people under the impression that his body was preserved in rum; it was actually brought home in a cask of brandy, as evidenced by a letter from the *Victory*'s purser Walter Burke, asking to be allowed credit for this in his accounts.[45]

Various mixtures based on rum were popular at the time. Rum, water, sugar and nutmeg was known as 'Bumbo'; rum or brandy mixed with beer and sugar and heated with a hot iron was known as 'Flip'; and in the officers' wardroom similar mixtures with lemon juice and hot water were made into punch.

Seamen on shore used their own slang to describe their preferred dilution of spirits: 'due north' meant plain spirit, 'due west' meant plain water, 'north westerly' meant half and half, and describing a glass as 'southerly' meant it was empty.[46]

When there was no beer, and wine or spirits were served, the men filled up with water. Away from a good watering place, there was always concern about replacing what was used, and most captains made a rule that while men could drink their fill at the scuttle butt, they could not take water away. To prevent this, a marine sentry would be stationed by the butt, the fear being that water taken away might be used for some frivolous purpose, such as washing their smalls (damp and salt-encrusted underwear being one of the tribulations of life at sea). Admiral St Vincent became quite incensed about this practice when women were on board, and issued a general order forbidding it.[47] When water was short, instead of an open butt at the scuttle, there would be a closed cask with a bung-hole in the head and a hollow tube would be provided as a drinking straw; there are even stories of this cask being put in one of the tops to make it even more difficult to get a drink, but these are probably apocryphal. When there was a real water crisis, it would be rationed out to each man at set times, and at such times rainwater would be collected by spreading sails like awnings, with a couple of shot placed in the middle to form a pool. This water might taste a bit odd, but it would serve to steep and maybe cook the salt meat or pease if nothing else. Pasley reported heavy rain when becalmed near the Atlantic Equator in 1782 when they collected a ton and a half for the cooks to steep the pease, 'being greatly superior to any other [water] for breaking the pease'.[48] The quality of the drinking water depended on three things: how long it had been kept, the state, age and cleanliness of the casks when they were filled, and where it came from. Plymouth had good sweet water from Dartmoor, piped in a conduit known as Drake's Leat; Deptford water was less dependable, sometimes being compared with the contents of London's cellars and cess-pits. Although there had been earlier experiments with distillation devices, it was not until 1810 when a new type of cooking stove was introduced that there was any facility for producing fresh water on a useful scale.[49]

Other officially issued drinks were tea and cocoa but only as substitutes for cheese: 'half a pound of Cocoa or a quarter of a pound of Tea, is equal to one pound of Cheese.'[50] Since one of the other substitutes for cheese was sugar, it would have been possible for a mess of men to have taken their tea or cocoa sweet, but either drink would have been without milk unless the captain was indulgent enough to allow the crew to keep their own goat on board. To the modern mind, tea and cocoa are odd substitutes for cheese; while it can be seen that there is food value in cocoa, there is none in tea, so one can only conclude that these substitutes were chosen as being roughly equivalent in cost to cheese. Even so, economy prevailed: in 1803, when contemplating a purchase of tea, the Victualling Board discussed the available types of tea and then recommended the cheapest.[51] This was not popular, and soon after this decision was made, Lord Keith wrote to report that there had been 'a murmuring in the fleet' and that the men had thrown the tea overboard.

Despite being a substitute for cheese, tea and cocoa were generally taken at breakfast, when hot water was available, although some men made themselves a drink called 'Scotch coffee' which consisted of burnt biscuit ground up with hot water added.[52] Tea was, by this time, a popular breakfast drink on land while cocoa had become not just popular but ultra-fashionable. The only source of supply for tea was the East India Company, which brought it back from China; it was 'black' tea, the sort made by fermenting the bruised leaves (of the camellia bush, *Camellia sinensis*) to allow oxidisation before drying. Cocoa, which is the powdery residue left after cocoa butter has been extracted from the beans of the cacao tree (*Theobroma cacao*), had been introduced to Europe by the Spanish after Cortes invaded Mexico. Originally found growing wild in Central America and the northern Amazon basin, the cacao tree was successfully cultivated in the West Indies and in the eighteenth and early nineteenth century most of Europe's supply came from the Caribbean, arriving in solid blocks which had to be pounded into powder by the mess cooks, each taking it in turns to do this job for the whole ship.[53] Popular then as now for its comforting nature, cocoa was also rumoured to be an aphrodisiac; it is perhaps best not to enquire too closely into how sailors found this beneficial!

Chapter 2

HOW IT GOT THERE – THE WORK OF THE VICTUALLING BOARD

ALL THAT FOOD AND DRINK did not appear on the ships by magic. Although the specific methods by which it arrived could vary, all were organised or controlled by the Victualling Board, which reported to the Board of Admiralty. Victualling had originally been administered by the Surveyor of Victualling; he was replaced in 1683 by the Board of Victualling Commissioners, which continued until 1832 when they were in turn replaced by the Victualling Department.

In its earliest days victualling was dealt with through a system of contracts, whereby the contractor agreed to supply, for a set number of men, the standard provisions at an agreed rate per man per day, delivering these to specific locations. For reasons of quality control and efficiency of operation this system changed over time, until by the end of the Napoleonic Wars in 1815 all but the most remote stations were fed under the direct control of the Victualling Board. The supply chain and the delivery chain were separated, with an intervening period when provisions went into Victualling Board warehouses, thus more easily achieving both accounting control and quality control.

HEAD OFFICE ADMINISTRATION

The Victualling Board received its day-to-day instructions from the Board of Admiralty, although many of these, such as instructions to supply victuals to individual ships, had originated with another sub-division, the Navy Board. It also had some dealings with the Sick and Hurt Board,[1] in such matters as providing meat to make portable soup, as well as with the Transport Board which arranged ships to send provisions to the British outports and the agents victualler and fleets abroad. The Victualling Board consisted of seven commissioners who met every day except Sunday, the day-to-day work being done by an establishment of clerks in the Victualling Office situated first at Tower Hill and then at Somerset House. This establishment consisted of about seventy people: in the secretary's department there was the secretary himself, a deputy secretary and up to sixteen clerks; in the cash department there was an accountant for cash, two chief clerks and a total of twenty clerks; in the store department there was one accountant, three chief clerks and up to twenty-four clerks; and finally there was a secretary to the committee of accounts.[2] During busy times – that is, those when Britain was at war – 'extra' clerks and other staff were taken on.

The chain of supply and delivery started with the Victualling Board receiving an instruction from the Admiralty, telling them the size and localised make-up of the navy for the following year and asking for an estimate of costs. The Victualling Board responded with a detailed figure; for instance, in 1797, the figure given for the following year for 110,000 men was £2,758,268.1.10½.[3] The Board of Admiralty, armed with these figures, then added them to the rest of the spending requirements that made up the 'Naval Estimates', which went before Parliament.

Working Conditions

As the eighteenth century progressed, as well as the move away from direct delivery by contractors to delivery by the Victualling Board itself, the Victualling department manufactured and packed increasing amounts of the food on their own premises. All this required substantial numbers of staff. At the manufacturing yards there were bakers, brewers and butchers; at all of the victualling yards there were storekeepers, 'hoytakers' (who organised boats to move provisions from the storehouses to the waiting ships), watchmen and gatekeepers, numerous labourers and not a few rat-catchers. The labourers were mostly paid by the day and engaged as and when needed; most of the other yard workers, as well as all the clerks at the outports and in the office at Somerset House, were engaged on a more permanent basis and, after serving faithfully for a great number of years, were able to retire on a superannuation or pension. With the clerks and the master craftsmen, when anyone retired, everyone below them moved up a step: the second clerk moved into the first clerk's position, the third into the second's and so on down the line, until the first extra clerk moved into the lowliest permanent position and the rest of the extra clerks performed the same upward dance. This, until 1800, was done in the same way as officers advanced in the army: except at the highest levels, government offices were a saleable commodity, so when there was a position available, everyone down the line bought the job above them and sold theirs to the person below them.[4]

Several of the more senior clerks and department heads decided to retire in 1799, at the point when it became obvious that the payment structure was about to alter. This had been on the cards for a long time and came about as a result of the beginnings of a change in the eighteenth century middle-class mindset. Previously the system of patronage and sinecures had resulted in a situation where people were put into high-level jobs not because they were efficient but because either it was felt they deserved a nice little sinecure, or because putting them there allowed a favour to be paid off or because other advantages would accrue to the patrons. To this was added the conviction that senior positions could only go to gentlemen, whose mere gentlemanly status rendered them capable of doing anything they set their minds to – as long as they were not expected to actually acquire expertise in the job (a trait which was far beneath them) or even spend any time in their office attending to it. This would not have mattered too much if the clerks had been given free rein, but they were restricted by the post-holders' conviction that what we would now consider to be office mail was actually their private property and should not be opened by anyone else. This would have been acceptable if the addressee had actually opened it; many of them could not be bothered. There are numerous reports of unopened packets of mail being found at these officials' homes, or their going off to the country for the summer and ignoring the calls of business. William Mark, a purser who served under Nelson in the Mediterranean, was called in to sort out the office of the Commissioner at Malta after his secretary had been sick for some months. The commissioner had made no attempt to deal with, open, or even note the date of receipts of any of his letters, just throwing them over the half door of the secretary's office; by the time Mark got to them, he estimated there was at least a wagon-load.[5]

Add to all this the fact that many of the clerks were deeply attached to the traditional ways of working and averse not only to doing things in new ways but also to doing new things, and you begin to see why eighteenth-century government administration was so inefficient and so expensive. There were one or two lights in this wilderness, including the talented administrator Charles Middleton, Comptroller of the Navy in the early 1780s. A typical example of incompetence was Middleton's complaint that the Navy Board clerks did not even sort the matters for Board meetings into topics, but presented them to the meeting at random. This level of disorganisation, which was repeated in all the various government departments, led in 1779 to a petition being presented in Parliament by the Opposition, calling for a committee to investigate public expenditure, the methods of accounting for it, the abolition of sinecures and the reduction of excessive emoluments. A committee was set up and between 1786 and 1788 produced a series of ten reports, two of which were on the activities of the Victualling Office.[6] As well as various recommendations on procedures, the committee recommended that the staff payment system should be changed from a small salary and the right to charge fees for various transactions (such as signing contracts or copying documents) to a larger salary and nothing else. The reports had gone through a prolonged process of comment and counter-comment on each of the committee's recommendations and at long last, in 1800, most of the recommendations were put into effect.

It was not that long before the combination of a fixed salary and inflation, caused partly by the length of the war and partly by several years of bad weather which led to crop failures, caused major dissatisfaction. In 1804 an anonymous petition was presented by the Victualling Office clerks requesting salary increases. This was considered by the Board of Admiralty and turned down. It was followed by another similar petition from the clerks at Portsmouth, which was also turned down. The Victualling Board secretary wrote again; he pointed out that the clerks were not allowed to work overtime and the press of business was such that they were falling more and more behind. The weekly lists of unanswered letters which the Admiralty demanded were getting longer because the clerks were unhappy and were leaving to go to other bodies such as the Customs where the workload was lighter and the salaries higher. This letter struck home. The Admiralty enquired what salaries the secretary felt should be paid. He responded with a long list and in due course the new salary levels were agreed and everybody in Somerset House got a pay rise.[7] Inflation continued throughout the rest of the war and these requests for pay rises continued, coming at irregular intervals from different groups of workers, from coopers to labourers to clerks, until in 1811 the Admiralty agreed to a new system which brought in regular pay rises linked to length of service.[8]

Apart from the six-day working week for everyone from the commissioners down to the humblest junior temporary clerk, the work itself was laborious. Almost every piece of paper which passed through their hands had to be copied at least once and all the accounting work had to be scrupulously correct. These were people who could nit-pick over a fraction of a penny and who would not only produce seven-figure estimates for the government of the cost of a year's naval provisions calculated down to the last farthing but also required that every account submitted matched every other that touched on the same items. This can be seen in the system of imprest accounts against the salaries of the pursers and captains whereby the cost of whatever foodstuffs passing through their hands was charged to their salary and not removed until a full set of information had been received and checked (see Appendix 5). This information might involve the pursers of other ships (if, for instance, swaps of provisions had taken place between ships) and since there were over 1000 ships in operation at the height of the Napoleonic Wars, it involved balancing a vast set of interlocked accounts.

Fraud, Corruption and Incompetence

Another of the ongoing tasks of the head office staff was that of fraud prevention. Like all government departments throughout history, the Victualling Board was seen as fair game by various types of predator, from the low-level clerk who earned a few extra guineas by colluding with contractors over tenders, to the serious money which could be diverted by the contractors themselves. Neglecting this policing task resulted in several public scandals. The most serious of these included those of Thomas Ridge, the contract brewer at Portsmouth, who was found in 1711 to have colluded with some pursers over false deliveries; the biscuit contractor Christopher Potter, who had a monopoly contract, and was accused in 1782 of using bad wheat and making short deliveries; and that of Christopher Atkinson, who used his political connections to obtain monopoly contracts, first for supplying malt for brewing beer, then as agent for the supply of all cereal products and pease.[9] After several years Atkinson was accused of buying supplies himself and selling them to the Victualling Board at a profit as well as taking his agency commission, and of 'padding' his expenses. The Victualling Board investigated and dismissed him. He had, by this time, been elected to Parliament and he attempted to clear his name by instigating a House of

Commons investigation. This found him guilty; he sued for libel and ended up being convicted of perjury and being expelled from the House of Commons. At about the same time, criticism of the Treasury's practice of awarding Army victualling contracts to Members of Parliament led to the so-called 'Clerke's Act' which excluded contractors from the House.

Another major fraud a few years later, concerning the dockyard and the victualling yard in the Leeward Islands, was reported to the Admiralty by Nelson himself. Nelson arrived in the West Indies in 1784 and discovered several dubious practices. The first of these was the way all the merchants and officials encouraged American ships to trade with the British islands; being no longer British subjects, Americans were forbidden to take part in this trade. Nelson was then tipped off about a series of fraudulent practices being perpetrated by the naval storekeeper and the agent victualler at the Leeward Islands; sums in excess of £300,000 were suggested. As so often in these situations, the story is convoluted and not made any clearer by the accusatory letter from the 'whistle-blower' Wilkinson, which is long, rambling, and tends to go off track as the writer fumes about the guilty parties: 'the most rascally and bungling Villainy!', 'a gentleman...perfect in the habits of Public Deception', 'famed for some time past in assisting bungling peculators', and 'where money is to be got by fraud and peculation, Mr Druce appears.' The basic story as far as the victualling side of it goes is that the agent victualler and his assistant, in collusion with various other parties, had for many years been falsifying the accounts with non-existent purchases and over-statement of everything else. For example, they hired a sloop to transport provisions at £4 a day and charged it at £5, they paid £150 rent for a store and stated it at £192, bought 13,911 pounds of meat at 15 pence a pound and stated it as 35,662 pounds at 18 pence. To try and prevent the truth coming out, the conspirators had had Wilkinson and his partner Higgins thrown into jail for debt, where Higgins contracted a fever and died and Wilkinson languished for over a year.

It transpired that Wilkinson really did have a debt problem, which he had sought to alleviate by asking the conspirators for £10,000 to keep what he knew to himself. They turned him down and so he took his story to the senior naval officer on the station, who at that time was Nelson. Wilkinson proposed to Nelson that he and Higgins would conduct the investigation for the navy, for a fee of £15,000 for the first £100,000 of the amounts recovered and 7½ per cent of the rest, and he gave Nelson some details which were duly passed on to the Admiralty in London. At the point at which the bundle of documents stops, the Board of Ordnance had agreed to this proposal, the Navy Board had put their file into the hands of the Attorney General, and the Victualling Board had passed their file to their solicitor with instructions to proceed to prosecution. The end result of these prosecutions has, alas, not come to light.[10]

Another interesting story is that of the victualling contractor for the East Indies station, Basil Cochrane. An uncle of the brilliant but difficult frigate captain Thomas Cochrane (later tenth Earl of Dundonald), who was found guilty of a Stock Market fraud in 1816, the Honourable Basil had taken over the victualling task from his brother John in 1796. Basil had gone out to India as a junior writer in the East India Company and had worked his way up to a senior position when he was involved in a scandal over the deaths of two Indian clerks who he believed to have been falsifying accounts. The story was that he had flogged them so badly in the attempt to get confessions that they both died. This turns out to have been a bit of an exaggeration, as one of them was found to be alive and well some time later, but the other had died several days after the flogging. The East India Company decided it was time to part company, and Basil, who by this time was already operating as Commissary to part of the army, moved over to concentrate on his personal business affairs, including that of victualling the Royal Navy on the East Indies station.

The terms of the contract under which he operated must, one assumes, have been acceptable at the time but to the modern eye they seem a masterpiece of charging not only very high rates for the provisions themselves, but very high rates for moving these provisions about and keeping them in stores. For instance, the price of a hundredweight of biscuit was 16s 6d at Calcutta, £1.14.0 at Bombay, and £2.10.6 at Prince of Wales Island (now Penang); and he charged two shillings per cask for moving casks from ships to his godown, the same for moving them from godown to ship, and one shilling per month while they were in the godown. His business went along quite nicely for ten years until he resigned and returned to England rather abruptly in 1806, when his friend Admiral Peter Rainier handed over the command to Admiral Edward Pellew. Whether, as has been suggested by C Northcote Parkinson, this was to evade an investigation into his victualling affairs is a moot point but on his return home he proceeded to bombard the Victualling Board with demands for payment. It took until 1818 to get his money out of them.[11] One small amusement in reading the Victualling Board papers relating to this ongoing saga is that the clerks who entered details of the incoming letters into the abstract books abbreviated 'Honourable' to 'Honble' with a flourish which makes it look, at a quick glance, as though the letters have come from 'the Horrible Basil Cochrane'; one hesitates to suggest that this was deliberate, but it could well have been the way those clerks thought of him!

One of the problems was that the Board had portioned out his accounts amongst several different clerks who had managed to lose half of the vouchers. He provided another set for the whole ten years' worth of transactions and offered to pay for a clerk to check them but this was refused. This saga included a court case over some £9000 which the Victualling Board said he owed them. This ended with a decision in Cochrane's favour: the Board actually owed him about £1000. Between 1818 and 1824, he published several long pamphlets, accusing the Victualling Board of incompetence on a grand scale. In the circumstances one can hardly blame him. The strange thing about this whole affair is that the Victualling Board could have dealt with the situation far less expensively by hiring its own warehouses in India and employing agents victualler to run them, because the East India Company had an agreement with the government to ship military supplies out to India free of charge.[12]

The Supply Chain

As well as using contractors to deliver provisions to the remoter victualling stations, the Victualling Board used them to supply raw materials and finished products to their British warehouses. Although they preferred to manufacture what they could, the Victualling Board was not in a position to cope with the fluctuating requirements of wartime and at the various times when the manning requirements increased substantially, they had to buy in beer, meat and biscuit from outside.

A system of competitive tendering was introduced to ensure the best possible prices; invitations to tender were advertised and as tenders were received, they were entered in a book and prices and quantities offered were compared; contracts were not necessarily awarded to one merchant for the whole of the annual requirement, but spread among several.[13] The conditions of tendering were firmly enforced. For instance, in April 1804 one of the largest firms of Irish contractors, Messrs Bogle, French & Co, headed a group which complained that they had not been awarded any of the contracts for that year. This complaint was rejected on the grounds that they had missed the required date for submission of tenders, as a result of which the contracts had already been awarded elsewhere. Later contracts also specified delivery in batches throughout the agreed period and this not only kept the amounts in store at a manageable level but also spread the payments over the year. This did not mean that provisions were never purchased outside the tender system. The minutes contain frequent reports of letters received from merchants offering supplies, which were sometimes accepted but more frequently refused because the Board had sufficient stocks or thought that the price was excessive.[14]

There was an ongoing concern over the development of monopolies and price-fixing and the Board was perfectly capable of deciding not to buy any particular item at all if the prices were excessive, as happened in the autumn of 1803 when there had been a prolonged drought. The normal tenders were invited for annual supply contracts of butter and cheese but when the tenders arrived the prices asked were all exceptionally high and on enquiry it was found that a group of speculators in Ireland had cornered the bulk of the supply on the assumption that the Victualling Board would pay whatever they were asked. The Victualling Board were not prepared to be taken advantage of in this way and recommended to the Admiralty that it would be 'expedient for the present wholly to suspend the issue of butter and cheese, and to substitute the issue of rice and sugar, tea and sugar, or cocoa and sugar…'. The Admiralty agreed, and an order was issued to this effect, remaining in place until the following autumn, when the Victualling Board suggested returning to an issue of butter and cheese, but at only half the usual quantity.[15] This particular incident shows another source of supply: when recommending that rice should be issued as a substitute, the Victualling Board remarked that they had 'a considerable quantity of East India rice' in store, bought from the East India Company at the Treasury's prompting.[16]

Manufacturing

Working on the premise that the best way to ensure quality was to manufacture provisions in their own yards, the Victualling Board brewed beer, slaughtered and packed meat, and baked biscuit at various locations in London and round the Channel coast. The three main manufacturing yards were at Deptford, Portsmouth and Plymouth, where at the busiest times there were up to 2400 tradesmen (brewers, butchers, bakers, coopers, storekeepers and labourers), all working away six days a week, and at various critical stages in the wars, being actively encouraged to work overtime.

Over half of these tradesmen were engaged in making casks, something the Board had decided they should do themselves after finding there was a monopoly operating amongst the main firms of coopers in London. Prices had risen at the onset of the American War when supplies of stave wood, traditionally imported from Virginia, were cut off. Attempts were made to obtain stave wood from Canada but with only minimal success and for some time there were complaints about the resultant casks. Either the heads were made of deal, which tainted the contents with the smell of turpentine, or the staves were unseasoned and warped as they dried out, making the casks leak. It was some years before the situation settled down, with stave wood eventually coming from various sources: the Baltic, Canada and Britain itself.

The general term 'cask' does not refer to a specific size but just means a wooden barrel, bound with iron hoops (or, for some smaller sizes, twisted withies). There were a number of standard sizes (listed in Appendix 1) but they were all the same shape: wider at the waist than the ends, which meant they interlocked when stacked. With the exception of bread, which was packed in bags, all the provisions were packed in casks, as were much of the ships' other stores; they were to the Georgian world what the shipping container is today. Unfortunately they did not last forever and although they were generally regarded as a returnable item, there was a constant need for new ones.

As with beer, the Victualling Board manufactured as much biscuit as it could but also had to buy a great deal from outside bakers. One of the largest of these was Moody and Potter of Southampton, conveniently close to Portsmouth; they also made biscuit for the army. Biscuit production is not something that can be increased overnight; new ovens have to be built and that takes time. Each oven was served by a team of five men who worked and shaped the dough, put it in the oven and took the cooked biscuits out, producing some seventy biscuits a minute. But that did not mean seventy per minute every minute of the working day. These were brick ovens, the principle of which is that they are heated by lighting a fire inside them to heat the bricks, then raking out the ashes and baking until the oven has cooled down, then starting again with another fire.

The fires were of wood. This was bought from outside until 1801, when an amusing little story unfolds in the Victualling Board letter files. The Victualling Board premises at Deptford were adjacent to the naval dockyard, where the Navy Board had been growing more and more annoyed over the years about abuse of the traditional shipyard workers' perquisite of 'chips'. Chips are offcuts of wood, and the workers were allowed to take these home for their domestic fires, but as inevitably happens, this privilege had come to be abused. A chip was defined as any piece of timber under three feet long, and just as happened with miners who sawed up perfectly good pit-props to take home, dockyard workers could be seen marching through the gates every evening with a neatly-cut piece of wood on their shoulders which measured exactly two feet eleven and three-quarter inches. It was said that most of the workers' houses near dockyards were built in multiples of this measurement. After a long struggle, the Navy Board had finally managed to put a stop to the practice. It was not many weeks before the Victualling Board received a letter from the Navy Board, remarking that they had some spare chips and wondered if the Victualling Board would care to have some rakes and peels made for the bakery? The Victualling Board would indeed like some, and shortly after another letter arrived to say the implements were ready. Then, a few days later, another letter arrived, this time nonchalantly remarking that the dockyard had rather a lot of chips to dispose of, and wondering if the Victualling Board would like them to fire its bread ovens.[17]

We do not know exactly how many bullocks and pigs passed through the hands of the Victualling Board's slaughtermen and butchers into barrels of brine at the depots, but some rough estimates can be made from the amounts of meat stated in the annual estimates: the figure given for 1797 of 110,000 men, gives about 23,000 bullocks and 115,000 pigs.[18] Even allowing for the fact that much of the beef (but not the pork) came from Ireland, the mind immediately turns to the sheer logistics of the task, given that it was a seasonal activity and thus compressed to about six months. It is not the actual saltable meat that makes the mind boggle, it is the by-products: the bits that would not salt down. The hides went off to make leather, the tallow was used for soap and cheap candles and the feet went to the glue makers. But the heads (less the ox-tongues), the bones and the offal, all had to be disposed of. The Victualling Board, of course, sold it, but that only shifts the problem; what did happen to it? The answer is that the bones and some of the offal went for agricultural fertiliser and the rest was made into cheap meat products: black and white puddings, sausage, meat pies, tripe and so on. But the suspicion lingers that a fair amount just got dropped in the river – hopefully when the tide was going out, when it would add to the richness of the estuarine mudbanks and help to fatten the crabs and oysters.

The last of the manufacturing activities in the victualling yards was brewing, which was done at London (at first at the Hartshorne Brewery at Tower Hill, then at Deptford), Portsmouth and Plymouth. It was particularly important that beer should be brewed at all three depots, as it does not take kindly to excessive shaking, and the additional handling involved in transporting it from London to the two Channel ports may have been too much for it, especially in bad weather. As with all other aspects of naval victualling, the Victualling Board received a steady stream of suggestions on different or 'improved' beers; for a while they toyed with the idea of replacing the small beer with the stronger porter which might have travelled better, and experimented with other schemes for concentrating the beer to save on space. None of these worked as well as had been hoped and so the idea was abandoned.

Storage

Having purchased or manufactured all these provisions, they were put into store at the various victualling yards to await ships' requisitions. As well as the three main victualling depots in London and the Channel ports, there were others round the British Isles, notably at Leith, Cork and Great Yarmouth, although the importance of the last waxed and waned as the locus of wars shifted. When the Dutch were the enemy, and when the Danes and other Baltic countries, including Russia, were involved, the squadrons operating in the North Sea and Baltic were augmented and Yarmouth became more important. In foreign parts, there were numerous victualling yards in locations which depended on the locus of any given war; Gibraltar was the oldest permanent yard, while others opened and closed as necessary.

All the British yards outside London were referred to as outports and these, like the main yard at Deptford and those on foreign stations, were run by an official called the agent victualler. This was an important man, earning a substantial salary – by 1800 between £400 and £600 per year, depending on the size of the yard he controlled, sometimes with an additional 15 shillings per day for 'table money' and sometimes with a house provided. Most of the clerks at Head Office earned £80 to £90 per year. The agent victualler had charge not only of the provisions in his stores but also the staff who ran them and the clerks in his office. However, at the home yards he did not control the manufacturing side. This was managed by the master tradesmen: the master brewer, master baker, master cooper and master butcher; they reported direct to the Board commissioner responsible for each type of product, as did the master hoytaker, who organised waterborne deliveries.

Not only were the different species of provisions stored appropriately (for instance, the butter and cheese were kept in cool cellars), they were all marked with numbers and letters which indicated where they came from and when. This was for two reasons: firstly so that any problems could be traced back to the origin and appropriate action taken; secondly so that nothing was kept too long; they had to be issued on a 'first in, first out' basis. The stories of salt meat many years old are exaggerations: the rule was a maximum of two years for meat and bread, six months for butter and cheese. We have already seen that the rule was enforced for butter and cheese; the same applied to everything else. The purser who tried to return to stores any item that he had kept beyond its 'use by' date was likely to be refused credit for it. This does not mean that no seaman was ever given very old food. The 'past use by' items were sent out of the victualling yards for sale by auction and it is quite possible that chandlers who supplied merchant ships bought it and sold it on to merchant captains and that is where some of the stories of ancient 'salt horse' originated.

The Delivery Chain

The best of the victualling yards were those where all the storehouses were close together and the items requisitioned by each ship could be assembled in one spot for collection. Some of the outports, notably Plymouth, had their victualling stores spread out over some distance, so collection parties from ships had to go to different locations to collect all their stores, or the agent victualler had to arrange for the hoytaker to organise boats to collect and deliver them. Of course, the larger the ship and the longer its intended voyage, the more of each item had to be provided and the longer it took to accept the full load and stow it all away. The picture of a busy naval port like Portsmouth with a large squadron arriving for restocking is one of potential chaos; in such circumstances the agent victualler had to be a master of organisation to avoid mistakes.

As well as the standard items of provisions, the agent victualler had to supply fresh meat and vegetables to ships while they were in port, and also to maintain and issue stocks of tobacco. He also had to provide pursers with 'necessary money', the cash with which they bought essential non-food items such as candles, stove fuel and turneryware for the men to eat off; and, if the ship was bound for places where there was no victualling yard, sufficient to buy small quantities of fresh food as well. All of this required a complex accounting system. Weekly details of stores received, issued and remaining had to be sent to London, quarterly accounts had to be prepared and submitted, and everything had to be ready for the annual commissioners' inspection.

The instructions to supply ships were of two sorts. Ships that were fitting-out were only allowed three days of provisions at a time, the purser putting in an application for sufficient provisions for the number of men on board during each three-day period, a number which increased as new batches of men joined the ship. This was known as 'extra petty warrant', and the rule still applied after the ship was commissioned and fully manned but still in the port, even if fully stocked with her 'sea' provisions. These sea provisions were specifically for use when the ship had left port; by using the extra petty warrant system it meant that when she did sail, it was with her main provisions still intact.

When a ship was newly commissioned (which term includes those ships which had a new commanding officer as well as those which were newly built or were coming back into use after being in Ordinary for a while), the order for her provisions started with the Navy Board. They sent an order to the Victualling Board for the named ship to be supplied with provisions for so many months for either Channel or foreign service. For Channel service the normal period was three or four months, for foreign service (never defined any more than that) it was usually six months. Sometimes the order just said 'all species of provisions'; sometimes it would be more detailed: 'four months of all species except for biscuit, of which three months,' or 'and as much beer as she can stow', or even 'as much beer as she can stow with due regard to her trim'. The main difference between supplies for Channel or foreign service was the type and amounts of alcohol: ships on Channel service were not meant to have spirits, ships for foreign service would only take three months' worth of beer, butter and cheese.

Having received this order from the Navy Board, the Victualling Board passed one copy of it to the appropriate agent victualler and one to the ship's captain, who produced it at the victualling yard. Once a ship was in commission and needed to top up her supplies, which they were encouraged to do at regular intervals, the paperwork was different and did not involve the Victualling Board head office or the Navy Board. Instead, a three-part form listed all the standard items, with spaces for the amounts required. The first part of the form certified that there was a want of those items, the second part ordered the agent victualler to deliver them, and the third part certified that they had been received on board. A different form, also in three parts, dealt with fresh beef, the difference between this and the previous form being that the agent victualler was required to furnish it 'from time to time, until further orders' with the third part certifying the total quantities received during the stay.

That worked well enough when ships came into port in small numbers and with time to spare. For the Channel Fleet, during the close blockade of Brest, the pressure to get large numbers of ships restocked and back on station led to a system where seven or eight merchant vessels, loaded with sufficient provisions for 15,000 men for one month, waited permanently at Dartmouth for the fleet to pass, then followed them in to Torbay and anchored by the fleet for transhipment. When St Vincent took over the command, he discouraged ships from returning to port for anything less than urgent repairs or seriously bad weather, instead arranging for victuallers to go to the fleet each month, carrying preserved provisions and supplies of fresh vegetables.

Victualling Yards Abroad

The task of the agents victualler on foreign stations was more complex than that at home. Unlike the agents at the British outports, who reported to the Victualling Board itself, the agents victualler abroad, although still employees of the Board and still obliged to account for stores and money under its rules, were under the immediate control of the commander-in-chief, through, if there was one, the naval officer or civilian commissioner in charge of the station. There was a fuss at the Victualling Office in 1811 when the agent victualler at Malta, Patrick Wilkie, had ordered a large quantity of bread and flour from a local supplier. The Victualling Board said he should not have done it and was personally responsible for the cost, some £5266. Wilkie replied that the new *Instructions for the Agents of the Victualling Establishments Abroad* said quite clearly that he must take orders from the senior naval officer on the station and that was what he had done. The Board had to back down and pay the Bills of Exchange which Wilkie had drawn and the senior officer, Admiral Boyles, had countersigned.[19] In such situations the agent victualler also had to provide full details, certified by three local dignitaries, of the current exchange rates. In a location such as Malta, where he had to supply necessary money for pursers to make purchases in various countries or small islands, he had to be able to provide this cash in several different currencies, each with its exchange rate listed in his accounts.

When the yard did any manufacturing, as several of them did, the agent victualler had responsibility for that operation. He also had to pay the wages for all the yard and office workers and see to the repair and maintenance of the yard premises. The final task for agents victualler, whether at home or abroad, was to take back into store empty casks and bread bags, and to accept, inspect and dispose of any returned provisions which had been condemned as inedible.

Transport Ships

One other way in which agents victualler on foreign stations differed from those at home, and for which there were detailed instructions, was in the necessity to deal with transport ships and 'victuallers'. In home outports, almost all the items which were not manufactured locally arrived by sea from Deptford, carried in transports which delivered their cargo and went away, usually back to London. The agent victualler would return empty casks and bread bags on them but that was all. On foreign stations, while some of the transports arrived from England and went back there, others would remain on the station under the commander-in-chief's command, and shuttle back and forth carrying supplies between the victualling yard and the more remote squadrons.

This was certainly the case in the Mediterranean. The main victualling yard for the Mediterranean station was at Gibraltar, at one end of a sea which was almost 2000 miles long end to end, and a minimum 400 miles across, and which was prone to some very contrary wind patterns. Add to this naval activities which might involve blockading Toulon (800 miles from Gibraltar), harassing the enemy in the Adriatic (some 1200 to 1500 miles from Gibraltar), convoying the Levant trade or supporting army activities in Egypt (1800 miles from Gibraltar), and you see why it was not feasible for ships to constantly return to Gibraltar to restock. There were supplementary bases at Port Mahon during the times when Minorca belonged to Britain and, after 1800, Malta, but these could also take many weeks of a ship's time for the round trip there and back to her operating station. So the commanders-in-chief used a system of rendezvous where the transports could meet them. This meant the agent victualler had to despatch bulk supplies on the transports as well as supply individual ships which arrived at the yard. Whether originating from the main yard at Deptford or from victualling yards abroad, it was the norm to load these victuallers with proportionate supplies of all items of provisions, thus ensuring that an accident or capture of one of a convoy of victuallers did not deprive the recipients of any given item. It was also normal, where the destination was one of the larger victualling yards abroad which employed coopers, to include sets of disassembled wine and water casks for those coopers to make up.

When the Royal Navy requires transport ships today, they use what are inelegantly termed 'STUFT' (Ships Taken Up From Trade), and much the same happened in Nelson's time. There had been a separate Transport Board between 1689 and 1714, but this had then been disbanded. In 1794 the Transport Board was reinstated to organise transports for all the different boards' purposes, but in the interim each board had arranged its own as and when needed, causing some confusion when the boards started bidding against each other for shipping. This had created major difficulties in the American War of Independence, when as well as the Navy Board and Victualling Board supplying the navy, and the Ordnance Board supplying both navy and army, the Treasury had been given the task of organising both food and other supplies for the army (and made a dreadful mess of the job, too), ending with a bidding war that pushed freight rates sky-high.[20]

Once the Transport Board had been set up again, it handled all the merchant shipping for all the other boards, and things went more smoothly. The Admiralty owned, or had on long-term hire arrangements, a few vessels known as store-ships, which were operated by naval personnel: for instance the *Hindostan* and the *William*, which operated in the Mediterranean after the Peace of Amiens broke down. However, in general the Transport Board chartered merchantmen as transport ships, under the same terms and conditions prevailing in the commercial market. These ships might carry a mixed cargo of naval stores and victuals, and often passengers (*Hindostan* carried numerous dockyard artificers out to the Mediterranean in early 1804, while others might carry some troops), in which case they were referred to as 'transports'. When their entire cargo was victuals, they were known as 'victuallers'. These ships were hired direct from their owners or through brokers, either on charter for the use of the whole ship at an agreed rate per ton, or on 'freight' terms (either weight or volume of goods carried) which theoretically meant the ship could carry other goods as well – an advantageous situation for the owners of the ship, as it was the Victualling Board's practice to give protection certificates to exempt the crews from impressment.

The Transport Board sent regular lists to the relevant commanders-in-chief of ships in use as transports for their station, showing which were on their way from England, which were already on station, and which were still loading. One of these lists, prepared for Nelson in 1804, shows eighteen ships already in the Mediterranean or on their way there, listing their tonnage, whether they were sheathed or coppered, and their charging rates per ton per month; the coppered ships were the most expensive. A secondary list shows sixteen others loading at Deptford, Woolwich, Portsmouth and Falmouth with a mixture of navy and army supplies. Accompanying these lists is a letter from the Transport Board asking Nelson to send home the ships on the first list as soon as those on the second list arrive, and retaining, if needed, 'the lowest priced coppered ships as generally most fit for the service'. Whenever possible, the returning ships were loaded with a useful cargo such as wine or lemon juice. All of this added yet another layer of tasks to the commander-in-chief's job, but it did allow him some flexibility of supply pickups.[21]

There were three other methods by which ships on foreign stations obtained provisions. The first was where the victualling was done by a contractor and where the man on the spot was an agent of the contractor rather than an agent of the Victualling Board. These contractors might be an individual, such as Basil Cochrane who supplied the navy in four separate locations (Bombay, Madras, Calcutta and Prince of Wales Island) as well as various sections of the army, or they might be a business firm based in London. As far as the pursers of the ships using these agencies were concerned, the procedure was more or less the same as for a Victualling Board yard: they produced the standard three-part form, the agent provided the provisions and the necessary paperwork for the pursers' accounts.

The second method applied at ports where there were no formal arrangements and where one or a few ships arrived needing provisions. Here, the purser took himself off to see the local British consul if there was one, or the local merchants if there was not, and bought what the ship needed. He had to provide certification that the prices he paid were the local norm, obtaining three signatures from local dignitaries (one of whom should be the Governor or Consul), or in situations where this was not possible, such as farmers' markets in towns where neither of these dignitaries existed, by taking some of the ship's officers with him to witness the purchases.

The third method was used, by the approval of the Victualling Board, on occasions when a large squadron was operating in an area of its station which was remote from its victualling port, and needed supplies of provisions which could not conveniently be provided by transports from that port. What was needed was someone who could go off and make arrangements for provisions to be assembled at a convenient place for the individual ships of the squadron to collect as and when required, or someone whose own ship was prepared to collect bulk supplies and take them back to the rest of the squadron. Sometimes this person was a senior purser, sometimes he was a special Victualling Board employee appointed from London to do the job.

Amongst the pursers who did this job were Thomas Alldridge, who was deputed to victual the squadron blockading Alexandria after the Battle of the Nile, Richard Booth, appointed by Nelson at Copenhagen, Richard Bromley, purser of *Belleisle* in the Mediterranean with Nelson, and William Fitzgerald, who was with Pellew at Ferrol. Alldridge bought various batches of provisions, including fruit and vegetables, from Cyprus, Syria and St Jean d'Acre, for a total cost of just under £3500; although he had offered to do the job 'without any profit', he was given an allowance of 2½ per cent on the total of the transactions (just about the equivalent of a year's salary for him). Richard Bromley also did a good job. In August, November and December of 1803, *Belleisle* collected bulk supplies of 987 cabbages, 42,201 pounds of onions, 272 bullocks and 142 sheep with 30 bags of fodder, first from Spain and then from the Maddalena Islands, each batch of which she had then taken back to the squadron cruising off Toulon.[22]

Richard Booth did not do so well. His appointed task was to buy fresh meat from Danzig for the fleet off Bornholm, having stated confidently that he could obtain this at a price of fourpence three-farthings per pound. Booth interpreted Nelson's instruction as meaning he could buy live cattle if necessary; he thought he had some 600 beasts lined up when he found that the local butchers had 'combined' against him to push the price up. He then went to a local firm of merchants, Messrs Solly & Gibson, and asked them to go to an inland cattle fair and buy some bullocks there. They did so, buying 744 beasts, but by the time these had been bought, driven to a pick-up point, fed and delivered to the ships, the price was higher than expected. Added to this, a combination of hot weather and ship manoeuvres caused the hides to become seriously maggoty and smelly by the time they could be got ashore and the agent who received them then had so many complaints from his neighbours that he had to get rid of them quickly at a give-away price. Apart from the annoyance to the captains of the ships, who rather unkindly blamed Booth for the nuisance to their ships of the maggots and smell of rotting hides, the end product was that meat which should have cost fourpence three-farthings per pound cost fivepence halfpenny. This was bad enough, but then both Booth and Solly & Gibson asked for a 2½ per cent commission on the deal, Booth because he said Nelson had promised it to him and Solly & Gibson because it was their normal commission. Nelson was all for giving it to Booth but the Victualling Board disagreed; they thought that since he had handed the job over to Solly & Gibson, they should have the commission and Booth should have no more than his 'reasonable expenses'. After much correspondence back and forth, the Victualling Board prevailed.[23]

William Fitzgerald's story is not a pretty one. He was sent to buy bread and flour, wine and cattle for the squadron in the countryside behind Corunna and Ferrol and took advantage of the situation to line his pockets. Among his little tricks was charging for 164 pipes of wine, when the receipts only showed sixty-six, and charging eightpence per pound for the cattle when the local going rate was fourpence halfpenny. He had falsified the certificates of market price by filling them in with invented names, and had persuaded the farmers from whom he bought cattle to sign receipts when they could not read English. The last document in this story refers to the file being passed to the Admiralty solicitor to start a fraud prosecution.[24]

Apart from this sort of thing, the main problem with using pursers to do this job was that not only did the purser have his own job to do (not something he could lightly hand over to someone else), his ship also had a job to do and could neither turn itself into a transport indefinitely nor hang around waiting for its purser to complete his transactions. The answer was a dedicated agent victualler attached to the squadron, or, as they came to be known, an agent victualler afloat. Nelson had asked for such a person soon after he arrived in the Mediterranean in 1803; this was not a precedent, as such dedicated agents victualler had been appointed before. There had been two in the eastern Mediterranean not long before – Nicholas Brown supporting the fleet of warships and troopships off the coast of Egypt and the Levant under Lord Keith, buying food from various places from Sicily eastwards, and William Wills doing the same job in the hinterland behind Alexandria. This was not the easiest of tasks, Wills explained when asking for a proper salary: when buying provisions he was at risk from 'the Bedouin and vagrant Turks who infest the desert around Alexandria', he was exposed to the plague and other diseases, and finally put to much expense by being quarantined at Malta and Gibraltar when he was trying to get home. The poor man had also had nearly £600 of the Victualling Board's money stolen from his house in Alexandria by a soldier, but since the culprit had been seen and was subsequently court-martialled (although the money was never recovered) and since there were no banks where the money could have been kept, Wills was absolved of responsibility. After some time, the Victualling Board agreed that he should be paid and awarded him a back-dated salary of £400 per annum.[25]

Although Nelson would have been aware of these two agents, and the many others who had done similar jobs, the precedent he quoted was 'Mr Heatley, who would find the Fleet in everything'.[26] Heatley was agent victualler at Lisbon, but had spent some time travelling round the western Mediterranean organising supplies for both the navy and the army during the Corsica campaign between 1794 and 1796. He seemed to be very good at this, writing in one letter of his success in finding food in Naples, Tuscany, Sardinia, Rome (where the Pope insisted neutral ships should be used) and Elba, where he had command of five biscuit ovens.[27] What he was not so good at was paperwork: by 1801 the Victualling Board was sending him sharp letters about his failure to produce proper accounts, which they complained was preventing them from passing the accounts of all the pursers he had dealt with.

Heatley replied that it was not his fault, but that of the clerk who should have completed them but who had absented himself from the office after a quarrel with another clerk; Heatley then asked to be relieved of his post and allowed to come home.[28] The Victualling Board agreed to this but sent out an audit team consisting of Commissioner Towry and a senior clerk, Richard Ford. With the exception of a few minor items, Heatley's accounts were passed, Towry returned to England and Ford stayed behind to take over as agent victualler at Lisbon (a short-lived appointment which ended with the Peace of Amiens in 1802). During the peace, Ford returned to work in the Victualling Office and at one point accompanied two of the commissioners on their annual inspection visit to the victualling yards at Chatham and Dover.

These experiences, together with his previous work in the Victualling Office in London, made Ford the perfect man to attach to Nelson as agent victualler afloat. The Victualling Board recommended him, Nelson's bankers Marsh & Creed reported to Nelson that he was well thought of, and he was duly appointed, given another Victualling Office clerk, John Geoghegan, as his assistant, and sent off to the Mediterranean to sort out Nelson's problem. In December, the Admiralty gave them a passage out on the storeship *Hindostan*, but for some reason she was delayed and Ford showed his initiative by changing ships, travelling as far as Gibraltar in the frigate *Diana* and then in the Third Rate *Donegal* for the last stage. He and Geoghegan arrived with the squadron off Toulon by the middle of February; *Hindostan* did not arrive in the Mediterranean until April, when she promptly took fire and sank in Rosas Bay near Barcelona (fortunately with no loss of life, but with a quantity of Nelson's personal supplies).

Ford took up the reins immediately, his first task being to take charge of the residue of public money which Nelson had been holding. This was 1050 'hard' or Spanish dollars (a currency which was in common use in the commerce of the western Mediterranean and which was currently worth just over $5 to £1 sterling); James Cutforth, the agent victualler at Gibraltar had supplied Nelson with $6000, most of which he had issued to the pursers of his squadron to buy provisions. Ford's accounts show that this was not reimbursements of specific sums spent, but small tranches of money for use when needed, varying from $200 for the frigates to $800 for the First Rate *Victory*.

Ford's next task, having received a further tranche of $12,000 from Cutforth, was to pass some $3000 to the pursers so they could pay the crews their long-awaited money for short allowances and savings of provisions over the past year. This was something which, as Ford pointed out in his first progress report to the Commissioners for Victualling, was not covered in his instruction letter, but Nelson had given him written instructions to proceed. Another difficulty with his instructions which he pointed out in this report was the requirement that receipts for purchases should be witnessed by two commissioned or warrant officers. His buying trips to the Maddalena Islands had already demonstrated that this was impractical as he had only been able to buy cattle in small lots from different sellers at places some five or six miles from where the fleet was anchored, and since payment had to be made at the time of purchase (without any warning of the sellers arriving with their cattle), complying with this instruction would have meant officers having to attend him all the time. He would, he said, therefore fall back on the alternative of providing certificates of market prices from the consul or local merchants. His final comment in this report was that as four victuallers had arrived, the fleet 'amounting to nine sail of the line' was 'now completed to five months victualling of all species'.[29]

This comment did not mean that his task was over for the time being. The nine ships he had referred to were only those with the commander-in-chief; there were a further thirty-three naval vessels in the Mediterranean at that time, and 'complete of all species' did not include wine or the desirable fresh food on which Nelson was so keen. There were also future supplies of beverages to be organised, so Ford now set off on a series of investigating and buying trips which continued throughout his service in the Mediterranean. His first trip, in March, was to Barcelona and Rosas, with a specific instruction to buy 200 pipes of wine, 30,000 oranges, 20 tons of onions and 50 sheep 'for the use of the sick and convalescent'. Ford carried a letter of introduction from Nelson to the Rosas merchant Edward Gayner, which also expressed concern over the difficulties being raised by the Spanish authorities over supplying bullocks, sheep and other items.

The obstacles created by the Spanish authorities ranged from rigidly enforcing export duties on various products and export restrictions on live animals to treating naval personnel with a level of insolence which caused Nelson to complain to the British minister in Madrid, John Hookham Frere. Ford could do nothing about the insolence, but he shared with the locally-based British merchants an ability to think laterally when dealing with Customs personnel. One of the merchants in Barcelona, Walsh, had suggested that if necessary he would deliver wine by neutral vessels and Gayner had remarked that even if Spain declared war against Britain, he was confident that the wine he was holding for the fleet would not be confiscated, which implies that he knew who was 'persuadable'. Ford, when reporting to Nelson from Rosas, remarked about cattle;

> ... they are in a great degree prohibited from exportation. The last that we had put on board the *Active* were without the public permission of the Revenue officers at Rosas tho' with their knowledge and coment [*sic*].

This may explain the entry in his accounts, after 'Duties on the live cattle' and 'Ditto on the slaughtered' of 'Paid Customs House officers'. On the matter of sheep, he said;

> The sheep sent by the *Niger* for the use of the sick were obtained without the knowledge of the officers of Customs, who refused my application to ship so large a number in consequence of [an] order from the Spanish government. It was therefore necessary to provide them by other means.

Gayner seems to have been the most useful of the merchants in Catalonia and Ford was in regular contact with him during this period. As well as organising live beasts, vegetables and lemons and oranges, Gayner supplied wine itself and organised the manufacture and repair of casks. In June, when Ford was having difficulty in obtaining a supply of water at Rosas, Gayner agreed to fill casks and get them out to the ships at a better price than any of the other offers. He had also gone to the aid of the crew and passengers of the transport *Hindostan* after the fire, finding and paying for their accommodation and food. Nelson made sure that he was reimbursed for his costs in that matter, and was moved to write to the Admiralty secretary William Marsden and suggest that for this and for the fact that he 'had on every occasion furnished us with articles prohibited by the Spanish government, without a motive of pecuniary reward' Gayner should be given some sort of official recognition; the Lords of the Admiralty agreed with this suggestion and Gayner was presented with a 100-guinea silver cup. Nelson did not mention in that letter that Gayner was also feeding him with intelligence information, but he was clearly a very useful contact in what was about to become an enemy country. Alas, poor Gayner was thrown into prison in Barcelona when the Spanish declared war against the British in late 1804; so far the author has not been able to find out what happened to him after that.

There was, however, the constant concern over whether Spain would declare war against Britain and it was therefore necessary to explore other sources of supply. Apart from Sardinia and the Maddalena Islands, where Ford did buy substantial supplies, he began to investigate Sicily and much later, Tangiers. There is no indication that he ventured further east than Sicily or attempted to obtain provisions from Naples, where there was a risk that the French spies who infested the city would pass the word back to Bonaparte, who was thought to be seeking an excuse to invade. While Nelson was alive, the majority of purchases arranged by Ford were from Catalonia and the Maddalena Islands, but later he rented a house and storehouses in Palermo and made some purchases from North Africa. He was buying on a far greater scale than Bromley had done; within five months of his arrival, he had bought 1627 cattle, 219 sheep and lambs with fodder, 70,416 gallons of wine, 30,326 gallons of brandy, 99 cases of lemons, 21,300 oranges, over 30,000 pounds of onions, 913 cabbages and various other small amounts of 'vegetables' (undefined), soft bread, fresh beef, rice and sugar.

He continued to perform at this level for the rest of his time in the Mediterranean. We are fortunate in having a lot of documentation about him: his detailed appointment letter, which runs to twenty-four long clauses and reads very much like the printed instructions for victualling agents abroad, his accounts and his letter book. We also have some personal information, including his will, which shows that he left his house and other property to his sister Susannah. Neither she nor Richard ever married, which would explain why he was happy to move out to the Mediterranean for several years. At the end of 1807 both Ford and Geoghegan left the Mediterranean, Geoghegan to be agent victualler at Rio de Janeiro and Ford to return to London where the post of Accountant for Cash had fallen vacant. Ford was next in line for this job, which carried the substantial salary of £750. He may, by this time, have grown tired of dashing round the Mediterranean; he may also not have got on as well with Collingwood as he had with Nelson, or perhaps he thought it would be too long before another similar vacancy came up again. He was obviously a man of comparatively humble origins: despite his elevated position, he was still referred to as plain Mr Ford, not the coveted 'Richard Ford, Esquire' which would have marked his rise to the status of gentleman, and his letter requesting a pay rise when he was in London with Nelson in 1805, is in terms which are just on the borderline between due deference and grovelling.

Nelson clearly liked Ford; he took him along on the dash to the West Indies after the French fleet in 1805, and he wrote his own letter to the Victualling Board supporting Ford's request for a pay rise. Knowing that Gayner was feeding Nelson with intelligence, it is not unreasonable to suspect that Ford, who visited Gayner regularly, may have been carrying that information back to *Victory* every time he returned to her. Ford was 31 years old when he joined Nelson in the Mediterranean, having joined the Victualling Board in 1790 at the age of 18; he retired in 1826 and died in 1836. We cannot be certain that he was multilingual, but it seems likely that he was, from the facility with which he dealt with merchants and farmers in Spain, Sicily, Sardinia and Morocco and the fact that at the end of the war in 1814, when it was decided to sell off the remains of Wellington's supplies at Corunna rather than bring them home, Ford was recommended to go out and deal with this, being 'well qualified' for the task. There are a few passages of standard contract phrases at the beginning of his letter book in Italian but these are as likely to be for the benefit of his clerk as himself. What does come across strongly from the information we do have is that he was a man of high business acumen and resource; one of the unsung heroes on Nelson's team who beavered away in the background and enabled the fighting teams to stay on station and do their work. There must have been many more like him.[30]

Chapter 3

ADMINISTRATION ON BOARD SHIP

LIFE AT SEA in the Georgian navy was conducted under four levels of regulations: those issued by the various departments of the Admiralty which applied to the whole of the navy; additional general orders issued by the commanders-in-chief of individual fleets which applied to all the ships under their command; additional general orders applying to ships in detached squadrons issued by the squadron commander; and additional instructions issued by the commanding officers of individual ships which applied only to that ship.

The regulations issued by the various subsidiary boards of the Board of Admiralty were known as the *Regulations and Instructions Relating to His Majesty's Service at Sea* (hereafter 'the *Regulations*'). At irregular intervals, these were gathered together and re-issued in printed and bound form under an Order in Council; each version built on what had gone before and as time went by, each became more elaborate and detailed. For instance, the thirteenth edition, published in 1790, consisted of 232 pages, with a few printed forms bound into the volume at the appropriate places; by 1806 the fourteenth edition had almost doubled to 440 pages with a separate section of 29 forms at the back. These forms, which included such things as muster sheets and pursers' accounting forms, were also available separately. It was, however, acceptable to use a hand-written version. Although it was the responsibility of each level of commanding officer to ensure that everyone below him adhered to the *Regulations*, separate chapters were addressed to the relevant commissioned or warrant officers.

General orders given by commanders-in-chief added to the *Regulations*, partly as a matter of that officer's personal views on discipline and partly to cover local conditions. These orders were usually issued in the commander-in-chief's name by the senior captain of the fleet; copies of these orders were entered in a separate letter book where they are typically shown as being addressed to 'the respective captains'.[1] For example, Nelson issued an order on procedures to be followed when obtaining provisions from locations where there was no agent victualler, this order stating firstly that it was the master's responsibility to check the goods against receipts or bills of lading and to enter details of these transactions in the logbook, which was then to be signed as correct by 'the Captain or other signing officers'; and secondly that all fresh beef coming on board was to be weighed 'in the presence of a lieutenant or the master' before the receipts were signed. A copy of each of these orders would be sent to each captain as it was issued, and a set of them to any new captains who joined the fleet. There were several of these orders immediately after Nelson joined the Mediterranean Fleet in 1803, with others following at longer intervals. This was the normal pattern when any commander-in-chief took over his new command.

One common general order from commanders-in-chief and squadron commanders referred to regular reports on amounts of provisions on each ship. These were usually required weekly and there seem to have been two basic formats: either the specific amount of each species of provision, or the number of days or weeks the items in store would last. Similar reports were required for other types of stores, such as cordage or sailcloth, the numbers of sick with their ailments, and finally the state of the ship itself. The object of this exercise was to allow the senior officer to decide when any particular ship should go into port, or when to organise transports to bring supplies. There are substantial collections of such reports for both Keith and Nelson and it is quite noticeable that the provisions reduce over the weeks and then suddenly increase for all ships at the point at which transports are known to have arrived. This checks out with the logs, and something else which is apparent is that somebody was organising transfers of provisions between ships in a squadron. Ship A's logs will show her receiving, say, bread from Ship B and giving beef to Ship C, and at the same time passing pease to Ship B and oatmeal to Ship D. The captains also did it between themselves when the rest of the squadron was elsewhere: Ship E sights a sail which turns out to be Ship F, a signal requests a lieutenant to come aboard and a couple of hours later, some provisions are received or sent across. Almost as often one ship will go off to port for some repairs and bring back supplies for the others; this will most commonly be fresh vegetables or livestock.

The Captain and the Provisions

Fictional ships' captains, when not playing whist or the violin, appear to spend all their time directing gunnery drill or engaging in bloody battles. Real ships' captains, although they did do these things, actually spent a lot of time dealing with administration and paperwork, including that relating to the provisions. As well as checking those weekly reports for the commander-in-chief, which would have been prepared by the purser and, where water was concerned, by the master, and making sure that the appropriate vouchers had been exchanged when stores were passed from ship to ship, he was required to ensure that the right amounts of provisions came aboard in port or from victuallers (but forbidden to stop a victualler bound for another ship). Of course he had a clerk to do the main part of this work but his was the ultimate responsibility and his the salary that could have an imprest placed against it if the paperwork did not tie up.

The principle of imprests was one which operated throughout the Royal Navy, from warrant officers to admirals and from agents victualler to major contractors. Every time a financial transaction took place, the cost was charged to someone's salary or business account and stayed there until their accounts could be passed. When the captain decreed an extra issue of wine for the sick, it was charged to his salary. When an agent victualler abroad made a local purchase and paid for it by a Bill of Exchange, as soon as the Bill had been presented to the Victualling Board and paid, that amount was charged to the agent victualler's salary. When a victualling contractor like Basil Cochrane bought supplies with his own money, that amount was the subject of an imprest to his account. The system operated on a 'guilty until proven innocent' basis, and proving your innocence could take many years. In the middle of the argument with Basil Cochrane, the Victualling Board remarked to the Admiralty that it was their practice not to finalise accounts until the agency was closed. Basil Cochrane's agency opened in 1796 and closed in 1806, by which time his account bore an imprest totalling £1,418,236.6.9. In that year, the total amount of imprests on agents and storekeeper's accounts alone (*ie* not counting pursers or captains) was almost £11,000,000.[2]

The same principle was applied to warrant and commissioned officers. Their account started when the ship was commissioned or when they joined her, and did not cease until the ship was paid off, which could be many years later. Everyone was meant to submit quarterly accounts, but because the Victualling Board insisted on seeing original documents, and because no-one with any sense was going to risk sending those off by another ship which might be captured or suffer other disasters, those accounts went off with copy vouchers and sat in the Victualling Office limbo for years until the originals could be produced. Add to that the Victualling Board's insistence on seeing and finalising both sides of every transaction and you get, as we saw with Heatley in Chapter 2, a situation where dozens of pursers' accounts were held up because those of the agent victualler were not finalised. Small wonder that barely a day went by without the letter files containing a plea from some officer (or his widow or executors) for his accounts to be passed despite missing vouchers. (For more information on Bills of Exchange and imprest accounts, see Appendix 5.)

Another little bit of penny-pinching from the Victualling Board was their reluctance to allow the possibility of accidents. If, say the *Regulations*, through the carelessness of the men handling it, some item of provisions was lost when coming aboard, it was to be charged to their wages. This happened on *Leviathan* in 1804, when a bag of bread was dropped between boat and ship, a common enough situation when two men were tossing it and one let go too soon. The fuss about this went on for days, while the rescued bagful was spread out to dry and inspected and a decision made on how much was still usable.[3] And all of this, of course, was the captain's problem, as he had to make the decision on who to charge and how much, and then pass a voucher to the purser who also had to account for it. It was also technically the captain's decision, when pork ran short, to declare that beef should be served instead; of course what really happened here was that the purser would report on the shortage and suggest the substitute and the captain would give him a written order to do it. The same applied when overall shortages occurred and food had to be rationed.

The final aspects of the provisions which required the captain's attention were those relating to quality and fairness. He had to see that certain items, such as biscuit, were checked over regularly and any incipient problems dealt with; to ensure that food was shared out fairly (especially fresh meat); and generally ensure that the men were fed properly. A common entry in captains' orders is one that says when a cooked meal is about to be served, a portion is first to be taken to the officer of the watch for sampling. Quite what should have happened if that sample was declared inedible is not stated but one can imagine the panic and demands for the keys to the cheese store!

The captain's orders were entered in the ship's order book, which was kept where it was available to anyone who wanted to read it – often attached to the binnacle. These orders expanded on the *Regulations*, and typically would state the times at which food was to be issued and who was to hold the keys to various storerooms. Officers were expected to be familiar with the whole and many kept their own copies of the portions which covered their personal responsibilities.[4] As above, there was typically a flurry of new orders when a new captain took over a ship, with the number and type of orders depending very much on the character of the captain. Those from Prince William Henry (later to be William IV), who was a real control-freak, run to many more pages than the normal and amongst other nit-picking, require everybody, including the senior lieutenants, to ask for permission every time they wanted to leave the ship.[5]

The Master and the Provisions

For the master, the *Regulations* which outline his duties with regard to the provisions appear, on the face of it, to be quite simple, covering the receipt and stowage of provisions and liquids, seeing them brought up from the hold and observing the quantities present when casks or bags were opened or fresh meat brought on board, having responsibility for the spirit room and making a daily report to the captain on the quantities of beer and water consumed and the amount remaining. The reality was far more complex.

The easiest of these tasks was checking that the quantities within casks tallied with the quantities marked on the outside. A group of officers assembled for this job: the master, a lieutenant, the purser and perhaps the boatswain. The cask would be opened and the contents carefully checked. With beef or pork it was simply a matter of counting the pieces and recording them in the purser's journal and the ship's logs: for instance 'opened 3 casks pork of 50 pieces, No 12 5lb short, No 13 5lb short, No 14 4lb short; opened 1 cask beef No 2154, 38 pieces, 12lb over'. This would be done in the vicinity of the galley and the pieces would go into the steep tubs under the cook's eye. Other provisions would be opened in the purser's steward's room, transferring them into different containers and weighing them in the process, using a steelyard suspended from a beam. Again, shortages or excessive quantities were recorded in the logs and purser's journal. Miscounts of contents in meat casks are very frequent, too many pieces in the cask being almost as common as too few. To take just one example, on *Triumph*, between July 1803 and June 1804, the master reported opening ninety-one casks of meat; only one contained the weight marked on the exterior; twenty-three were overweight (by up to fourteen pounds for the pork, thirty-two for the beef) and sixty-seven were underweight (by up to twenty pounds for the pork, thirty-two pounds for the beef).[6]

Exactly how liquids were measured when casks were opened has not been recorded; it could have been with a dip-stick, or by emptying the cask from the bung into a measuring jug. There might have been some temptation to broach beer casks and steal the contents; there would have been far more with wine or spirits. One sequence of reports of wine in *Triumph* does cause one to wonder just what was going on. In December 1803, after receiving a sequence of complaints about faulty casks delivered by one particular transport, Nelson had issued a general order that the contents of every cask was to be measured and recorded in the log book when it was opened.[7] Between 3 February and 4 July 1804 *Triumph* reported twenty-six faulty casks with losses of between four and eleven gallons. The reasons given, although acceptable at first, begin as time goes on to sound rather like the increasingly unlikely excuses of 'food poisoning' or 'migraine' which alcoholics offer as a reason for not turning up at work on Mondays: 'split stave', 'broke stave', 'bad joint in head', 'bad knot in stave'. After a while, you begin to wonder whether Nelson's warning about faulty casks had provided a convenient excuse for pilferage. Most of the losses were under six gallons, and they did not increase consistently as time passed as one might expect from casks which were faulty when received. Equally, one might expect after the first few were found that the master and purser would have had the whole lot up to inspect and measure, but there is no indication that this was done.

Spirits were less easy than wine or beer for the unauthorised to get at. A clever petty officer could, however, organise himself a supply of extra grog by taking charge of the empty spirit cask after its contents had been issued. Filled with fresh water and left for a couple of days, the remains of the spirits in the wood would permeate the water and produce quite a strong liquor. A wise purser would see the empty casks rinsed out with salt water and left on deck to air; there was otherwise a risk of explosion from the vapour if the bung was removed with a candle close by.[8] Fully aware of the risks, both to the spirits from thieves and from the spirits themselves as a fire risk, the *Regulations* required that they were kept in a separate spirit room which, like the powder room, was fully lined and plastered and lit from a separate light room, and that it was kept locked except at the specific times stated for issue. No lights were allowed in the spirit room itself, and spirits were only allowed to be served on the open deck, in daylight and with no candles in the vicinity.[9]

It was at this point, of opening up containers of provisions, that most of the quality problems would be found. The procedure in such cases was that the container would be set aside, or if spirits, marked and returned to the spirit room, until a survey could be arranged. The term 'survey' was used in several ways: it could mean a stock-take; it could mean inspecting something to see if it was worn out and no longer usable, as in the case of an old sail (or even a sick human being), or defective and unusable, as in the case of provisions. In each case, the survey would be carried out by three commissioned or warrant officers, usually from other ships. For such things as boatswains', carpenters' or sailmakers' stores, it would be three of that sort of warrant officer; for the sick, it would be three surgeons; for a purser's stores it was more likely to three masters, perhaps because it was felt that they would be less sympathetic to misdemeanours. Whatever the type of item to be surveyed, its nominal 'owner' would ask the captain for a survey to be carried out and he arranged for the relevant officers to come aboard and do the survey. With provisions, if they agreed the items were inedible, they signed a formally-worded statement to that effect. Occasionally, when these provisions were so bad they were 'stinking, rotten and a nuisance to the ship', they would be thrown overboard, but otherwise they were supposed to be returned to victualling yard stores at the next opportunity. Some items, such as butter or ox-hides from beasts slaughtered on board, were meant to be offered for the boatswain's use.

The next part of the master's duties with provisions was to see them brought on board and check quantities against the receipts or bills of lading. Sometimes they would be delivered to the ship by a hoy, other times a boat or party of men had to be sent to collect them, under the charge of a lieutenant or midshipman. Small casks and bags of bread or vegetables could be carried in a pinnace but for larger casks and large quantities of supplies, the launch or longboat would be used.[10] Logs frequently report receiving provisions by the launch or sending the launch to transports for provisions.

It has been suggested that seamen's skills were adequate to make direct ship-to-ship transfers of provisions; this is theoretically possible, using cables and 'traveller' blocks. It would, however, require a level sea, a high degree of seamanship and two captains with nerves of steel and the certainty of a forgiving commander-in-chief.

Stowing the Provisions

Spirits, as we have seen, were kept in a separate locked room. This was usually situated aft, under the cockpit; as well as being locked it would also have a marine posted to guard it. In the days when salt or dried fish were carried, this would be in a separate room, also aft. Even after fish was dropped from the official ration, the fish room retained its name, although it tended to be used as a coal store. Bread (*ie* biscuit) was kept in the bread room, right aft, where the shape of the hull kept it sufficiently high up to be clear of bilge water.

Everything else, from water to raisins (with the exception of fresh meat and possibly vegetables and fruit) was kept in the hold; exactly where required the master to exercise some skill if the trim of the ship was not to be adversely affected. Consider the weight of provisions and beverages that had to be carried, and the not inconsiderable weight of the casks themselves (tare weight), and you can appreciate the magnitude of the problem.[11] The basic ration works out at about eleven pounds per man per day, but to this you must add the weight of brine in the meat casks and the water needed for steeping and cooking. These are difficult to calculate, but a total per day, including these, of fifteen pounds would not be unreasonable. Multiply this figure by the number of men on a ship and the time for which they must be provisioned, and you get this result:

Ship	*No of men*	*Tons daily*	*Tons weekly*	*Tons monthly*	*Tons three-monthly*
First Rate	850	5.7	39.9	159.6	479
Third Rate	640	4.3	30.1	120.4	361
Frigate	250	1.7	11.9	47.6	143
Sloop	120	0.8	5.6	22.4	67

NB.1 ton = 2240 pounds. The Royal Navy used the lunar month of 28 days. It was customary to stock with water for only half the period for which food stocks were loaded.

These are speculative figures, but can be more or less confirmed by a list of provisions carried by the frigate *Doris* when she set off for the west coast of South America in 1821. Stored for 240 men for four months, she carried 107 tons of water, 14 tons of biscuit, 12 tons of salt meat (plus, of course, an unspecified amount of brine), about 4 tons of pease, oatmeal, sugar, cocoa, lime and lemon juice and tobacco, and just short of 6 tons of spirits; a total of 141 tons. She also called at Madeira *en route*, where she picked up 10 pipes (4 tons) of wine.[12]

Although the figures for the sloop are considerably less than those for a First Rate, the comparative sizes of the ships made them just as important. The master's problem is two-fold: keeping the ship trimmed, and at the correct draught, both essential to preserving the ship's sailing qualities. The problem of trim required everything to be stowed so that each day's removals balanced out over the course of a few days; for this the master would direct exactly what was stowed where, keeping in mind the rule of 'oldest to be used first', and then direct which items were to be taken out each day. They must all have drawn up plans of this stowage; some of them copied these plans into their logs.

The draught problem could be extreme. Consume too much of the hold's contents and the ship will lighten and rise in the water, becoming, since she carries a lot of weight in her guns, top-heavy and at risk of capsizing in rough weather. However, there was plenty of handy stuff to correct the problem: seawater. Many logs report filling water casks with seawater when the fresh water is getting low. One wonders to what extent they then flushed out these casks after emptying the salt water, or whether they just drank it slightly brackish. It cannot have tasted any worse than some of the stuff they got from Deptford Creek (although they did finally pipe water in from the Ravensbourne, a small river which ran into Deptford Creek above the tidal level).

The basic rule on stowage was to keep the largest casks at the lowest level. The bottom of each hold was ballasted, first with pigs of iron and then with a layer of shingle, deep enough for the bottom tier of casks to nestle in. The ideal was 'bung up and bilge free' (the bung being in the widest part of the cask), but the shingle would inevitably become wet and often foul. Quite apart from the water continually making its way down the ship (and consider the state of the water that came off an anchor cable which had been lying on the bottom of a harbour where every ship's head vented into the water), there must have been many men who, although this was strictly forbidden, found shingle ballast more inviting than the seats of ease exposed to the weather. There are stories of noxious gases being generated, so powerful that men in the hold would be overcome by them. It was another of the master's responsibilities to ensure that the shingle ballast was 'clean and sweet'. There were only two ways to do this: let in seawater and pump it out again, as many times as it took to flush all the foulness out, or remove all the shingle and replace it with fresh. This laborious task, which involved shovels and baskets, was slow work. On one occasion when the master's log for *Victory* reports this operation (emptying first one hold completely and reballasting, then moving the stores before repeating the exercise with the other), she dumped almost seventy tons of shingle ballast overboard before restowing her holds, and the operation took five days to complete.[13] At the same time, she refilled all her water casks to the total capacity of 315 tons.

Casks were stowed in rows lengthways down the hold, with perhaps a few crossways at either end. Once the bottom tier was in place, a second tier of smaller casks could be put on top in between the rows, wedged in to stop them shifting. There would be three or four rows in the bottom tier and there might, on larger ships, be a third tier on top. The smaller ships may not have used the larger sizes of casks.

Despite the 'bilge free' ideal, that bottom tier of water casks would be almost permanently lying in wet shingle. This must have led to early deterioration and would explain the constant plaint from commanders-in-chief on all stations of the difficulties of maintaining stocks of water- and wine-casks, this despite the rule that ships going on foreign service were to be supplied with new casks. The Victualling Board were very fussy about casks; water- and wine-casks were never to be 'shaken' (*ie* taken to pieces) except in 'absolute necessity' and then must be bundled with their hoops and labelled so they could be reassembled easily. It was undesirable to shake other casks, but often necessary to make it possible to get at the middle row of water casks. It is often suggested that food casks were automatically shaken to save space but on reflection, with the exception above, space may not have been an issue. You mainly need space to put supplies in, those supplies are going to come already packed in casks, in which case you can dispose of the empties and get

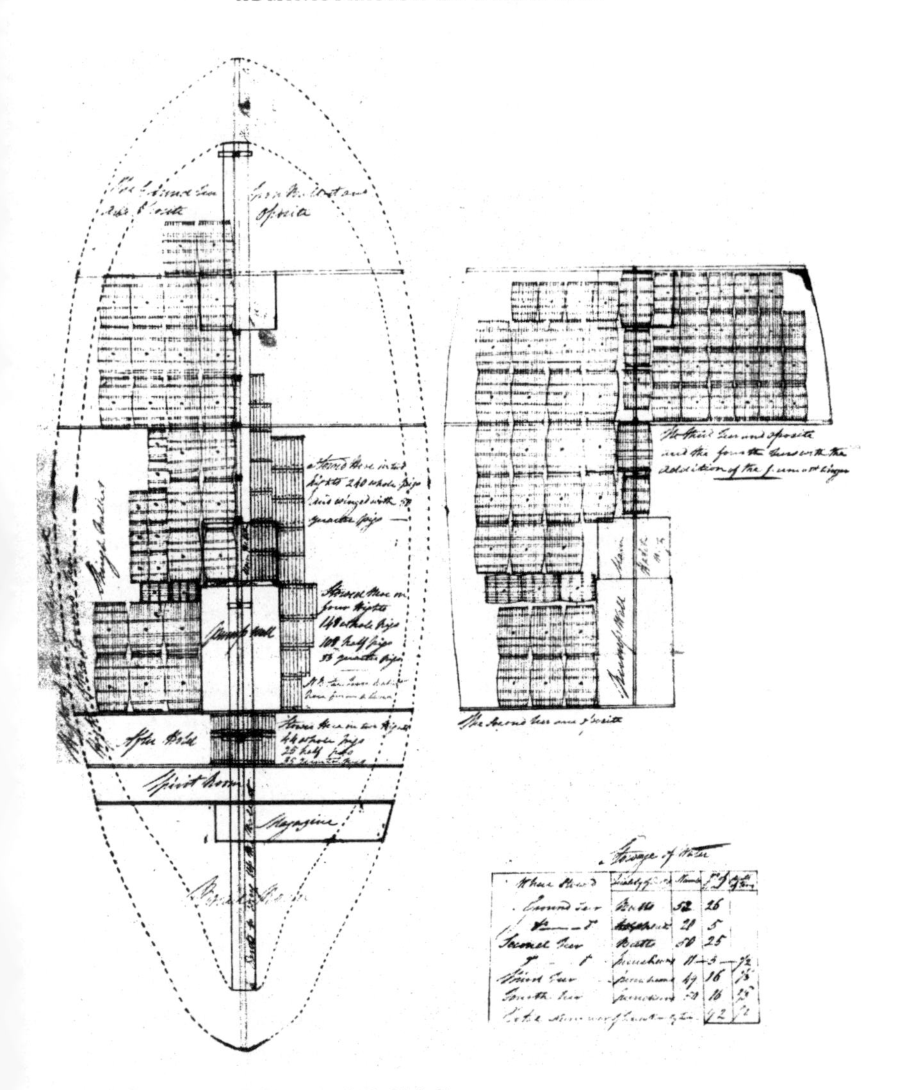

The traditional method of stowing the hold (left) and orlop deck in the frigate *Galatea*, December 1802. Stowage was clearly dominated by the weight and volume of the laden casks – in this configuration the ship stowed a total of 92½ tons of water – which was vitally important for the trim and stability of the ship, and hence its sailing qualities. (*PRO Adm 95/41*)

a bigger credit for them if they are whole and the recipient does not have to pay a cooper to reassemble them. Of course, ships which were carrying such large quantities of supplies that they could not fit them all in the hold (for instance those going on very long voyages, or carrying troops) would store these on the decks, use these first and then shake them; others might do it when needing space to clear for action.

Theoretically, most ships, especially the larger ones, had a cooper on board. There is a special pay rate for them shown in the *Regulations* and sometimes a commander-in-chief mentions them in his correspondence; for instance, Sir James Borlase Warren offered to lend the flagship's cooper to the victualling yard for a few days when he was on the North America station in 1808.[14] However, there are also some remarks in the Victualling Board papers about the difficulty of persuading coopers to volunteer, given that they were in a 'reserved' occupation on a high wage, and a survey of muster and pay books for line-of-battle ships and frigates found them listed on less than a third of the ships, and those not necessarily First Rates.[15] This does not mean no-one ever touched the casks when there was no qualified cooper on board – any competent carpenter can do what is necessary to remove the head from a barrel and put it back, and shaking a cask is simplicity itself – but it takes a very skilled man with special equipment to put a set of staves and hoops together to produce a watertight cask. Perhaps the rule was to provide coopers in only sufficient numbers to do this for a whole squadron, although a cooper's duties would have included making small tubs and buckets for use in the sick-bay and elsewhere.

One other thought which comes to mind about water casks is the business of 'starting' the water as a method, much loved by writers of naval fiction, of quickly lightening the ship when chasing or being chased. The theory of this is that you start the casks in the hold and then pump the water out using the ships' main pumps. However, given that the casks were stored, as we saw above, bung up, one suspects that there was only one way to empty them quickly and that was to take an axe to them. Because they were stowed end to end, it would not be possible to knock in the heads, so it would have to be the staves that went; however, this could only be done with the specific (*ie* documented) instructions of the captain.[16]

Each ship had two or more holds, although these would not necessarily be

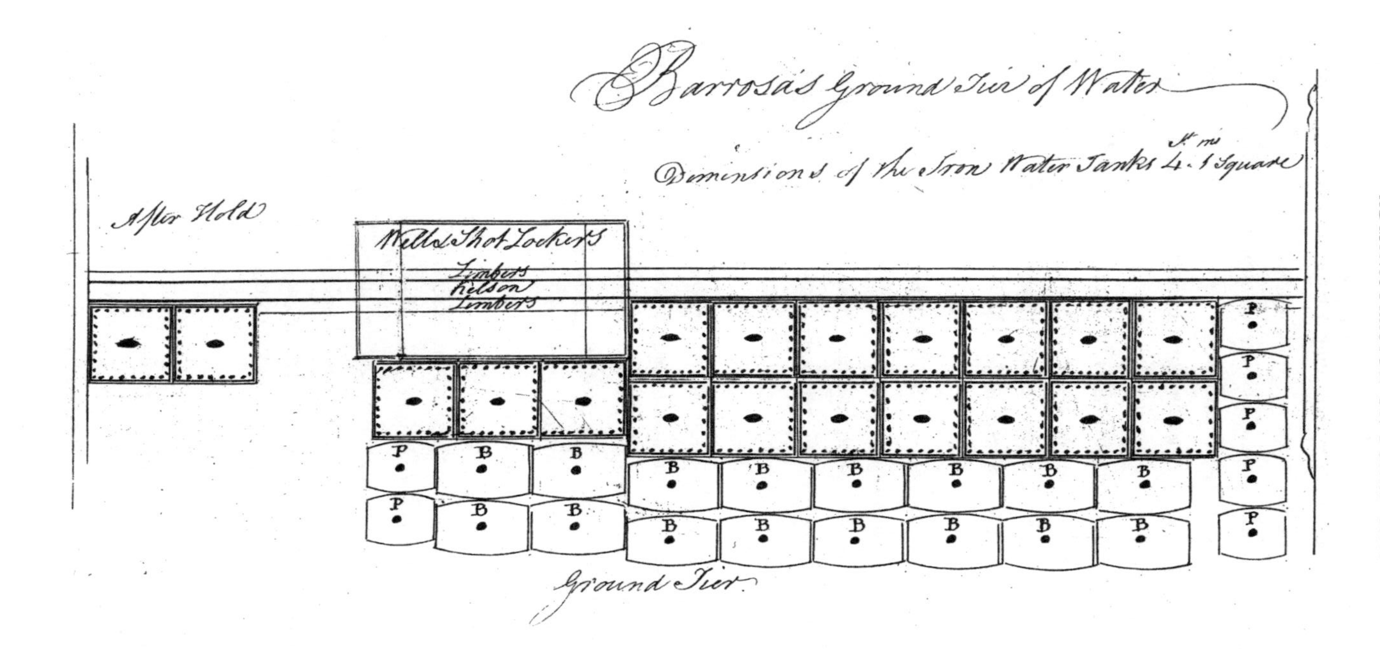

The stowage of a frigate's hold after the introduction of iron water tanks, 1812. The tanks held about 400 gallons, far more than even the largest cask, but the real advantage was the lack of wasted space in a tier of close-fitting iron cubes, unlike barrels which even when nested left much of the overall volume unused. *(PRO Adm 106/3122)*

partitioned off. Goods access was through a series of hatches one above the other, through which casks in slings could be lowered by a system of pulleys from the yards or booms above. The general assumption is that water casks came up when they were empty and either new full ones went back down (certainly this happened when a transport brought water) or the empty ones were taken off in boats to a watering place. However, whilst it is all very well to hoist a 250-gallon leaguer into the hold with the aid of pulleys, it is quite another matter to get that full leaguer into a boat from the shore, although there were various methods of doing this. Wybourn reports a watering party at the Maddalena Islands using a triangle to hoist the casks into boats,[17] while other possibilities were rolling them up a plank, or 'rafting' (*ie* towing them) out to the ship. Given the ever-present risk of hernias one wonders if watering parties used smaller casks and decanted the contents into the leaguers with pumps and pipes. They certainly had to do this once iron water tanks were introduced, as these were too big and too heavy when full to think of moving them.

There is a slight mystery about water tanks. The concept appears to have been suggested to the Victualling Board for the first time in March 1809, when Messrs Richard Trevithick and Robert Richardson sent in a printed abstract of their patent, dated 10 February 1809.[18] This does not include any drawings, remarking instead that the tanks could be of any shape, but goes into great detail of how much space and weight they would save when compared with wooden casks, not to mention solving the difficulties of obtaining suitable wood for staves. They are also, they say, proof against rats, weevils, cockroaches and thieves, and they advocate their use for all sorts of cargo and dry foodstuffs as well as liquids. The Victualling Board reported on this to the Admiralty, remarked that they had consulted Sir Joseph Banks who approved the idea, and suggested that trials should be conducted. The endorsement (one of those delightful scrawls on the back of a turned-over corner of the page) from the Admiralty Secretary Sir William Wesley Pole, shows that the Admiralty agreed with this suggestion and instructed the Victualling Board to carry on.

All this indicates that water tanks were a new idea to the Victualling Board, and yet in 1796 Samuel Bentham designed two experimental ships, *Dart* and *Arrow*, which, as well as being fitted with solid bulkheads and drop keels, had large iron water tanks. (Bentham was awarded a Gold Medal of the Society of Arts in 1800 for this innovation.[19]) These may have been too troublesome to consider seriously at the time; in June 1804, Nelson wrote to Captain Vincent of *Arrow* that while he was in Valetta, 'If the tanks cannot be repaired, water casks must be substituted in their room.'[20] Unfortunately no detailed documentation of the problem with these tanks has survived, but we do know that there were eight of them, each holding 40 tons of water and that they were fixed in place; this may have been why they were not generally adopted. *Arrow* did not make it home in 1804, falling victim to a larger French ship, and so there are no dockyard records of the repairs needed.

When they were accepted as a good idea, water tanks superseded the old wooden casks in the hold quite quickly, the Victualling Board ordering them in batches of one or two hundred at a time, a transition that was speeded up in 1812 when Truscott's pump was officially introduced. This pump, or one like it, had been in use since at least 1805 and as well as merely getting water in and out of the tanks it could be fitted to a system of flexible leather tubes so water could be pumped straight to the galley coppers or into a tank on deck. This was not entirely good news: these wooden deck tanks, which replaced the old scuttle butt, were lined with lead, but despite the protests of some captains that this was a health hazard, the Admiralty could see no reason to discontinue their use.[21] Another of those details which, irritatingly, are never mentioned is how they got water up for use before suction pumps were available. It can only have been done by hoisting the casks up in slings and then, perhaps, they had some sort of rigid stand for them to sit in while the contents were tapped off for the scuttle butt or the galley boilers.

Gradually all ports organised water pipes out to jetties where ships could tie up and use their pumps, but until then there was still the task of getting water on board from *ad hoc* watering places; this could only be done with wooden casks and manpower. There were other hazards for these watering parties besides muscle strains and ruptures. Other than at the occasional spring which flowed out of a cliff-face, watering places tended to be marshy and infested by mosquitoes. Despite a merchant captain having remarked on the connection between mosquito bites and malaria as early as 1572, the medical profession had ignored or forgotten this; but without realising that it was the marsh-dwelling mosquitoes which carried malaria and yellow fever, naval surgeons were aware that marshes were unhealthy places.[22] Dr Snipe, Physician to the Mediterranean Fleet, had told Nelson that the men were at risk and recommended that 'as a preventative against the disease which the men are subject to [when watering in marshy places]' they should be given 'a dose of Peruvian-bark [quinine] in a preparation of good sound wine or spirits' and Nelson issued a general order to this effect. Another hazard was the local inhabitants: elsewhere in Sardinia the peasants made a practice of plying the watering parties with wine in the hopes of getting them so drunk that they would not notice the casks disappearing.[23]

The last of the provisions tasks falling to the master was to observe, with a lieutenant and a mate, the cutting-up of fresh meat. Whether this was meat bought on shore or from beasts slaughtered on board, the *Regulations* specified that it should be cut up 'in some convenient and publick part of the ship, open to the view of the company'.[24]

It is not known exactly where vegetables and fruit were stowed. They might have been put in empty casks in the hold, where the casks would keep the rats out. Most would have arrived in nets or bags, in which case they might have been hung up near the galley. In general they do not appear to have been acquired in such large quantities that they needed stowing at all, as they would have been consumed in a few days. Some log entries show onions being 'served out to the men' within a few hours of arriving on board.

Livestock

Although not specified in the *Regulations*, the master would have had some involvement when livestock was brought on board, especially when large numbers were involved. Even a small live bullock would weigh about half a ton, so sixty or seventy of them would need careful positioning. The matter of getting them on board would, in itself, require some expertise where no jetty was available. With a jetty they could be herded up an enclosed gangway; without one, they would have to be slung on board, which means you first have to get them onto a boat, while leaving enough room to row it, or swim them out to the ship, having first attached some ropes to facilitate fixing the slings under their bellies (one hopes they did not lift them by their horns) and to keep their horned heads under control during the whole procedure. Alas, there was no way to control the other end, given the propensity of alarmed beasts to void their bowels, the only consolation being the availability of plenty of water to sluice down the decks.

Sheep and pigs, of course, are much easier to deal with because they are smaller and lighter than a bullock. A strong man can pick up a sheep or pig fairly easily, especially if he can catch it unawares. Several could be carried on a boat, confined under a net and at a pinch they could be hoisted on board in a strong net. By the same virtue of their size, these smaller animals were easily accommodated on board. The carpenter built pens for sheep on the centre line, usually between the capstan and the main hatch, made so that the lower section of the pen could be pulled out for easier deck cleaning (not a major problem with sheep whose droppings are fairly dry and small).[25] There are also several references to sheep being kept in the boats, although this cannot have been on a long-term basis. Pigs needed a more solidly constructed sty. This was traditionally under the forecastle but in 1801, at the instigation of the surgeons, the pigs were moved to the waist and the sickbay took over the space vacated. The pigs seem to have been allowed out for a run at intervals; there are journal reports of them wandering the deck and even eating clothing which had been left lying about. With the exception of such ships as Pasley's *Sybil* (see page 19) there were probably never that many of them but they tended to be kept longer than other beasts, often purchased as piglets and kept until they were big enough to make a series of good meals. Since they were not the ship's property the logs do not record their acquisition or their food, although on one occasion in the Mediterranean, when a merchant ship with a cargo of acorns was captured, the acorns were shared out among the squadron. In this situation the acorns are most likely to have gone to the pigs, but they were probably being carried by the merchantman to sell for human consumption; it is difficult to think that they had sufficient value for any other purpose to make it worthwhile carrying them. They were probably acorns of the holm oak (*Quercus ilex var. rotundifolia*) which are prized for their chestnut-like flavour and are cultivated in parts of Spain and Portugal.

Many ships also had a goat, kept for its milk. There are pictures of these loose on the quarterdeck during the day, but they probably spent the night with the sheep. Poultry were also kept on most ships, or at least at the beginning of the voyage. They belonged mainly to the officers and were kept partly for eggs and partly to eat. They were kept in coops which were brought up on deck during the day; they can be seen in old pictures, fitted with vertical bars in front and a trough below, so the birds could put their heads out to peck. In 1815, new instructions were issued to the dockyards to construct permanent poultry coops in the waist 'in lieu of the moveable coops now in use'; captains of frigates could site theirs on the quarterdeck.[26] The poultry would have fed on corn, crumbs and, no doubt, the beetle larvae known as bargemen. There are a couple of stories of cockerels escaping when their coops were shattered in battle, one at the Glorious First of June and another during the Battle of St Domingo; each took up a perch to crow throughout the battle, and thereby no doubt managing in the process to change their status from potential meal to much-loved ship's mascot.

It is possible, but unlikely, that sheep or even pigs might be housed in the manger, the area round the hawse-holes where the anchor cables came inboard. The manger was separated from the rest of the deck by a solid barrier whose purpose was to prevent water from the cables swilling round the deck. Because this area, to the uneducated eye, seems a likely place to confine animals, popular opinion believes this is where they were kept. It would, however, be dif-

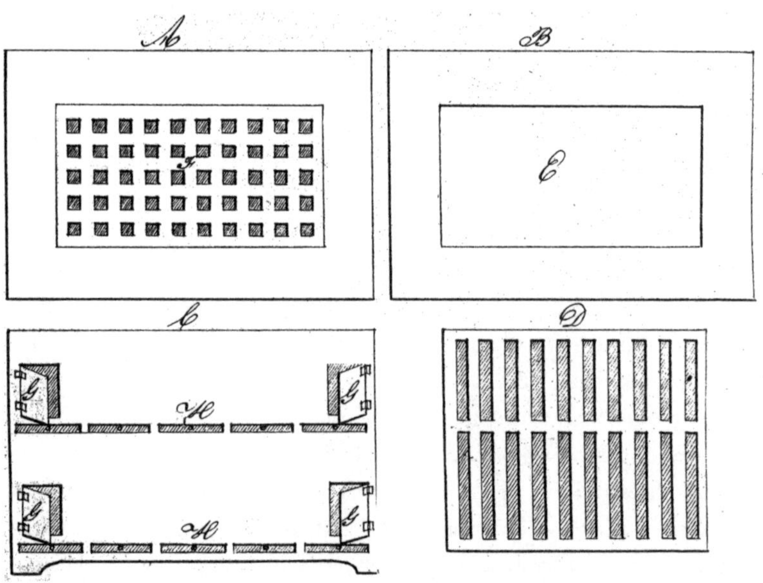

The new standard pattern of poultry coop introduced in 1815. (*PRO Adm 106/3574*)

ficult to get cattle into the manger without hoisting them in, and even more difficult to keep them there, quite apart from the question of what you do when anchor cables are in motion. Some pigs do seem to have been kept in the manger, although probably only on a temporary basis: Liardet remarked on the pigs '[disputing] the right to the manger with the fore-topmen when working the cables', the agile topmen being chosen to pass the nippers when heaving in the cable.[27] Another suggestion is that the manger was used to store fodder, citing the case of the *Boyne*, which is supposed to have caught fire when the hay in the manger spontaneously combusted, but this is not correct.[28] Another case where a ship was destroyed by fire was that of *Queen Charlotte*. In her case the fire was caused by loose hay coming into contact with a lighted slow-match in a match tub outside the admiral's cabin (*ie* aft). Of interest here is that the hay was being moved to be bagged and 'pressed', thus compressing it to take up less space. (Also of interest, although perhaps a *non sequitur*, is that one of the officers, when reporting events at the court martial, stated that on being informed that the ship was on fire, he replied 'God bless me, where?'. One suspects that what he actually said was something quite different!)[29] As a regular practice, storing hay, or anything else, in the manger, once again ignores the question of what you do when you need to weigh anchor.

So where did they keep the cattle? One or two could be tucked away in a number of places, ideally, one assumes, close to a scuttle where the deck could be swilled down. Large numbers were another matter. The accounts of Thomas Alldridge, arranging cattle for the fleet off Egypt in 1798, include an entry for wood and battens and the fees for carpenters to nail them 'to prevent the bullocks falling to leeward'; this indicates that they may have been amidships somewhere. But the best indication of common practice is the story of the unfortunate *Amazon* in 1804, when Nelson asked her captain, William Parker, to collect sixty cattle and thirty sheep for the squadron off Toulon. 'Unfortunate' because Parker and his crew took great pride in their ship and she had just been in port for repairs, finishing off with a repaint. But when Nelson asks for a favour, how can you refuse? The cattle were taken on board and tied between the guns, heads to the ship's side and tails to the centre, and there they stayed for several days until they could be shared out among the squadron. Glascock also reports a seaman yarning about the Glorious First of June and remarking, 'we'd three or four bullocks twixt the guns on the main deck', so perhaps that was the standard solution to the problem. They would have been able to secure the bullocks fairly tightly, thus solving the problems of keeping them upright in rough seas and preventing their milling about dangerously in a panic (undesirable behaviour from animals armed with horns). It would also explain why cattle were thrown overboard before going into action, as *Zealous* did before the Battle of the Nile.[30] There are several unanswered questions attached to this: if the men usually ate at mess tables between the guns, what did they do when there were cattle there, how did they practice gunnery, and did they use cleaning the deck as a punishment duty?

The final question about cattle and sheep on board is that of feed and water. Some of the log entries which report taking on cattle also mention fodder, as do some of the accounts of the agents victualler afloat. But since they use such vague terms as 'bags of fodder' or 'bundles of hay' it is impossible to know how much fodder was bought and how long it lasted. Nelson once testily enquired why so much fodder had been bought for cattle that were soon to be slaughtered but in general the amounts listed do not seem like a lot: two or three bundles for twenty or thirty beasts. There must have been a fine line to draw between common humanity, restless hungry cattle, and the hope that reducing input will also reduce output.

Another area on which information is sparse is that of slaughtering animals on board ship. What follows is, therefore, a resumé of the processes on land, with some suggestions as to how the process might have been done on board ship. With pigs or sheep, you restrain them, pull back their head and slit their throat, then hoist them up by the back legs to drain the blood. On board ship, there were plenty of beams high enough for this purpose, and one assumes that a piece of old sailcloth would have been spread out to protect the deck and a tub used to catch the blood. Bullock carcasses, being bigger, would have needed something higher than a deck beam to hang from, so this was probably done on the weather deck using a yard or tackle from the main stay. With bullocks, the process starts with pulling their head down and hitting them, very hard, on the forehead with the blunt end of a pole-axe, then once they are down, using the sharp end to finish them off before cutting their throats. Once the bleeding has stopped, the next step with a pig is to immerse it in scalding water and scrape off the bristles before hoisting it up again. After this, all the beasts were gutted (as with the blood, presumably into a tub) and the sheep and cattle were skinned; this is most easily done when the carcass is warm. The carcass was then left to cool for several hours before cutting it up. Pig skin stays on the meat; as we will see in the next chapter, they had facilities for roasting and would not have wanted to forego the crackling.

The tallow was scraped off the skins and collected to be sold, with the ox-hides, at the next opportunity. These hides were obviously only rudimentarily dressed, as there are many reports of their becoming maggoty and stinking. Sometimes they became so noisome that they were declared 'a nuisance to the ship' and dumped overboard. Although not specifically mentioned in any of the logs or accounts the author has seen, the sheepskins may also have been sold on shore. On the other hand, there are many things you can do with a sheepskin, from making warm waistcoats to padding a damaged limb, assuming that you have someone on board who knows how to dress the skin. There are other usable by-products; the horns of the cattle could have been used for powder-horns or to make drinking mugs, and sheep's knucklebones are traditionally used as gaming pieces or dice.

To what extent they had experienced butchers on board is not known but at a time when many beasts were killed on the farm it would not have been difficult to find a crew member who knew what to do; the author has not seen any listed as such in muster or pay books. How much of the offal was used would also depend on whether anyone knew how to deal with it, and, perhaps, weather conditions; cleaning-out intestines to make sausage skins without damaging them would not have been easy in a rough sea. Mentions of any specific pieces of meat are rare but Jack Nastyface mentions feasting on bullock liver fried with salt pork and St Vincent ordered his officers to take the heads as their share, as a good example.[31] This makes one wonder whether the crew were inclined to refuse this sort of meat; certainly most of it needs more complicated preparation than simple boiling.

The Purser

Captain, master and lieutenants had some involvement with the handling of provisions; the purser spent most of his time on them and was responsible for them financially. He was a combination of paid employee and entrepreneurial businessman, allowed to sell certain items to the crew. He was appointed by warrant, which meant that unlike the commissioned officers, who could move from one ship to another comparatively easily (often following the senior officer whom they regarded as their patron), he tended to stay with one ship for many years. The main reason a purser would want to move ship would be to get into a higher-rated ship and thus increase the magnitude of his 'business' as well as his salary. Until 1782 they had been allowed to go straight into the higher-rated ships, but Sandwich, as First Lord of the Admiralty, put a stop to this, insisting that pursers started their career in a sloop.[32] In 1813 an order was issued that pursers had to pass an examination by three experienced pursers before obtaining their warrants.[33] In theory the purser's accounts from one ship had to be passed before he was appointed to another; in practice the Victualling Board would not block his appointment unless they suspected him of fraud or he had a big debt with them. Even then, if they saw no other way of recovering his debt they would allow him to go to a new ship.

Before obtaining his warrant, the purser had to find two other people to stand as surety for him, in amounts relating to the rate of the ship: starting at £1200 for a First Rate and reducing to £400 for a Sixth Rate or sloop. However, 'For encouraging him to a zealous and faithful discharge of his duty', after his accounts were passed, in addition to the wages for himself and his servant he received a commission based on the amounts of provisions he had dispensed, ranging from tuppence per pound of cheese to three shillings per bushel of pease. His wages were not over-generous: he received an amount related to the rate of the ship; in 1790 this was set at £4 per lunar month for a First Rate, reducing to £2 for a Sixth Rate, then in 1806 this was increased to £4.16.0 reducing to £3.1.0. In all Rates he was allowed a steward, in First to Fourth Rates his steward was allowed a mate.[34]

As well as accounting for all the food that came onto the ship, the purser had to account for its use on a 'per man, per day' level. He had to keep a copy of the muster book, noting when each man joined or left the ship and why; when they were away on duty (perhaps manning a prize) and when they were taken to the sick bay, at which point they were fed on a different basis. The purser also had charge of slop clothing, beds and tobacco; the men had to pay for these, by deduction from their wages. If they wanted more tobacco than their normal ration, the purser was allowed to sell it to them from his private stock. All of these items, except the private stock, had not only to be noted against each man's name in the purser's muster book, but in a sequence of other books: an appearance (*ie* joining the ship) and discharge book for all men, a book of all sick men sent out of the ship, a slop book, a tobacco book, and a book detailing every cask or package of provisions brought aboard, with full details of the identifying marks on each so the origin of defective items could be identified, and separate lists of all these defective items together with the formal certified documents of survey condemning them as 'not fit for men to eat'.

Finally he had to keep receipts for, and details of, purchases and issues of 'necessaries'. This term covered all items which were either not supplied through victualling yards or for some reason had to be bought on the open market, such as candles, 'lanthorns', turneryware (wooden utensils for the men to eat from) and coal. For all these items he was allowed a sum of between fourteen and seventeen pence per man per lunar month, depending on the size of the ship and the categories of men involved. He could either draw cash for necessary purchases from an agent victualler, or when away from a victualling port, could draw Bills of Exchange on the Victualling Board if supported by his captain, using the same method to purchase fresh meat and vegetables.

All of this was comparatively easy when in home waters, where most of a ship's requirements could be obtained from the outports and the rest purchased in sterling. It was when abroad that the documentation became more complex. Victualling yards were fewer and thus more items would have to be purchased from local merchants, each transaction requiring certification from two or three 'principal inhabitants' (one of whom would ideally be the local governor or consul) that the amount paid was the current market price. In addition, full details had to be given of the currency used and its exchange rate at the time of the transaction, this also requiring certification. For larger transactions and where the seller was amenable, the purser could pay by drawing a Bill of Exchange on the Victualling Board. The preferred format for these and an explanation of how the Bill system worked is shown in Appendix 5.

Finally, whether in home or foreign waters, the purser had to keep full stock records. When he joined or left a ship, a 'survey' or full stock-take of all his stores had to be performed and certified by three warrant officers; when the commission was completed and the ship laid up, all the remaining provisions had to be returned to the victualling stores and he had to accompany them to see them properly received and accounted for. And of course, whenever ships passed provisions between them, both pursers had to prepare and exchange 'warrants' and 'distinct accounts' of those transactions.

If for any reason any species of provisions were not available, or were refused by the men as being bad, or if provisions were saved for other reasons such as the boys receiving less than the full allowance of wine or spirits, the purser had to keep track of the value of these provisions and pay it over to the men in cash, theoretically at no greater than quarterly intervals. This 'short allowance' money was considered sufficiently important to warrant its own chapter and printed form in the *Regulations*. It was to be paid in cash, at sterling value but in local currency, with the men having the benefit of the exchange and the money was to be paid to each individual in person, regardless of debt notes or other financial obligations. This is probably how the men obtained the money which they would spend on shore or when the bumboats came calling.

This makes it appear that the purser's life was, if complex from an accounting point of view, at least safe financially: provisions were either expended by issuing them to the men or declared inedible and the subject of an accounting credit. Alas, poor purser, the Victualling Board were not that generous. Even after the Spithead mutiny, when he was officially allowed a margin for wastage, he only received that allowance after his accounts were passed, not before to make up any shortages. There were also various situations in which he did not receive any allowances. Leakage of wine or spirits or oil once the casks had been checked on receipt were considered to be his personal problem and he might even be refused credit for items which had been legitimately surveyed and condemned: one unfortunate purser produced survey certificates for a large quantity of bread which had been eaten by cockroaches, but the Victualling Board refused him any credit, on the grounds that this might create a dangerous precedent. Nor, if he was bulk-buying at a non-victualling port and needed to store his purchases, could he claim for the cost of that storage, or for hiring boats. Small wonder that albatrosses, with their propensity for following ships for days on end, were said to be the souls of dead pursers, desperately seeking a ship that would allow them to recover their losses.

Many pursers, no doubt, did resort to sharp practice to make ends meet.

It is not unusual to find them being court-martialled for fiddling their vouchers or even being prosecuted by the Victualling Board for various frauds. There are many time-honoured ways of building up a 'reserve' stock of items to replace those lost by accident: for instance, one wonders what quantities of items which were reported as damaged in battle were reserves of this sort. A good purser who was a competent book-keeper did not have to resort to such things, and could rise up the career ladder from small ship to large one; a few made the next step from purser to agent victualler at one of the victualling ports; some even made a further step by acting as prize agents to the officers and men of the ships on their station. If he was astute and entrepreneurial, a purser could make quite a bit on the side by stocking and selling various small items to the officers and men, from crockery to pepper and from warm socks to boot polish. Many would have anticipated a retirement career as a ships' chandler on shore.

Of those who failed – and judging by the volume of the Victualling Board's letters to the Admiralty suggesting write-offs of irrecoverable pursers' debts, there were many of these – some may have had bad luck but many more were the victims of their own incompetence and bad judgement, sometimes with a dash of ill-health thrown in. Samuel Grant was probably typical of this latter sort. The son of a merchant in Aberdeen, he had been purser of various ships, ending up in *Pembroke* and then *Goliath* between the late 1790s and 1803; some of his papers have survived and they tell enough of his story to give a picture of the whole. His journals are a mixture of brief personal diary entries and notes of money lent and borrowed. He was not well and mentions this frequently, once remarking that he was a little better and had been able to leave off the flannel from his throat 'and to prevent catching cold, tyed a lock of my dear Jeannies Hair round my Neck in its stead'. Then he says that the commander-in-chief has written to Admiral Campbell to call him to account for neglect of duty, and adds 'He may be Damn'd'. After a while, the ship came back to England and Grant went home to his Jeannie, leaving his steward to sort out the remaining stores but it transpires that the steward had been lining his own pocket.

After a sequence of letters to and fro, Grant wrote to the steward accusing him of selling the ship's stores and embezzling the stocks of candles; the steward returned this letter with a cheeky note scrawled on it, which basically says

'Hard Luck'. Then there is a statement from Grant's bankers, Thomas Coutts & Co, and an instruction to them to sell some stocks. A tiny piece of paper, from the constable of the parish where he lived, summoned him to appear and bring details of his income; a copy of the statement prepared for this meeting shows that his income for the year was his net pay of just over £30 and investment income of £65. It is clear that he was in money trouble as well as ill-health. He tried to find someone to take his place on *Goliath* but failed; he had to go back to sea and his health and spirits suffered again. In the last file, a letter from a friend tells him to buck up and a copy letter from him shows he wrote to the Physician of the Fleet saying that his health was getting worse and begging to go home by the first possible ship. The final, poignant, letter is a formal one from the secretary of the Victualling Board to Grant's bankers, asking if they want the various documents found in the trunk of 'the late Samuel Grant, purser of *Goliath*'.[35]

Vermin

Rapacious stewards were not the only vermin to bother pursers. To the modern mind, the idea that ships should be constantly infested with varying levels of rats and insects is horrific, but at that time, although it was possible to control these pests, it was impossible to eradicate them. Wooden ships were full of havens where rodents and assorted insects could hide away and breed and when there had been a major blitz to reduce numbers, others could get on board easily enough. Mice are rarely mentioned. They were, perhaps, less likely to climb the mooring ropes, and there were few stores brought aboard in the forms which usually carry mice, except the occasional fodder and bedding for cattle. Perhaps the rats killed them.

We do not know exactly what sort of rats they were. They could have been the common brown rat (*Rattus norvegicus*) or the black rat (*R. rattus*), both of which have the alternate name of 'ship rat'. It is the latter which brought the bubonic plague to Europe in the fourteenth century. Rats were ever-present on ships and a constant nuisance. They breed at an alarming rate, producing litters of eight or more every couple of months. They gnawed their way into storerooms, bread bags and even casks, and once in they fouled much of what they did not eat. They also damaged other things besides food: sails, clothing and paperwork. *Bittern*, in the Mediterranean in 1803, has a note

Right: Method of suspending a small barrel. This is how the officers' beer or wine would be kept in the wardroom, with a tap fitted to facilitate pouring.

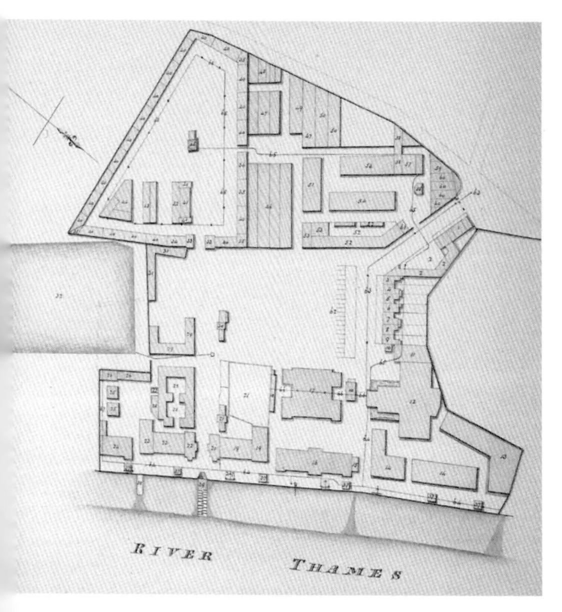

Left: Plan of the victualling yard at Deptford as it was in 1813. The size of the establishment can be gauged by some of the statistics quoted in the key: the slaughter house could accommodate up to 260 oxen, and the hog hanging house 650 pigs; the bakehouse had twelve ovens; and the spirit vats held 56,000 gallons. Besides the large storehouses, there were ranges of houses for the yard officers and craftsmen. (*PRO Adm 7/593*)

Below: A mess table on the *Victory*. Note the square plates, cow's horn drinking mugs and 'half-barrel' mess kids. The hammocks would not normally be slung during mealtimes. (*Photographs of HMS* Victory *by kind permission of the Commanding Officer*)

Above: Detail from a contemporary print, showing the use of a 'triangle' to lift a heavy object – here a gun, but it was also used to lift barrels from beach to boat.

Right: The preparation area in the galley on the *Victory*. The long wooden object next to the half-door is a peel for moving bread and dishes in an[d out] of the oven. Note the ever-present rats.

ve: Side view of the replica Brodie stove on the *ory*. Note the buckets and the chain for driving spit. This was operated by a smoke-jack in the nney. The square open container is a salt box, ch housed two ready-use powder cartridges, so presumably only kept in this position when the was in action (when the stove would be doused).

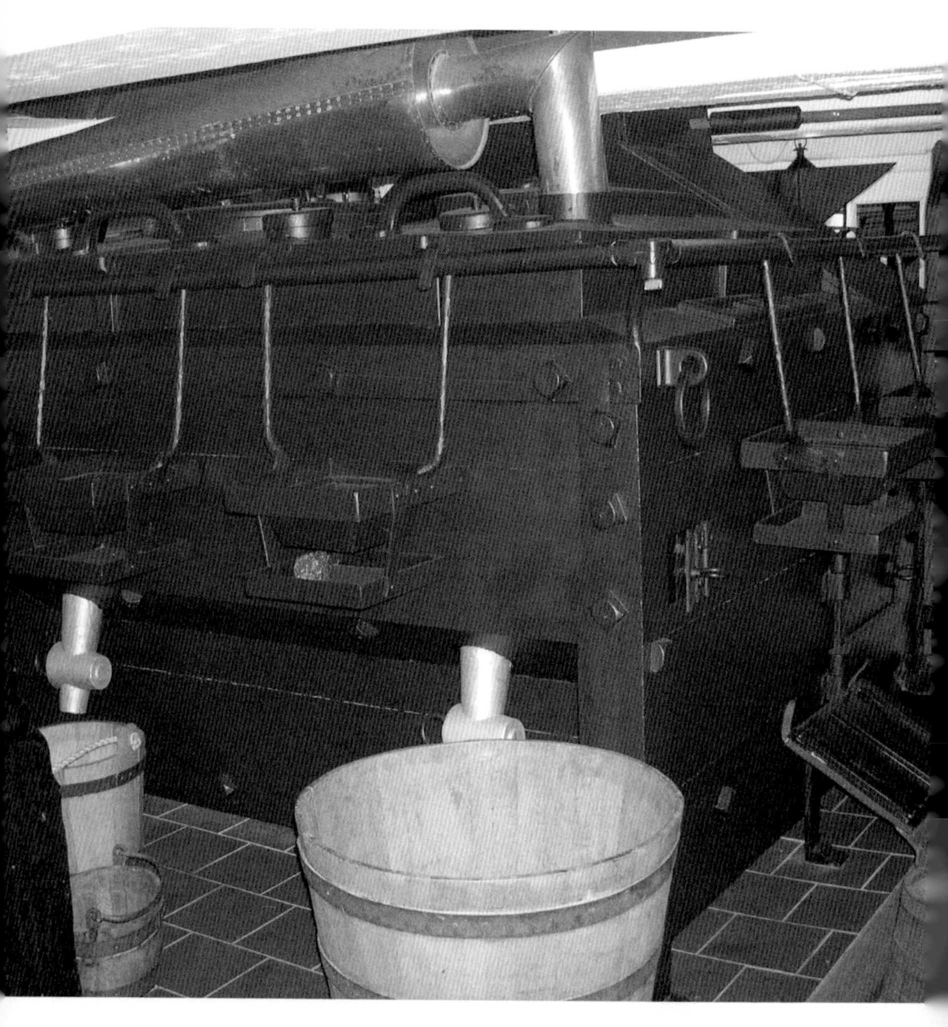

Above: Another view c
the replica Brodie stov
on the *Victory*. Note t
condenser (top left), t
large tubs for steeping
salt meat and receivin
liquids from the boile
and the cocks (bottom
left) for pouring these

Left: The open fire at
front end of the Brod
stove on the *Victory*.
Note the different
facilities for standing
hanging cooking pots
and kettles.

e: Side view of the replica Brodie
on the *Victory*. From top right,
.wise, note the lids of the coppers and
extreme proximity to the beams
:, the hanging stoves on the rail, the
fire-box (this is underneath the
:rs), the closed door to the oven and
ıpports on which the spit would be
ıted.

Above: Casks stowed in the hold of the *Victory*, with the bottom tier nestling in shingle ballast.

Left: Cheese racks in the purs
steward's room on the *Victory*

Below: A close-up of the
preparation area in the galley
the *Victory*. Note the stonewa
bottles and the wooden pestl
and mortar for grinding spice

in the master's log explaining that a twelve-week gap was due to 'vermine' having attacked the rough log 'being all cut to pieces so as to render it impossible to copy it with any degree of correctness…'. This conjures up a picture of the clerk opening the box or bag and discovering a family of little pink ratlings, all cosy in shredded paper; it also gives an interesting insight into the system of 'fair' copying. None of the logs for *Bittern* cover this missing period and it is common on many ships for all the logs (lieutenants', masters' and captains') to be in the same hand and almost identical wording; some sets have identical doodled enhancement of capital letters. There was no report of what *Bittern* did about the rats, but the storeship *William*, when in Malta dockyard, reports 'smoked the ship with charcoal to kill the rats which had done a great deal of damage to the crew and ships stores': the next day they found fifty-two dead rats and the following day 'upwards of 20 dead rats in different parts of the ship'.[36]

However, rats were not entirely bad news. There are many reports of rats being caught by wily sailors and offered for sale to the hungry (an almost permanent state for the numerous growing boys on board most ships); peppered, salted and grilled, they were declared to be good to eat. They taste rather like rabbit and like all fresh meat, contain small amounts of Vitamin C; the Arctic explorer Elisha Kent Kane who spent one winter trapped in the ice believed that his willingness to eat rats was the reason he was the only one of the crew to avoid scurvy.[37] Many people cringe at the idea of eating rat but this is totally irrational; they are considered a delicacy by aboriginal peoples in much of the developing world, as are their close relatives the grey squirrel (*Scirius carolinensis*) in North America; every nationality (except those whose dietary laws forbid it) eats shrimps, lobsters and crabs, all of which have far nastier habits than rats.

The other ship-borne pest which everyone thinks they know about is the weevil: the cause of biscuits which moved like clockwork was supposed to be black-headed maggots which tasted metallic. This comes from Smollett; he probably got it from Antonio Pigafetta who sailed round the world in 1520 with Magellan; and it was then repeated by Masefield and so on down to the present day, many of the stories embroidered to the extent that it is assumed that all biscuits were like this. Some real accounts of damaged biscuits tell of 'cockroaches' having reduced the biscuits to powder, assuming that because 'cockroaches' were present, they were the culprits. They were wrong on several counts, as was Pigafetta, Smollett and everyone who has repeated these stories ever since.

The reddish-brown beetle which was taken for a cockroach was actually the Cadelle Beetle (*Tenebroides mauritanicus*), and its larvae, up to 20mm long, are those black-headed white maggots called bargemen by sailors because they crept out of the biscuits into the bread 'barge', the small tub used to hold biscuits on the mess table. These bargemen did not eat the biscuits themselves, but instead ate the minute Bread Beetle (*Stegobium paniceum*) or its larvae. The Bread Beetle (no bigger than 4mm) is not a weevil either, but a relative of the woodworm. It is the larvae of this creature which eat the biscuit; these are even smaller than the adult (no more than 0.5mm) and since they cover themselves in a mixture of saliva and flour dust, to the naked eye they would be indistinguishable from that dust. This means that no-one would have been aware of their presence in the bread bags; if they had not got onto the bread in the bakeries, they would have done so when they were packed in the reused bags. Weevils, which are a different type of beetle with a very long snout (belonging to the family *Curculio*) may also have been present in the flour, as there are several varieties which live on grain. These are also very small and would have been almost impossible to see in their larval stage. All of these little brutes lay tiny eggs and all of them breed and mature more quickly in warm, damp conditions. They would have been in or on the bread from the moment it came on the ship, but as long as the bread stayed cool and dry no-one would have noticed, or not until the bread was very old.

This might explain Nelson's letter to the agent victualler at Malta, ordering more bread to be sent, and remarking 'I sincerely hope that no weevily bread will be sent, as the Fleet is free from those insects at present…'. This letter was written in November 1803 and despite Nelson's propensity for exaggeration, may have been true, or as true as the invisibility of the 'weevils' allows. If it was not an exaggeration, and given that Nelson had a fleet of over 30 ships under his command, this is an indication that the weevil problem was certainly not as bad as the 'oh weren't it awful' brigade would have us believe. Alas, the situation did not last: between March 1804 and August 1805 ten batches of weevily bread, one of oatmeal, three of flour and five of rice were condemned. But there are no such condemnations before that.[38]

There are a couple of interesting letters in the Victualling Board papers in 1813, referring to a method of clearing weevils from flour and biscuit which had been suggested to them via the Admiralty. They duly tried it out, and reported, sadly, that it did not work: they had put a live lobster in each of three casks of flour or biscuits, but after three days the lobsters were found to be dead and there was no diminution in the number of weevils; they were even crawling over the bodies of the lobsters. They declined to repeat the experiment, as the workers in the warehouses were complaining about the smell of dead lobsters.[39]

Other small beetles might have appeared in the pease or dried beans; the author once had the unhappy experience of putting a saucepan of allotment-grown haricot beans to soak in hot water and finding on her return that the water was full of small black beetles. Organically grown and air-dried fruit even today often harbours various tiny insects which proliferate in warm cupboards; these, or other more visible insects were probably the reason that 130 of the 165 messes on *Victory* refused to accept the raisins in 1798.[40]

The warmer the environment, the more insects there are. Dillon tells of the occasion when, in the West Indies in 1796, they suffered an invasion of black ants. It is probable that some queens had flown on board and set up their nurseries, as the annoyance lasted several months, with the food covered in ants; and cold pies, when cut, looking more like ink than food. Eventually the ants, Dillon said, grew larger, sprouted wings and disappeared, leaving the way clear for the cockroaches.[41] Perhaps he should have been grateful that they had not acquired any bananas complete with stowaway tarantulas.

Chapter 4

HOW THE MEN ATE

WE KNOW A GREAT DEAL about what the seamen in the Georgian navy ate and how it got to them. What we know less about is how they ate; it is one of those aspects of naval life which no-one seems to have thought important enough, or perhaps different enough from land-borne life, to describe in consistent detail. Compared with the number of letters and journals written by various levels of officers there are very few written by lower-deck men and of those few, hardly any mention of food or mealtimes. So, we must piece the story together with what has been documented from naval and other writings on food history and what we can reasonably surmise.

Issuing the Food

Unlike the modern military mess, which term tends to mean the place where you eat, to the Georgian navy a mess was a group of men who ate together. We will come back to this concept in more detail later; for now we just need to know that one man from each group was designated 'mess cook' and he went along every day to collect the food from the purser or steward. The steward's room was usually aft, on the orlop deck next to the bread room. It would be equipped with bins or casks containing the biscuit, flour, pease, suet, raisins and so on, racks for cheese and the small firkins of butter, a counter and several scales. The atmosphere at issuing time would have been somewhat dusty, especially when flour was being served. For this reason the steward was known as 'Jack-in-the-dust'; it was clearly not a job for asthmatics.

The Admiralty, through the *Regulations*, laid down the official ration for each man, and some rules to ensure fairness in issuing and what was to happen with poor-quality provisions. It was up to the captain of each individual ship to decide when the food was to be issued; typically, captains' orders give a twice-daily, two- or three-hour, period for issues (7 to 9 or 10am, 4 to 7pm).[1]

It is when you contemplate the number of messes in a ship and think about the length of time it would take to physically weigh out and hand over the day's food to each mess, and make a note of what they had received, you realise why it needed a generous time slot.

Remembering that the purser had to account for the food on a 'per man' basis, and that the men were entitled to cash payments for what they did not receive, it is obvious that there must have been some foolproof way of doing this. Messes were normally identified by number (hence the expression 'he's lost the number of his mess', meaning 'he's died') so each mess cook would arrive at the head of the queue and sing out 'Number whatever, all present today' (or 'Fred Bloggs absent'), and the steward would make a note, perhaps by moving a peg in a tally board or ticking each number on his list. Unfortunately no full sets of pursers' books seem to have survived, so we cannot see the detail of these issues – whether half the messes went in the morning and the others in the afternoon, or whether different items were issued at different times. What we can reasonably infer, from the fact that we know there was little secure storage space on the mess decks where the men lived, was that they would probably only have received one day's food at a time. So, each mess cook would take one or two mess 'kids' (small tubs with rope handles) along to the steward's room and collect the day's biscuit, pease, butter and cheese, or whatever substitutes might be required. If it was a pudding day, that would include flour, raisins and suet. Other items were dealt with elsewhere.

As well as its mess kids, each mess would have a pudding bag and one or more nets, each of these with some sort of tag or button bearing the mess number (small tally sticks with carved Roman numerals which have been recovered from shipwrecks may have been used for this purpose). As well as being for suet puddings, the pudding bag would be used for cooking the pease; the nets were for cooking meat and vegetables. The advantage of using a system of nets and bags is that you can put different items in to cook at different times. The cloth for the bags was a regulation issue: 'And there shall be supplied, once a year, from the Victualling Office, a proportion of canvas for pudding bags, after the rate of one ell to every sixteen men.'[2] We do not know the shape of the bags made with it; these may have been cylindrical but were more likely to have been round, perhaps with a draw-string to close them. Certainly the round bag would have been easier to get the pudding out of as well as to clean. There is no mention of nets in the *Regulations*, but a net is an easy enough thing to make with some twine and nimble fingers.

The method of allocating meat was known as 'pricking' and it was done by the ship's cook. He had a large fork called (officially, not just colloquially) a tormentor, with which he would prick a piece of meat, doing this in such a way that no favouritism could be shown. Either the cook could see the waiting mess cooks but not the meat as he pricked for it, or he could see the meat but did not know who was going to get it, sometimes standing behind a screen, sometimes calling out 'Who shall have this?' and his mate picking a mess number at random. There is one report of this pricking being done after the meat was cooked but this begs the question of how, with no more than a big fork, the cook was able to prevent the meat falling apart in the process. The pricking process included the officers as well as the men; there was a rigid rule that 'all are to be equal in the point of victualling'.[3]

The problem attached to this process is how they coped with messes of different numbers of men when meat came in standard-sized pieces (four or eight pounds for beef, two or four pounds for pork). Some of the meat must have been cut while raw to ensure that each mess got the right amount; perhaps it was all cut into one- or two-pound pieces, which would have had the added advantage of shortening the steeping time. No-one has mentioned that this was done, but nor has anyone said anything to indicate that it was not. Another thought: how did the ship's cook know how much meat each mess should have? He could not take the mess cook's word for it and he could not be expected to know how many men there were in each mess even when they were all there and all having the day's meat ration in full, let alone know that one or two men were away from the ship or in the sickbay, or that the mess was having half meat and half duff. Perhaps the purser's steward gave the ship's cook a list (assuming that he could read) or, more likely, the steward gave the mess cook an appropriate number of counters or tally sticks which he then gave to the cook in exchange for the meat.

When the meat was fresh, there were traditionally vegetables to go with it. This was normally when the ship was in port and they had more for the first two weeks than after: on the North American station in 1813 this was expressed as 'for fourteen days at the rate of ⅘ pound of cabbage and ⅕ pound of onions per man per day, thereafter until quitting the port, ½ pound of cabbage and

1/10 pound of onions, or fruit in lieu'.[4] Sometimes the amount was specified as 'such as will satisfy the men' and this, as well as the fact that it was sometimes referred to as 'vegetables for the soup', makes one wonder if it was cooked in a separate copper and ladled out, rather than being issued raw and cooked in a net or bag. Alternatively, some of the men may even have preferred their vegetables raw, relishing the crunchy texture as well as the more intense flavour.

Having said that provisions were issued on a daily basis to each mess, this did not apply to the oatmeal. The only feasible way to make porridge on a large scale would be to put it all in a large pot where it could be stirred and watched, and then to serve it out with a ladle. Although Jack Nastyface says that each mess had its own hook-pot for burgoo, the *Regulations* say 'when [the cook] serves out soup or burgou [*sic*] he is strictly charged to do it without any partiality, giving to every man, as nearly as possible, an equal quantity'.[5] Nor is it likely that they had porridge for breakfast only on the three days shown on the official table of provisions. What must have happened here is that the purser issued one-seventh of the week's total oatmeal ration to the cook each day.

The final item which was collected by the mess cook was the drink, and tradition gave him an extra share as a reward for his efforts. The rule here was that it should be served on an 'open deck', where all could see fair play in both the serving and, where spirits were involved, the mixing of grog. When lemon or lime juice was issued as a scurvy preventative, this, together with its accompanying sugar, would be served at the same time, either mixed into the grog or with water as 'sherbet'. Captains' orders typically required the drink to be served in two halves, one during or just before the midday dinner break, the other late in the afternoon. The captain could also restrict the amount of alcohol to be issued to particular individuals or classes of people. The most likely class would be the boys, who would then be paid for their unused portion. The individuals would be those being punished for some minor crime; in this case they would not receive the value as they could have used that to purchase drink from someone else. In such a situation the 'no drink' order would probably have involved their being moved to a separate mess for the duration to prevent their usual mess-mates sharing with them. Those who, for their own reasons, did not want alcohol, could refuse it and receive credit; it is likely that many of them took it and used it, as would many others, to pay debts or purchase favours from their shipmates. The same would have applied to tobacco: alcohol and tobacco have always been valuable commodities in closed communities.

Cooking

Every ship carried a cook, that is to say, a man with the title of cook – the only qualification he required was that he must have a warrant and be a pensioner of the Chest at Greenwich, which meant that he would often be short of a limb. This qualification was, until 1806 when the fourteenth edition of the *Regulations* specify it as an absolute requirement, merely advisory, dating from an order in 1704 which says that pensioners of the Greenwich hospital were to be given precedence when appointing a cook. Depending on the size of the ship, the cook had at least one able-bodied assistant and the services of a boy, who would prepare vegetables and clean out the coppers and other utensils for the daily inspection by the officer of the watch.

As well as his pension and salary, the cook had the perquisite of the 'slush', the meat fat which rose to the top of the coppers during cooking, and which had to be periodically skimmed off. Dudley Pope refers to it as 'unappetising fist-sized lumps of yellowish fat', but this is not correct.[6] Not only would no self-respecting mess allow the cook to have the benefit of large amounts of such useful stuff from their piece of meat, what we are discussing is fat which has come out of the meat in liquid form and risen to the top of the cooking liquid. When it has cooled and set, slush is little different to suet or dripping. The slush had first to be offered to the boatswain for lubricating the running rigging, gun trucks and so on, but the rest was the cook's to sell, theoretically to the tallow merchants on shore but no doubt also to his shipmates. As well as being useful for waterproofing boots, it could be used for frying fish, onions or, according to Jack Nastyface, a mixture of ox liver and pork.[7] Beef slush would be in demand for making puddings. Although allowing the men to eat slush was forbidden in the *Regulations* on the grounds that it was unwholesome and caused scurvy, this rule was probably ignored on a grand scale if the captain and surgeon were prepared to turn a blind eye. It is, however, another situation where the *Regulations* were actually correct, although as with so many of these things they could not have known the reason: eating rancid fat can lead to malabsorption of other foods by the gut.[8]

With rare exceptions, any actual cooking skills would be minimal and learned along the way. There was certainly no training in the culinary arts for these ships' cooks. Their main duties, as specified in the *Regulations*, were: to have charge of the steep tub and be responsible for the meat put into it; to ensure it was properly secured in stormy weather to prevent it being washed overboard; to 'see the meat duly watered, and the provisions carefully and cleanly boiled…'; to see that the vegetables were 'very carefully washed' before cooking; and to be frugal with fuel. This last was either coal or wood, and part of the 'necessaries' bought by the purser.

Other than the possibility of a friendly cook allowing occasional frying or grilling, as far as the men were concerned all their food was boiled in large boilers or coppers. At the beginning of the eighteenth century there was little facility for anything else, just a brick-built hearth with a single riveted copper boiler on top and a chimney venting to the upper deck. In 1728 iron fire-hearths were introduced as preferable to the weighty brick hearths; in 1757 the Navy Board issued stove dimensions for each rate of ship.[9] These also included a double boiler with two lids and other refinements such as grilling racks and a small oven. One version had a spit operated by a fan in the chimney.

Then, in 1780, the Scot Alexander Brodie patented a new type of stove.[10] Almost square, it came in several sizes (each adequate for feeding a specified number of men), the biggest of which was just over six feet square and about five feet high. It was made of wrought iron with cast iron for the fire boxes, with a ventilator and hood of copper. The whole thing was put together with nuts and screws so that it could easily be taken to pieces and individual parts replaced if damaged in battle. It had two separate fires, one of which was open at the front and was divided into three separate sections, each of which could be used independently of the others. In front of these was a facility for one or two spits extending the full width and thus large enough to roast a whole sheep or pig, a significant joint of beef or several fowls. The spit was operated by a system of chains and pulleys connected to a smoke jack in the flue. Level with, and extending across the top of the fire, was a hotplate on which pots would stand. Other larger pots could be swung onto the fire on what the patent calls 'cranes': simple hinged arms with cut-outs for the pot handle to rest in. Behind the fire, also extending across the whole width of the stove, was an oven and behind that was a separate, closed, fire. Above the oven and the second fire were two lidded boilers, with (for the largest-sized stove) a capacity of 100 and 150 gallons respectively.

Along the two sides and the back of the stove were rails, on which were hung separate 'stewing stoves'. These stewing stoves could also be free-standing; if the replica examples on *Victory* are correct, they can best be described as small barbecues, each about a foot square, with a grill for pots to stand on over a shallow fire-box. These could have held either hot coals taken from the main fire or charcoal when the main fire was not lit. As seen on *Victory*, they could have been used for frying or grilling but would be more effective for keeping a saucepan of food warm than cooking large quantities. The number supplied varied according to the rate of the ship: seven stewing stoves for First or Second Rates, five for a Third Rate, three for a frigate and one for the smallest ships. According to a Navy Board directive, these stoves may have been rather larger than those to be seen on *Victory* and they also seem to vary in size according to the ship's size, having a variable number of grates, trivets, furnace bars and 'plates in the additional bottoms'.[11]

The closed fire had a ventilator under the firebox 'for carrying off foul air', intended to go through the deck below the stove from where it could 'be conveyed to any part of the ship, or where the sick people are kept'. The boilers vented through a condenser which produced a small amount of distilled water for use in the sick-bay. The whole thing stood on short legs to raise it from the brick or flagstone surface which protected the deck timbers. Given this clearance and the height of the stove itself, it cannot have been easy or comfortable to reach into the boilers when the fires were lighted. *Victory*, as those who have visited her will know, has a replica Brodie stove which sits so close to the beams above that it would have been extremely difficult to remove the boiler lids and fill or empty the boilers, and virtually impossible to reach inside and clean them. One hesitates to suggest that this replica stove is incorrectly fitted or over-large; perhaps there used to be a hatch above so that these essential operations could be done from the deck above. The boilers do have large cocks underneath for drawing off liquid, and it would have been possible to use a pump to fill them with liquid. Equally, an agile boy might have been able to wriggle onto the top of the stove and swab them out with some sort of mop, but this operation would have to be left until the stove was cold. Nor can one imagine the mate of the watch, who was meant to inspect their cleanliness, being anxious to perform such contortions. (The captain's orders for *Amazon*

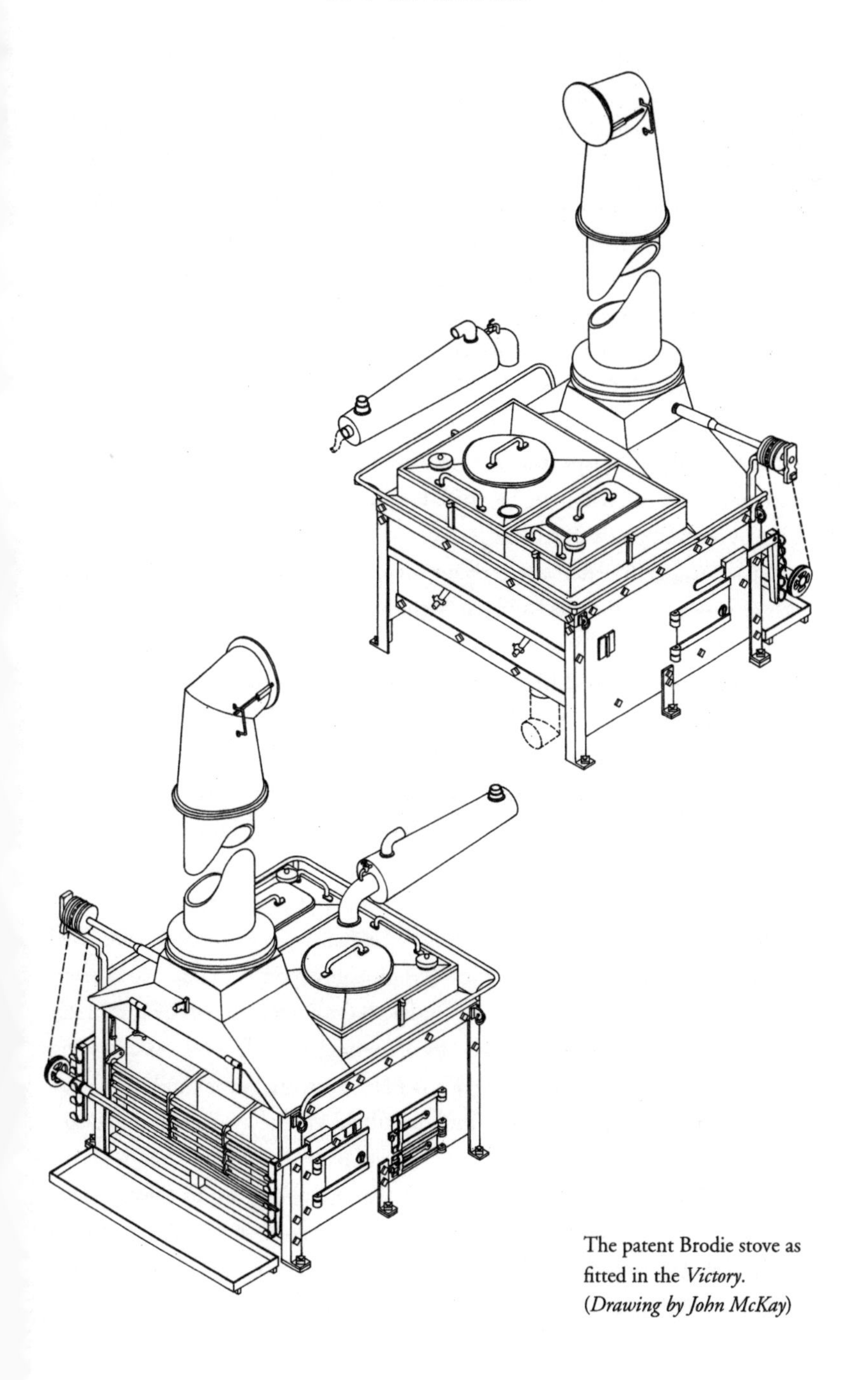

The patent Brodie stove as fitted in the *Victory*. (*Drawing by John McKay*)

required this inspection to take place at 3pm.)[12] It would have been impossible to stir porridge in these boilers, unless that hatch was fitted above. Porridge making was more likely to have been done in very large pots on the open hearth at the front, or on separate stoves. On ships where the range was lit early in the morning, the first option is the easiest, but St Vincent's orders in 1796 on the timing of range-lighting remark on 'the stoves being sufficient for breakfast'; however, if those stoves were like those to be seen on *Victory* today, one doubts their being big enough to provide enough for her 837 men.[13]

By 1810 a new stove, patented by Lamb & Nicholson, had been adopted. This was larger and had three boilers, making it possible, said one of the captains who performed trials, to cook potatoes separately. He had also, he remarked, when transporting troops to the Schelde, been able to feed 1164 men at a time; other captains reported feeding 1200 and 1300 men. But the biggest advantage of this larger stove was its ability to produce significant quantities of fresh water: up to twenty-five gallons per hour if all three boilers were used. Indeed, the Lamb & Nicholson patent was as much about providing fresh water as cooking for large numbers.[14] The Lamb & Nicholson stove was fully enclosed (*ie* no open grate) and looks much like a giant Aga or Raeburn. As well as the boilers, it had an oven and 'warming plates' on the top where saucepans, frying pans and griddles could be placed.

To a certain extent each captain could influence the internal arrangements of his ship. There was not much scope for doing this with the stove itself but there may have been some with the rest of the galley; a captain who took pride in keeping a good table would have wanted more preparation space for his cook than would a captain who just regarded food as fuel. Even so, space was restricted and the reconstructed galley on *Victory* is probably typical. Situated amidships behind the foremast, the front (*ie* the end with the open grate) of the stove actually faced aft. Apart from 'stable' doors on either each side for access, this end of the galley is enclosed, consisting of a workbench with drawers and cupboards underneath and some windows at the back; these would have gained the advantage of any light coming down the adjacent stairway. The bench extends for the whole width of the galley (about eight feet) and is about two feet deep. Made of deal, it could be scrubbed clean and holystoned smooth. On the solid sides of the galley is space for hooks where utensils and nets of food could be hung. This preparation area was reserved for officer's and sick-bay meals; the crew mess cooks did their preparation at their own mess tables.

The Messes

Most captains allowed their men to chose their own mess and change it if they wanted. These changes were allowed once a month, after asking permission from the first lieutenant. A new captain, coming to a ship for the first time, would be able to gauge the nature of the crew by studying the purser's mess-lists. Few changes would indicate a settled crew; several changes which were not associated with drafts of new men or battle losses might indicate some short-term problem; a lot of changes continuing over a long period would indicate general unhappiness which might flare up into trouble.

Given the tendency of different trades to form cliques, it is likely that men who worked together would eat together, in a mutually self-supporting team of mess-mates. Such a group would probably include a boy, taken under the wing of one of the older men, but it would have been difficult for adult newcomers to find a place except with other newcomers. In fact, such newcomers, especially groups of newly-recruited landsmen, would tend to stick together for some mutual support against the scorn of experienced seamen. But there must also have been some anti-social men who made themselves obnoxious to everybody and who were refused entrance to established messes, ending up eating alone or with other misfits. One captain, Anselm Griffiths, made a practice of designating some punishment messes: a 'thieves' mess or a 'dirty' mess, in which those found guilty of those crimes, remarking that 'placing a man in one of these messes ... had more effect on his conduct than corporal punishment'.[15]

The marines, part of whose purpose was to protect the officers from mutiny, were never encouraged to mix with the seamen and were also required to eat in their own messes. Petty officers were usually forbidden by captains' orders to mess with the other men, for obvious reasons of discipline, and thus would eat together. The actual location of the mess tables for these men is not known, but since some had reserved hammock spaces under the cable tier on the orlop, it is possible they may have eaten there too.

Although some reports do occasionally suggest larger numbers, most messes consisted of between four and eight men; *Victory*, with her complement of 800-plus, had 165 messes, which gives an average number of five men to a mess. The size of messes may have been related to the size of ship, the higher-rated and thus wider ships having room for longer tables. Basil Hall mentions messes of ten to twelve men in a frigate, each at a separate table, then remarks that the line-of-battle ships had larger tables which seated two messes, one each side. However, twelve does seem rather a lot and most other reports give lower numbers and also say that each mess had its own table.

The mess tables were either suspended from the beams above at both ends or resting against the side (sitting on a batten) at the outboard side and suspended at the other. Originally the suspension was by ropes, later by rigid Y-shaped bars – whichever, the tables could be rapidly drawn up to clear for action. It is generally stated that the mess tables were between the guns, which some of them undoubtedly were (this was in the larger two- and three-decked ships; frigates had no guns on their mess deck), but when you do the arithmetic on the number of inter-gun spaces, the number of men to a table and the size of the complement you realise that unless they ate in shifts (which we are told they did not) there must have been some other tables. A print of *Vengeance*, dating from 1796, shows two sets of tables on either side of the ship, one between the guns and one inboard, with some others on the centre line between the hatches: eighty-seven tables in all for a complement of about 600 men. This print is the only available evidence for this practice but that does not mean it was not common.

A Cruikshank cartoon of men drinking and yarning at their mess table shows a rack on the ship's side containing plates. This has been taken to indicate that this was the norm and has even been extended to assume that cutlery was also kept there; both these assumptions are dubious. The cutlery is the easiest to deal with, for there would have been little. Each man would have owned an all-purpose knife, which he used for everything from cutting his meat to working cordage or whittling wood; he would have carried this with him all the time. They would also have had a spoon, made of wood, tin or horn, and would have been more inclined to tuck this away in their ditty-bag than leave such an easily-stolen item on a rack in clear view. The mess as a whole might have had a large spoon for serving soup and gravy but equally might have used a mug for this. Stirring, when called for, can be done with any piece of dowel and does not need a spoon as such. The plates and bowls also belonged to the individual men, who would be more likely to stow them away when not in use than leave them out where they could be filched. There is also the problem of putting such things away in a hurry when clearing for action. So perhaps Cruikshank's plate racks were an artistic shorthand for 'this is where the men eat as well as drink', or perhaps they were used to let the dishes dry off before they were stowed, rather than as permanent storage. It must also be remembered that the mess decks were also sleeping decks; hammock space was cramped enough without such things as plate racks intruding.

The men's plates and bowls would only rarely be ceramic, even the strongest stoneware being too vulnerable to breakage in rough seas. The better-off men might have pewter, purchased on shore; the others would have wood, either purchased from the purser or made by the owner. The square plates consisting of one or two flat pieces of plank with nailed-on batten rims which gave rise to the expression 'a square meal' were probably made by the men, as the items stocked by the purser were referred to as 'turneryware', which means they were made on a lathe and therefore round. The purser would also stock spoons and, for those who felt the need, forks. Each man would also have his own mug, bought from the purser or made up from wood or horn, or a combination of both: horn sides with a wooden bottom. To what extent the mess kids were supplied or privately owned by each mess is not known; there is no mention of them in any of the Victualling Board documents. They needed to be watertight, so would have been made by coopers; it is possible that the ship's cooper, where there was one, made them up as part of his duties.

Mess Cooks

The members of each mess took it in turns to act as mess cook, each serving for a week at a time and presumably to an unofficial rota. Although there may have been some men who did not want to do it and others who would prefer such work to the alternatives, the inevitability of a permanent mess cook being considered idle by both officers and crew rendered such a scenario unlikely. The only men officially exempted from this job were those belonging to the boats when the ship was in harbour.

The mess cook's duties were those which would allow the others to do no more than come to the table, eat, drink, and go away again. So as well as collecting the food and drink when it was issued, he did any pre-cooking preparation, such as mixing the flour, suet and raisins for puddings (whistling while doing so, as it is impossible to clandestinely eat raisins while whistling), taking such items to the galley in their labelled bags or nets and seeing them placed in the boiler. There are, incidentally, other things besides raisins which you can add to a suet pudding to make it a bit more interesting, and this is where the private bumboat-bought stocks come in. Any sort of dried fruit (including apples) will swell to softness in the cooking process. Chopped bacon (or some of yesterday's salt pork), carrot or onion will give a savoury version. There are even recipes using mussels for those occasions when a watering party had been ashore at low tide.

The mess cook then collected the food when it was cooked and served it out to his mess, having in the meantime lowered the table into place, fetched the benches and generally made everything ready for the meal. When serving meat, he carved it and handed it out at random, again using the question 'Who shall have this?', with someone else, with his back to the table, singing out a name. When the meal and the socialising was over, the other men went back to work and the cook tidied up. One assumes that any edible crumbs went to the poultry or pigs and the rest went overboard in the approved manner; the order book for *Superb* says that bones, dirt and dirty water are to be disposed of down the heads and not thrown out of the gun-ports.[16] This order book also says that the mess cooks were responsible to the officer of the watch; Jack Nastyface says he might also be subjected to the judgement of a 'court' of other mess cooks, called by hoisting a mess swab or beating a tin dish. 'Crimes' might include failing to prepare the food properly or not keeping the table and utensils clean; the obvious punishment would be for the culprit to forego some of his drink ration.

Timing of Meals

Although theoretically the time and duration of meals was at the captain's discretion, when a squadron was working together such things were laid down by the senior officer. Sir Edward Pellew took over the East Indies squadron in 1805 and put out a general order that said 'The commander-in-chief...will hoist a red pennant at the main when he makes it noon, that all the crews may dine at the same time...[they] are to breakfast at eight bells [in this case, 8am] and sup at half past five pm.' This makes good sense: a commanding officer who is contemplating mass manoeuvres wants people available to perform them and since mealtimes were sacrosanct he would want to know when they were. The norm was forty-five minutes each for breakfast and supper and an hour and a half for dinner.[17] Pellew stated this and went on to say that 'the meal times of the people are not [to be] broken in upon'; Nelson remarked in one of his general orders about turning the men up for muster when demanded by the senior officer at a port 'meal times excepted', and many captains said much the same in their own order books.[18] So we can accept that with the exception of essential watch-keepers such as lookouts or steersmen, who were known as 'seven-bell men' because they ate half an hour early, all the crew (*ie* everyone except the officers) ate together. Mealtimes were piped by the boatswain.

At this point one begins to wonder whether they ate their meat dinners hot. This doubt comes from contemplating the length of time it would take for the meat to cook, and the time it would take the cook and his assistants to serve each mess cook. Obviously this varied according to the size of the ship and the number in her crew – a large ship bearing less than her full complement having less of a problem than one which mustered nearly 100 per cent of her complement – but since we do have some actual figures for *Victory*, we will continue to use her as an example. During the first year when Nelson had her as his flagship in the Mediterranean (July 1803 to June 1804) she was carrying an average of 811 men, so although the officers would not be eating from the main boilers we can say that roughly 800 were. Whether there were still 165 messes, as five years previously, is not known, but it seems likely. On a pork day one boiler would contain pork, the other pease; on a beef day one beef and the other vegetables or pudding. We can say that with fair conviction because the pease, vegetables and pudding would not take as long as the meat to cook and would anyway be awkward to cook in the same pot. Even so, the boilers were going to be pretty full of nets and bags, each of which had to be given to the right mess at serving time.

The cook also had to skim off the slush. Because the boiler was full of nets, because the lid was high up and because the slush was suspended in the water during cooking, this could not be done during the cooking process. Another consideration here was the danger of dripping wet greasy liquid down the outside of the hearth and onto the deck in the process; one of the earliest things any cook learns is that the floor should not be allowed to get wet and slippery around stoves (even more dangerous when you are short of a limb).

So the best time to remove the slush would be when the cooking was complete and the liquid could be drawn off through the cocks into tubs; the fat would then rise to the top and could be removed easily. However, the cook could not leave the meat in the boiler as without liquid it would stick and burn; it had to come out straightaway.

The cook had another problem, which was ensuring that each mess got its own net and bag. Without some organised way of doing this, he would end up with a time-consuming gridlock at serving time and many of the messes would have had a long wait for their dinner. What follows is pure conjecture, but would work: to start with, he had to put the nets and bags into their respective boilers in number order. He did this by arranging them in batches before they went in the boiler, perhaps using a spare tub, and then he had a set of hooks on the rail which went round the stove and attached each batch to one of these, still in order and perhaps having previously tied each five or ten nets together, or even put them into a larger net (not too many in a batch as he would end up with too much weight to handle).

By serving time, he had emptied both boilers and he then had one tub full of meat nets, one full of pudding/pease bags, and a tub full of soup/gravy, lining these up across the back of the galley, with himself and an assistant standing by each. He needed to have this operation completed a good half-hour before dinner time. Meanwhile, the mess cooks had lined up, in mess number order, kids in hand, and as soon as the cook was ready, they filed past the tubs, collecting their own net/bag and some ladlesful of soup and off they went to their messes, getting there before the general stampede that followed the boatswain's pipe for dinner. In the interests of fairness, the cooks would have to change the mess number order from day to day. Maybe one day they started with the lowest number and worked through to the highest, the next starting in the middle and the next starting at the end and working backwards. To prevent confusion, they would always do it in a particular order on certain days of the week. But even so, the food was not going to be very hot. Actually, that would not matter too much with the meat, which tastes just as good and may be easier to cut when cold. Cold soup is not pleasant, but the tubful could be reheated, either by returning it to the boiler until the last minute, or by dousing some hot irons in it. What about those seven-bell men? It would cause considerable confusion if they ate anywhere other than in their usual mess, so the cook kept a separate hook for the seven-bell messes, the mess cooks announced that status when they brought their food to be cooked and they came back to collect it a good 35 minutes before dinner time.

One other piece of evidence for cold meat (or possibly reheated meat, although that raises the question of where it was kept in between cooking and reheating) is another part of St Vincent's order quoted above:[19] '[to save fuel] no fire to be lighted in the ranges of the ships of the fleet until 11 o'clock in the forenoon and [to be] put out as soon as the captain's dinner is served...'. This means a total of three hours of fire, and given that it would take at least half an hour for the water to boil, leaves no more than two and a half hours for the meat and other items to cook. One suspects that this particular order was either ignored when St Vincent was not in sight of the galley smoke, or that someone pointed out its impracticality and it was countermanded.

A few more questions to which we have no definitive answers but which inevitably come to you when you start thinking about all this. Did they really have three 'Banyan' days each week when their dinner consisted of no more than biscuit, pease (on two of those three days) and a little butter and cheese? Such rations would not go far with a hungry man. Perhaps they saved some of their meat and duff. Maybe these were the days when they had soup; there are numerous references in Nelson's and other commanders-in-chief's letters and orders to 'the men's soup'. Or perhaps, since those three Banyan days are the days when oatmeal features, they really did only have porridge on three days, and then in such quantities that it kept them going through dinner time. Or maybe those who were on good terms with the cook were able to do something with the remains of their porridge. Thick porridge, when cold, can be sliced and fried like polenta or baked into a sort of oatcake.

And for that matter, were those days of the week shown on the ration table meant to be absolute or merely advisory? Were they the days when specific items of food should be eaten, or just when they should be issued, keeping in mind that salt meat would have to be steeped for many hours before cooking? One would hope that masters' logs, which in Nelson's fleet at least were meant to record the opening of casks of meat, would throw some light on this, but they do not. Many do not mention opening meat casks at all; others mention it but show it to have been done on different days of the week, with no discernible pattern; others show both beef and pork casks being opened on the same day.

How long did it take to cook the dinner? This is something that has a number of variables, not least of these being how well done they liked the end product. To the modern eye, the cooking times given by some Georgian cooks for vegetables are far too long; Hannah Glasse remarks 'most people spoil garden things by over-boiling them' but then goes on to say that cauliflower should be boiled for fifteen minutes, which is more than enough to reduce it to mush. She also advocates boiling young spring carrots for between half an hour and an hour, and 'Sandwich' carrots (which probably means large main-crop) will take, she says, two hours. From all this it seems that the vegetables would cook for about an hour. Suet and pease puddings take quite a bit longer, from two and a half hours depending on the size. Porridge takes about twenty minutes once the water has boiled and the oatmeal is thrown in.

What takes longest is the meat; in the author's kitchen a piece of rolled salt brisket about six inches in diameter gets four to five hours of very gentle simmering, longer if it has been loitering in its brine for over six months. A large ham takes about the same time. Which means that if the meat has to be cooked by 10.30am to allow an hour's cooling before taking it out at 11.30am, it has to start cooking at about 6am. We know that on most ships (ignoring St Vincent's odd order quoted above) the cook lit the stove soon after 4am; he probably did so with some water in the boilers, topping them up after all the meat was in and it would then take half an hour or so to come back to the boil.[20] After this point, the cook would then need to watch his fire carefully, feeding it just enough to keep the water simmering rather than boiling hard.

And finally, what did they eat for supper? Other than the second part of the day's alcohol ration, which was issued late in the afternoon, there seems to have been no official preparation of food for this meal. They must have saved some of their biscuit, and could have eaten this with some meat saved from dinner, a little cheese, or whatever they had in their private stock. Perhaps, in cold weather, this is when they had the soup which several commanders-in-chief mention; otherwise, since the galley fire would have long since been extinguished, it had to be something cold.

Bad Weather and Battles

There were some occasions when it would have been impossible to light the stove and cook. One of these was the days in port when they were loading powder and the rule was 'No fires, no lights'. Any given ship would have very little, if any, control over exactly when it loaded, so on such days it would have been cold dinner and catch-up on another day. Such catching up was within the remit of the purser and since everyone would see the sense of it there would be no grumbling.

In bad weather it would have been impossible to cook. Not only would the contents of the boiler slop about with some inevitable spillage, the fire itself would shift and be difficult to control. Even the closed fire under the boilers would be a problem as the cook would not dare open the door to feed it. There are several reports of ships going round the Horn being unable to light the fires for weeks on end. It would not even have to be rough weather to create such problems; a ship moving, say, across the Trades could develop quite a heel even on a calm sea. This may not carry the fire risk of a ship lurching about on rough water, but it would restrict the amount of water they would want to put in the boilers.

The battle situation creates a problem of timing. The general thinking was that 'Englishmen would fight all the better for having a comfortable meal' beforehand; such a meal would not only be comforting to the belly but provide essential fuel for the coming exertions. So convinced were senior officers of the necessity for this that Howe incorporated a signal in his new system that read 'There will be time for the men to dine', hoisting this signal on the first of the four days that culminated in the 'Glorious First of June'. But they needed to ensure that the fires were out before powder started coming up from below and the enemy started firing. This would not, in most situations, have created much of a problem; unlike land fights, where the enemy could often hide and pop out unexpectedly, sea battles, whether major engagements or single-ship actions, were usually preceded by a long chase or prolonged manoeuvring for position. As long as they could see three or fours hours clear, there was time to light the fires and cook some meat; if, when it was ready, there was obviously no time to eat it at the tables, it could at least be issued and eaten from the hand. If there was no time for that, it was a case of biscuit, cheese and a mug of wine or grog taken at each man's action station.[21]

Personal Extras

It has often been said that the British seaman was a very conservative eater. Perhaps he was, but there can be little doubt that any mess of men who liked their food would take whatever opportunity presented itself to buy some little extras to perk up their rations. One man might be delegated to do the buying, with the others stumping up their share in cash or kind. The surgeon of *Daedalus* remarked that while on the Moluccas station, the men exchanged their unwanted rice for yams, pumpkins and sweet potatoes.[22] And of course, anyone who came across something good while on his own would naturally share it with his mess-mates; this has always been the norm when groups of men eat together regularly.

Whenever they touched land, even if away from a town, the locals would want to make the most of the opportunity to sell their wares. Wybourn remarked of watering at Sardinia, when 'hundreds of the Natives [*sic*] flocked down bringing quantities of provisions, Animals, Vegetables, fruit, etc.,' and when Keith's fleet was assisting the army in Egypt in 1800, the army quartermasters regulated the market by keeping the Arab sellers on one side of a stretched rope while the army and navy buyers stood on the other. Here, as well as sheep, poultry and pigeons, the Arabs sold spinach, lettuce and onions.[23]

Even if the men could not go ashore, bumboats would come out bearing local produce, including both fresh and dry fruit. In European waters, dry fruit would include figs, dates, prunes or apricots, even apples and pears. All of these were actively traded into England; some 'dry' grocers in London specialised in them as early as the mid-1600s and most sailors who had ventured near the Mediterranean would have been aware of them; they would also have been familiar with the various types of dried sausage. All of these would have been among the wares available on shore or brought out to the ships by bumboats. Any sailor with a sweet tooth and a few coins in his pocket would also have bought some dried fruit (and nuts) for long-term keeping as well as some of the equally available fresh fruit. Exactly what this was depended on where they were: in the Mediterranean, grapes, melons, pomegranates, figs, apricots and peaches, fresh dates, lemons and oranges (Malta was famous for the red-flecked blood orange); further south at Madeira and the West Indies, bananas, limes and pineapples and sometimes 'alligator' or avocado pears; and in the East Indies, all of these plus guavas, mangosteens and mangoes. In northern

Europe and round the Mediterranean basin, nuts would range from hazelnuts, almonds, walnuts and chestnuts, and further afield there would be more exotic nuts such as Brazils, cashews and coconuts. The bumboats would also bring sweetmeats, cakes, jams, pickles and even, for those who had a taste for them, spices and other seasonings.

Depending on the captain, they might be allowed to buy alcohol. Captain Parker of the *Amazon* said in his orders that liquor might be brought onto the ship by messes who first obtained permission and 'who know how to make proper use of it.'[24] However, allowed or not, no doubt plenty did make its way aboard one way or another.

Although there are few records of below-decks men keeping poultry, it is likely that many did, for eggs if nothing else. As long as the entire ship did not degenerate into a chicken farm, a reasonable captain would not object; they did, after all, allow such pets as parrots, so why not a chicken or two?

Another interesting question on how the men ate is how did they eat their onions? This might seem an odd thing to wonder about, given the obvious thought of putting them in to boil with the meat or adding them to the soup, but there are some clues pointing in another direction. Nelson put out a general order, chiding the pursers for using the onions to put in the soup when they were intended 'for the recruiting the health of the ship's company' and some of the logs of his fleet report receiving onions, then serving them out to the men more or less straightaway.[25] The men could indeed have put them in the net with their meat or added them to their duff, or even roasted them on the stove. On the other hand, this was in the Mediterranean, where big mild Spanish-type onions could be had, and those can be eaten raw, either with biscuit and cheese or chopped and dressed with oil and vinegar, both of which were available. Consider the taste range and texture of the rest of their diet: bland, boiled, soft (unless their teeth were good enough to crunch the biscuit without soaking it), and you can see how those men would have relished the sharp strong taste and crisp texture of a raw onion. And if they did this in the Mediterranean, they would have done the same elsewhere. There is an alternative possibility, and for this we also have some evidence: Richard Ford reported to Nelson on one occasion that because of the season, the onions were too small for anything but pickling. They had onions, they had vinegar, and before they were far into a commission, they would have had empty casks and the small butter firkins. It does not take many weeks before small whole onions are ready to eat, and if the big ones are sliced, they are ready in a week or so. There are worse ways to spend your off-watch hours than preparing something tasty to eat, especially if you do it with your mates and make a social occasion of the job, yarning while you peel.

Yarning is thought to be a major part of the social life below decks and the main opportunity for it, apart from such situations as above, was at the dinner table. Greg Dening believes that yarning takes on a ritual function, tales demonstrating experience serving not only to establish hierarchies among each group of men but also to create little areas of privacy between groups.[26] One can well imagine the kudos attached to having a man in your mess who had fought at one of the famous battles or served under one of the famous admirals.

One final thing about below-decks eating which no-one has mentioned is what they did when there were women on board. And there were, it seems, quite a few. There were the women who were in some quasi-official situation, such as the tradesmen warrant officers' wives, and those who did not exist as far as the Admiralty were concerned but were there with the full cognisance of the captain: one or two are known to have signed on with men's names and did a man's job; others did not pretend to be men but may have been in the muster book under a man's name to get them a wage and victuals. The question arises firstly for those who were not on the list but stayed with the ship when she sailed; these may just have 'belonged' to a mess and shared its food. The second sort are those who came on board when the ship was in port and stayed there for some time. Some of these would have been genuine wives and likely to bring baskets of goodies with them. But what about the others, the 'Portsmouth brutes' and 'Spithead nymphs' and their foreign equivalents? Was their price 'Sixpence and me dinner'? Did they bring food as well as liquor on board? Did the men share their rations or lay in a stock of food from the bumboats? Alas, we may never know.

Chapter 5

HOW THE OFFICERS ATE

As far as the Admiralty and the Victualling Board were concerned,with two small exceptions, there was no difference in the way officers and men ate. The official ration was the same, as we have seen there was to be no preferential choosing for the officers, and they were, exactly like the men, provided with no mess 'traps' beyond what they chose to buy for themselves. Officers were not provided with these until 1856 and then only when a ship was newly commissioned; they had to provide their own replacements. It was another forty years before anything was provided free for the men.[1] The two minor exceptions were that captains were traditionally supplied with a cask of ox-tongues on commissioning a ship, a practice which was referred to as 'ancient' in 1703 and which carried on until 1915; and that commanders-in-chief were given 'table money' as an acknowledgement of their need to entertain.[2]

By the social mores of the time, officers, as gentlemen, were expected to eat in a better way and on a different level than the 'people'. The obvious way to set themselves apart was to eat at different times. Although they breakfasted at 8am, as did the men, they supped at 6pm and dined at least one hour later than the men. On some ships, the captain ate an hour later than the lieutenants and warrant officers; Nelson's dinners were served at 2.45pm. There were some practical as well as social aspects to these different timings: the officers would be available to take over some of the essential watch duties while the men ate, the younger and more agile of them (probably midshipmen) going aloft as lookouts. And since the officers' cooks, stewards and 'waiters' also had to eat, they would do so with the rest of the men and be free to attend to the officers in due course.

Officers' Messes

Captains and admirals kept their own tables, while other officers formed their own messes, where they clubbed together to buy their own wine and food, or at least some embellishments for the ration food. This must have created quite a financial problem for the more impoverished officers, who would be almost unable to resist the social pressure to pay up. One can imagine the embarrassment for a man who declined to join the 'club' and was forced to eat ration food at a table where everyone else was eating something better.

One of the members of the mess would be appointed 'caterer' for an agreed duration, of several months if not indefinitely, and he held the mess's money and bought whatever they needed when they touched shore. In the commissioned officers' mess this was unlikely to be the first lieutenant, whose executive duties would have kept him too busy, but there was no hard and fast rule. They chose the most suitable, and on a foreign station the choice might well have fallen on someone with a gift for languages. In *Gloucester*, when Edward Mangin sailed in her in 1812, the mess caterer was the marine captain. His abilities where food was concerned were adequate but with wine they were not; Mangin reports that his fellows 'swallowed the nauseous and pernicious liquids, nick-named Port and Sherry, with wry faces both at its flavour and its costliness'.[3] For this dubious privilege, each of the twelve members of the mess contributed £60 a year, a not inconsiderable sum when a junior lieutenant's salary was barely more than that.[4] £60 a year seems to have been fairly standard for that year; the purser Thomas Peckston paid the same on *Volontaire*.[5]

There were two officers' messes on a ship of the line: the wardroom, where the commissioned naval officers, the marine officers and certain of the warrant officers such as the surgeon and master ate; and the gunroom, where the other officers ate. In frigates and smaller ships there was only a gunroom, which might have included both sets of officers or might not, depending on the individual ship. Pursers, masters and surgeons were considered 'wardroom officers' and joined that mess. Where there was a chaplain, he would be included, as might the admiral's secretary in a flagship. Various people of appropriate rank taking passage as supernumeraries to join their own ship or diplomatic post would also dine in the wardroom. The 'tradesmen' warrant officers (the boatswain, gunner, carpenter and sailmaker) would form their own little mess in the gunroom or elsewhere; other 'not-quite-gentlemen' such as the captain's clerk, the schoolmaster, the surgeon's assistants and any supernumeraries in transit of the same type, such as Richard Ford's clerk John Geohegan, would form another, each mess in its own little stratified world. One wonders what the financial arrangements would have been for Richard Ford. Once he had joined *Victory*, his important task and high salary (more than a post captain's) should have given him a place in the wardroom despite his 'trade' status; the same applied to his numerous buying trips in other ships. Presumably he made arrangements to pay his share of each mess's expenses, and no doubt returned from each trip ashore bearing useful contributions to the mess's storeroom, not least of these being wine. Ford's peripatetic work was probably rare outside the ranks of diplomats; there were few other people with such a need to move around so frequently.

In a ship of the line the wardroom occupied a substantial space on the lower deck, extending right aft to the stern. It had roundhouses for the officers' toilets, flimsily-constructed cabins on either side where the officers slept, and a long table down the middle where they did all the other things which required a table. Other than the first lieutenant in a line-of-battle ship, who might have a large enough cabin to include a desk, the other commissioned officers only had enough room in their cabins to sleep and keep their sea-chest, often sharing the meagre accommodation with a gun. So at this table, they read, played cards, wrote up their journals and ate their meals.

The table, and presumably also the chairs, were supplied by the dockyard when the ship was commissioned; those tables would have been constructed in such a way that they could be taken apart rapidly when clearing for action. Alexander Dingwall Fordyce regretted that they were not fitted with drawers, but the ship's carpenter could have added them if desired. There were various methods of keeping the dishes in place in rough weather: Fordyce recommends baize-covered wedges of different sizes for keeping dishes upright (especially those containing gravy, he says) or pudding bags filled with pease and fitted with beckets and lanyards at either end. An alternative was to put several layers of wet cloths on the table to prevent plates and dishes sliding. For decanters and glasses a 'fiddle' was used, this being a sort of lightweight railed enclosure, again with beckets and lanyards from each corner, and a gridwork of yarn to hold the individual items in place.[6]

The wardroom might have had two sets of tableware: good glasses and porcelain for Sundays and visitors, tumblers and pewter or earthenware crockery for other days. Thomas Peckston reports that they ate off Delftware, a reasonably priced soft clay pottery coated with a thin opaque whitish glaze, most popularly decorated in blue. There was plenty of earthenware or porcelain to choose from; by 1770 the potteries in Staffordshire were in full swing, and the opening of the Grand Trunk Canal in 1777 connected the pottery towns with Liverpool and the coasters which would take their goods to London, no doubt pausing at Plymouth and Portsmouth *en route* to supply the shops in those naval ports. In London itself, the East India Company had been importing Chinese porcelain in enormous quantities since the late 1600s, using it as flooring (*ie* ballast) for their tea cargoes. Tableware of all sorts was readily available, though then, as now, the best quality was not cheap. Moneyed captains and admirals could have it made with their own designs; Nelson's personal collection of china included a set of 'Baltic' pattern china from the Coalport factory, each piece of which included his crests and coat of arms and the inscription 'Nelson 2nd April Baltic'. It is not known whether this was used at sea or at Merton, but it does indicate what was available to those who could pay for it. Nelson also had some silver serving dishes, some of these chased with his arms and crests, delivered in their own wainscot chest, fitted and lined with green baize. These came from the big City firm of silversmiths Rundell & Bridge, and cost a total of £627.0.2.[7] He also had solid silver cutlery in a set for twenty diners, again kept in a compartmentalised sea-chest.[8] Cutlery might be made of steel, pewter or Britanniaware, sometimes with ivory, bone or wooden handles. Well-off senior officers might also have had some silver tea- or coffee-pots and cream-jugs.

Some other evidence for the type of crockery used at sea comes from a recent excavation of the wreck of *Swift* in Argentinean Patagonia in 1770. Items found at the stern, where the wardroom and captain's cabins would have been, show 'a clear predominance of high-quality ceramics and porcelain', including numerous ornamentally edged white English plates and bowls and some fine Chinese porcelain bowls and plates with blue decorations of a pagoda and trees. There are also many square 'case' bottles (so-called because they fitted into a lockable case), and many semi-glazed stoneware jars and jugs.[9]

There are no published reports of tableware at the lower warrant officers' messes, or details of where they actually ate on smaller ships where they were not included in the gunroom. Each of them would have some sort of office desk for their paperwork which they might have used as a dining table, either on their own or perhaps in pairs, desk size permitting; or the carpenter could have organised a trestle table so they could eat together. There are one or two reports of captains' clerks or schoolmasters being disgruntled at having to eat with the midshipmen for lack of any alternative.

The midshipmen ate in their own berth. Depending on the makeup of the group (age-range, family background, etc), conditions varied from the civilised to the squalid. Where there was a responsible older midshipman he would be the most obvious mess caterer. The very young 'young gentlemen' (also known as 'squeakers') were put under the charge of the gunner, although the captain usually took responsibility for their money and expenses, doling out pocket-money as appropriate and writing to their fathers for more when necessary. Admiral Cuthbert Collingwood wrote to his friend Walter Spencer-Stanhope of his son, William, 'Your son's debts are not enormous yet – you cannot think how cheap salt water is, and there is nothing else to buy.'[10] No-one seems to have reported what happened with the older midshipmen, at the age between squeaking and financial responsibility; perhaps the captain delegated the task of mess caterer for these boys to one of the other officers. William Dillon reports joining the *Alcide* (74) in 1790 as an eleven-year-old and paying a 5-guinea entrance contribution.[11] Jeffrey de Raigersfeld reports having 12 guineas when he joined his first ship and says it did not last long. He also took 'plates and spoons of pewter, a dozen knives and forks, two cooking kettles, a frying pan, a copper tea kettle, a dozen tumbler glasses, two decanters, a dozen cups and saucers of the old blue dragon fashion and a tin teapot.' One can imagine his loving mother buying all of this; little could she have suspected that these items, together with his stock of tea, sugar, onions and celery seeds ('to add interest to the pea soup'), would immediately be seized 'for the common good'. However, the common good did at least involve members of the mess taking it in turns to wash the dishes 'lest the blackguard boy should be the cause of breakages'.[12]

Raigersfeld's list of food supplies suggests enhancement rather than replacement of the official ration. He does remark later than they had their Saturday meat ration roasted for Sunday dinner, a diet also borne out by Dillon: 'One o'clock was the dinner hour, fresh meat in harbour with vegetables and salt at sea [with] potatoes and such, puddings and pea soup...we might have a slice of cheese and biscuit previous to turning in.'[13] However, they seem to have had some of their ration issued on a larger than daily scale, unless butter was something they bought for themselves. Raigersfeld tells of the tub of melted butter which started with some small hairs in it and grew progressively hairier as they used it up, eventually to discover a bald dead mouse at the bottom.[14] He does not say whether they threw the rest of the butter away; knowing the propensities of growing adolescent boys, one is left with the horrid suspicion that hunger may have overcome squeamish scruples. Nor would most of them be over-nice about the table linen: Frederic Chamier reports a midshipmen's mess where the table cloth, changed once a week on Saturdays, was used as a towel when not on the table and bore the marks of dirty hands and fingers. It was also used to wipe spoons and to clean the tines of forks by the simple method of poking them through the fabric. Chamier also throws some light on the methods by which hungry midshipmen acquired extra food, although in his case the plan misfired: he and a fellow midshipman stole some tripe from a dish intended for the captain's dinner; when the captain found out, he turned them before the mast (relegated them to the status of common seamen).[15] Like the wardroom officers, the midshipmen had servants to wait on them, a number which might only theoretically be expressed in the plural. Abraham Crawford reports 'notwithstanding the berths of the midshipmen were so numerously furnished with inmates, from the reduced state of the ship's crew, the idlers list could not be conveniently increased; and one wretched boy allotted to each berth had alone to perform the three-fold functions of steward, cook and attendant.'[16]

At the other end of the scale, captains and admirals ate in considerable style. The young 'commander' captains of the smaller ships might not be able to afford much beyond the basic ration, but they ate it at their own table in their day cabin. In the larger ships the captain had a separate dining cabin. Unless they chose to invite a guest, they ate in solitary state, although it was traditional for them to be invited to dine in the wardroom once a week. Most captains made a point of regularly entertaining the wardroom officers, in small groups if not *en masse*, and would include at least one midshipman at such meals, deeming it part of their duty to the boy's parents to show him how to behave on social occasions. Some, including Nelson, often took a midshipman with them when they were invited to dine ashore. An impoverished captain could fulfil at least part of his obligations by inviting the officer and midshipman of the watch to join him for breakfast.

The same situation of dining up and down happened with admirals: in their flagship they would invite and be invited by the captain of the fleet and the ship's captain and the wardroom; when the weather and the movements of the squadron allowed, with the captains and higher-ranking lieutenants of the other ships. In one letter home Nelson remarked that he was to have entertained William Elliott (son of Sir Hugh Elliott, minister at Naples) in *Victory* 'but a fair wind came and that cancels all invitations'.[17] In squadrons where there were sufficient freemasons (and this may well have applied to Nelson himself) such dinner parties would have coincided with a lodge meeting. Admirals, while in port, would also have to entertain diplomats, local worthies and other senior naval personnel such as the port admiral and dockyard commissioner. On many of these occasions, ladies would join the party.

Officers were allowed a number of personal servants dependent on their rank, these servants being men or boys carried on the ship's books. Marine officers' servants would be marine privates – Glascock mentions that while negro boys waited on the naval officers, the marine officer's servant was a tall marine, 'whose head and the beams above were in perpetual collision'.[18] All levels of admiral and commander-in-chief were allowed fifty servants, captains were allowed four for each hundred men of their complement, the wardroom officers of ships of more than sixty men had one each, and the boatswain, gunner and carpenter had two on ships of over sixty men, one on ships with less.[19] Some of these captains' and admirals' 'servants' were actually young gentlemen being taken to sea to oblige their parents, others would be adult seamen, while some would not be seamen at all but personal servants whom the officers kept with them on shore as well as at sea. These latter servants would include a steward to perform the duties carried out by a butler on land, and also a cook. A moneyed captain who liked his food, and an admiral or commander-in-chief who entertained a lot, might have more than one cook.

Officers' Stores

Officers had their own storerooms for wine, comestibles and table accoutrements. This would be a personal store for captains and upwards, a group store for wardroom officers, and perhaps another for midshipmen. The better-quality table settings, especially if they included silver, would be kept in the storeroom and returned to it after each meal, to avoid 'disappearances'. On some ships one of the roundhouses off the wardroom might be fitted up to serve as a steward's pantry, where everyday mess traps could be stored. James Anthony Gardner mentions such a pantry 'fitted in the wing to stow our crockery and dinner traps with safety.'[20] A small sink, draining out through a pipe, would facilitate the washing-up. Otherwise, the mess traps would have to be carried away for washing. Although no-one has mentioned this, the cook may have refilled one of the boilers with water for this purpose after the men's dinner was served.

The tradesmen warrant officers were actually better off for private storage space than the lieutenants. They had, as did the purser and the surgeon, lockable storerooms for their trade equipment and stores and would be able to stow some personal edibles in them as well; the wardroom probably had a single private storeroom on the orlop. The content of these stores, as well as wine, would mostly be preserved foodstuffs and tracklements. These were freely available. There had been a thriving trade in spices from the East into Europe as far back as the eleventh century and by the seventeenth century food retailing had divided into salters, who dealt in wet goods, and grocers, who dealt in dry goods. As well as salted foods such as bacon, ham and other preserved meats, salters sold such things as anchovies, oil, pickles and vinegar. Grocers stocked sugar and molasses, dried fruit, rice, oriental spices and other dry foods such as pease and flour.[21] As well as the big outlets in London, there were shops in the main naval ports to cater for naval officers.

Receipts for St Vincent, Nelson and other officers show a wide variety of spices, pickles, chutneys and flavoured vinegars: white, black and 'Chyan' (cayenne) pepper, ginger, cinnamon, allspice, cloves, nutmeg and mace, mustard and curry powder; lemon and mango pickle and 'yellow Indian pickle' (piccalilli), mushroom ketchup, pickled onion and walnuts, cucumbers and cabbage; soy sauce; tarragon, chilli, herb and elder vinegars; anchovies and French olives; capers and celery seed; and horseradish. Many of these would be served with the cold meats: hams, tongues and, listed in one of Nelson's requests to his agent Alexander Davison, 'Hamburgh Beef'. (Although Germans, possibly inspired by the Tartars, were already eating finely chopped raw beef at this time, this is more likely to have been the dried and salted beef which was also known as 'Dutch' [Deutsch] beef which features in several contemporary cookery books.)[22] That same request also included twelve 'Gloster' cheeses and four kegs of 'sour crout'; on other occasions Nelson's purchases included forty-two pounds of Parmesan cheese, 'sallad oil',

Brunswick sausages and pickled tripe.[23] Much of this would have been intended for his guests. Nelson himself was a very moderate eater; according to his surgeon William Beatty, '[he] often contented himself with the wing or liver of a fowl and a small plate of macaroni and vegetables'.[24]

On the sweet side, St Vincent bought milk chocolate and candy, currants, raisins and muscatels, Jordan almonds, 'moist' sugar and loaves of sugar, with a pair of sugar nippers to break pieces off the loaves. In the summer, during a return visit to port, he bought cherries, raspberries, currants and gooseberries. Nelson bought macaroons, dried cherries, raspberry and apricot jam and 'currant' jelly (whether red, white or black is not specified). Other officers took strawberry jam and marmalade; these fruit preserves would have made a considerable contribution to their Vitamin C intake. Midshipmen (or their mothers) would probably have packed cakes or sweet Naples biscuits. The biscuit manufacturing firm of Carrs started up towards the end of the Napoleonic Wars, making a refined version of ships' biscuit called 'Captains' Thins' (an even thinner version of these is still for sale and popular for eating with cheese: 'Carrs Table Water' biscuit). Other firms whose names are still to be found on the supermarket shelf, in Britain at least, include Huntley & Palmer and Jacobs, who all started by supplying ships' captains and then moved on to other and sweeter biscuits.

As well as preserved meats, officers bought fresh meat (beef, pork and mutton) and prepared poultry. Nelson received a reminder in 1791 from Mary Saunders of the Isle of Wight that he owed her a total of £7.10.0 for two-dozen fowls, a pair of ducks, and four crocks of butter.[25] Officers sent each other gifts of food and when operating reasonably close to home often received hampers of food from their wives or friends. Nelson, at Copenhagen in 1801, took the opportunity of one of his sailors catching a fine turbot to patch up his relationship with Admiral Hyde Parker by sending the fish to him.[26] Admiral James de Saumarez, when off Ushant in 1800, had been sent a fine salmon and a sucking pig, and when in the Baltic between 1808 and 1812 was sent a haunch of venison and a turtle by friends; his wife sent some porter, some hearts, pickled oysters, butter and biscuits, and arranged for a Guernsey cow to be sent. The cow was a great success, providing cream for the breakfast table and, reported Sir James to his wife, becoming 'a great pet on board...there is no fear of her starving'. He also reported receiving salmon, turbot and cod when off Gothenburg, and elsewhere 'plenty of fine mackerall'. Peas and other vegetables came out on the packet from Harwich and some of the officers cultivated a small garden on one of the islands; for a while they had great hopes of salad, spinach, new potatoes and green peas, but alas, the peas fell victim to thieves.[27] Such gardens were not new: Saumarez and other officers had cultivated small gardens off the French coast while serving in the Brest blockade in 1800.[28]

Other islands in the Baltic provided partridges, hares and other game, shot by the officers and occasionally contributed to the admiral's table. Raigersfeld reports shooting pigeons at St Helena and feeling guilty afterwards on thinking the survivors were mourning their dead companions. Other officers have reported shooting various birds, including doves, wild duck and snipe, and even peafowl on the Javanese islands; no doubt they also bagged the odd wild pig, goat or sheep when the opportunity presented itself.[29] The difficulties of such activities are explained by William Stanhope Lovell, who was a midshipman in *Renown* in the Mediterranean: when visiting Sardinia he took part in shooting parties, but these were ineffective without dogs to flush and retrieve, and 'Although some species of game were numerous, and flocks of blue pigeons, to the amounts of thousands, were seen, few were brought on board for no person would dare to follow them for fear of the wind changing, when we knew the fleet would sail immediately to regain our station.'[30] Basil Hall reported that when in *Leander* in 1802, at Bermuda, many of the officers kept pointers for their shooting expeditions ashore.[31]

And of course, the officers had their own livestock on board. They kept a full range of chickens, ducks, geese and turkeys, but the author has seen no mention of tame rabbits, although these are very efficient converters of food into meat. They may have been too temptingly pettable; as it was, many captains found the poultry-keeper (known as 'Jemmy Ducks') had to be changed regularly, lest he grow too fond of his charges. Cows for milk were rare but goats were common, as were sheep and pigs, both of which would provide a series of good meals, starting with the offal.[32] That intention could not always be realised, as Basil Hall found out on one voyage to China. Jean, the last of a litter of piglets had become very tame 'cruising along among the messes, poking her snout into every breadbag and often scalding her tongue in the soup-kids'. She even took her grog but was rarely seen to be drunk. Then, when halfway across the China Sea, Hall decided it was time to kill her. 'Let us have the fry today, the head with plenty of Port wine as mock-turtle soup tomorrow; and get one of the legs roasted for dinner on Saturday,' he told his steward, who listened to this and went off, only to return shortly to announce that the ship's company had begged for Jean's life. She had been trained to keep off the quarterdeck, but 'if the captain will only call her, she will show how tame she is'. Hall duly called Jean, she came gambolling up to him (tripping the first lieutenant as she passed him) and Hall relented. As time went on, Jean became fatter and fatter, until she could only lie on her side with her upper legs up in the air, grunting for food to be brought to her. When they arrived at Whampoa, visiting Chinese were much impressed by Jean, but then a horrid realisation set in: the Chinese were only waiting for Jean to die and be thrown overboard, so they could scoop her up as they did any other dead creatures that were thrown over. This was not acceptable to the crew, so when Jean did die, they sounded the river for a really muddy place and having bound some pieces of ballast rod to her snout, dropped her over at night in the selected spot, where she went straight down, deep enough to evade the grappling hooks, to great Chinese disappointment.[33]

And, just as did the men, officers bought fresh produce whenever they had the chance. St Helena provided vegetables for ships going to or from the East Indies and was famed for its watercress; one officer bought bunches of bananas in Madeira and slung them from the boats' davits, another had netsful of grapes, oranges, peaches and nectarines hanging from his cabin ceiling.[34] Admiral Rainier, commander-in-chief of the East Indies station from 1794 to 1804, was reputedly so fond of mangoes that he was said to have delayed his seagoing activities so that he did not miss the mango season on the Malabar coast.

To drink, as well as wine and the stronger sherries, ports and Madeiras, officers bought cider, porter and stout. Claret was very fashionable, bought in casks for general drinking and, after the last quarter of the eighteenth century when cylindrical bottles and long corks were introduced, the better sorts in bottles for special occasions. Admiral Bartholomew James recalled that as a midshipman he and some colleagues were in charge of some prizes, one of which had three cases of the best Bordeaux. His captain directed these to be sent to him, but Christmas intervened and the midshipmen drank the Bordeaux, refilled the bottles with cask claret, replaced the original corks and sealed them carefully. When the wine came to be drunk by the captain and his guests, they remarked that while it might be very good claret, it tasted little different from the cask claret.[35] Champagne, and its non-sparkling 'cousin' Sillery, were also drunk when the exigencies of the war allowed, and as well as the latterly ubiquitous rum, they drank gin, brandy or arrack, depending on the station. Punches were popular, cold or warmed with a hot poker and often spiced; this may have been one of the uses for the stores of nutmegs, ginger, cloves and cinnamon. Many of these punches included juice or slices of lemon; all were strong and involved mixing at least two kinds of drink, as a sort of precursor to the modern cocktail.

On the non-alcoholic side, officers bought the better sorts of tea and coffee. Souchong seemed to be the favourite tea, but St Vincent also had Hyson tea, Nelson had some other unspecified 'black' tea as well as Souchong and 'Turkey' coffee, while Hoste's coffee preference was for 'Moka'. Those on the East Indies station would have had their choice of all the teas coming back from China.

Cooking for the Officers

As we have seen, commanding officers could, and many did, bring a suite of personal servants with them. For those who cared about food one of these servants would be a professional cook, but those who saw food as mere fuel and were not too concerned about providing 'fancy' food for their guests would have someone called a steward. Nelson certainly knew the value of keeping a good table but did not seem terribly interested in food for himself. Rainier and Pellew came into the first category if their portraits are anything to go by: Rainier's portrait by Davis is rather dominated by his pebble glasses but when you look more closely you see a very large stomach jutting forward; Pellew changes from an early portrait which shows him as a post captain, substantially built but not desperately overweight, to a later portrait showing him as an admiral, considerably wider and with every garment bulging. He remarked himself when in the East Indies that it was time he went home as he was getting as fat as a pig. One suspects that both these admirals had professional cooks. At a slightly lower level Thomas Pasley, when a captain in 1778 to 1782, kept a delightful series of journals of his several convoy-escorting voyages, where a running theme is the food and dinners with his fellow captains. He refers to making 'the Hungry Signal' to invite guests to dine, dining sumptuously on Indiamen, sending milk and hot rolls for a lady's children and receiving in return six geese, being invited to share a turtle, sending a quarter of mutton and some fowls across to a fellow officer, and so on. His portrait also shows him to be distinctly chubby.[36]

What level of cook the wardroom officers had is not clear but no doubt any new intake of landsmen was eagerly scanned in hopes of finding someone skilled in the culinary arts. A well-off wardroom could, like the moneyed captains and admirals, hire a professional cook. Such a professional cook, engaged to perform his art, would arrive on the ship with his own 'batterie de cuisine', the pots and pans and everything else he felt he needed. Many of these cooking utensils would have been made of copper (for its good conduction) but well tinned inside to avoid poisoning by verdigris, the green cupric acetate which forms on bare copper. This would be for the pots which stood by the fire; those which stood or hung directly above it would be more likely to be longer-lasting iron. St Vincent's shopping list when he went back to sea in 1806 gives a good idea of the level of cooking he enjoyed: fish kettles, several stew pans and saucepans of different sizes (one described as 'a steam saucepan'), a 'hamlet' pan and other frying pans, soup pots, two sausage fillers, a Yorkshire pudding pan, a 'rooling' pin, some tartlet pans and a box of pastry cutters, an oval pudding mould and a cheese toaster, plus cooks' knives, ladles and a 'hand chopper'. This last was probably one of those half-moon knives with a handle at each end which we now call a 'hachette', invaluable for chopping the meat for sausages.[37]

It has been suggested that the type of cooking possible on board ship was restricted by the cooking facilities offered by the stoves, but this is faulty thinking. The Brodie, and then Lamb & Nicholson, stoves and their predecessors were each in their turn pretty much what the land-bound kitchen of the time had to cook on, the only difference being that the land-bound kitchen did not cavort about. The professional and experienced cook would deal with this problem by modifying the menu according to the weather, keeping the dishes simple when it was rough, more complex when it was calm, and taking advantage of the calm to prepare cold dishes for the rougher days to come. It is not the facilities of the cooking stove which make for good food, it is the expertise and care of the cook. What is done nowadays by turning the heat up or down was done then by moving pots closer to or further from the heat source, or moving them about in the oven. Equally, a practised wrist and a balloon whisk work just as well as an electric beater, and a set of sharp knives as well as any number of gadgets. The two secrets of producing good food (added to practice and good recipes) are having a well-stocked store cupboard and being prepared to stay in the kitchen and attend to what is going on, not having numerous gadgets and a fancy cooker.

They had butter and flour, so they could make pastry for tarts and pies; they also had eggs, dried fruit and sugar, so could make cakes; add milk to eggs and flour and you can make pancakes or batter puddings; with beaten egg whites and jam added to those other things you can make all sorts of tarts and puddings. They had plenty of varied meats, and whether using the spit of the Brodie stove or the closed oven of the Lamb & Nicholson, roasted meat means fat and juice for gravy and soups, as do bones; if all else failed there were the ubiquitous pease or onions for soup. Those onions would brighten up any savoury dishes, as would cheese. About the only thing they do not seem to have used was tomatoes, which, like potatoes, took a very long time to gain acceptability. And of course, given the right patch of sea, there was any amount of fish.

They could also, given those ovens, make bread and rolls – not every day, perhaps, and not on a grand scale, but enough to keep the cabin, the wardroom and the sickbay supplied (the oven on the Brodie stove was supposed to be big enough for eighty loaves). Until the process of making dried yeast as a brewing by-product was mastered, the leaven would have been some dough saved from the last batch. This is confirmed by A Edlin, the author of *A Treatise on Breadmaking*, writing in 1805, who quotes from 'The Hon Captain Cochrane's *Seaman's Guide to Making Bread*' '...which advocates retaining some dough from the last baking'. The same author also mentions the possibility of making bread with 'the artificial Seltzer water prepared by Mr Schweppe'; this would give a result more like the later Irish soda bread than yeast bread.[38] The main problem for an on-board baker would be maintaining an even and draft-free temperature during the rising stages but this could be more or less achieved by shutting the access doors at the front of the galley. This would not inconvenience anybody, as this end of the galley belonged preferentially to the officers' cooks. Finally, as well as the main stove, the senior officer's cook/steward had a small serving pantry close to the cabin dining room, where one of the hanging stoves could be mounted and where there could also be a spirit lamp for last-minute preparations or late evening tea-making or cheese-toasting.

The above is informed comment on what might be produced in the way of food, but we do have a fair amount of information on what was actually served. Crawford reports eating a 'three-decked sea-pie' much enhanced by onions: delicious but unwise, as he and his companions then went on shore to a dance, where the young ladies recoiled from their oniony breath.[39] Lovell recalled a pair of rather superior young Guards officers who begged a lift; arriving on board hungry but too late for wardroom dinner, they were presented with beef-steak, potatoes and port which was eaten to grumbles about 'roughing it'. Lovell, writing many years after the event, commented that their stomachs would have been glad to get worse if they had lived to serve with Wellington in the Peninsula.[40] On the East Indies station, while Rainier enjoyed local produce, Pellew displayed the classic English suspicion of foreign food; writing home to a friend, he remarked on the heat and his conviction that his good health was due to wearing flannel next to his skin and avoiding curry. His junior officers were not so fussy, eating their share of the ubiquitous rice, which substituted for biscuit, in the form of curry, even at breakfast.[41] On an Atlantic crossing at the beginning of 1813, the marine major T Marmaduke Wybourn reported their New Year dinner as including roast beef, mutton, pork, ducks and a turkey, boiled chickens, a ham, pumpkin pie, ' raspberry pudding [and] plum duff'. Alas, he gives no definition of the raspberry pudding; had he not followed it in his list with 'plum duff' one might suggest it could have been jam roly-poly but even so we can be fairly confident that the raspberries, at that time of year and in that location, would be in the form of jam.[42]

Hannah Glasse, whose *The Art of Cookery Made Plain and Easy* consists of recipes which she plagiarised from other writers, devotes a whole chapter to food for ships' captains. As well as suggesting that the head of an ordinary pig can stand in for a boar's head at a feast, she offers several recipes for globe artichokes 'fried, ragooed and fricasseed', ketchup to keep for twenty years, and a complicated recipe for what she calls 'sea venison' which is mutton marinated in wine and vinegar, served in a rich gravy under a pie crust.

Perhaps the most valuable of the available documents is Admiral Digby's menu book, kept by his steward John Gulivar in 1781.[43] Admiral Digby was at the time *en route* to New York in *Prince George* and one of his midshipmen was Prince William Henry (the future William IV), who dined with the admiral several days a week. This little book is doubly valuable, as it lists not only the dishes served, but also the guests on each occasion and thus allows us to see the relationship between the number and status of the guests and the number and type of dishes served. For a simple Saturday dinner, with only four guests (all of them described as 'Mr', so probably lieutenants or perhaps civilians) there were three meat dishes (boiled mutton, mutton hash and roast pork), a fricassee of duck, potatoes and French beans, pickles and butter, and tarts and pancakes: a total of four entrées with side dishes and two puddings. For a Monday dinner with 'P W Hinery' (Prince William Henry), one captain and seven misters, there was sea pie, roast mutton, salt fish, sliced ham and 'boild foul', potatoes, pickles and butter, fritters (whether they were sweet or savoury is not defined), tarts and fruit puddings: five entrées with side dishes and two (or possibly three) puddings. Then for a Sunday dinner with Prince William Henry, five captains and five misters, there were boiled ducks, boiled fowl, roast goose, boiled beef, roast mutton, bacon, and albacore (preparation method not defined), with side dishes of potatoes, French beans, carrots and turnips and beaten butter, and puddings of Spanish fritters (these would be dredged in sugar after frying), 'apil pye' and fruit fritters, with two dishes of whipped cream: a much richer and more elaborate feast for a more important occasion.

It is, perhaps, a little unkind to laugh at the quaint and varied spelling of the entries, for it is obvious from some practice sentences at the back of the book that Gulivar was comparatively new to the art of writing, but one cannot but smile at finding three versions of potatoes (potatos, potetos, purtatos) and two of gooseberry tarts (gosseboory tarts, gusebery torts), and such delicacies as 'pilches', 'cabges', 'hareco', 'carits', 'stud inyons' and 'grins', not to mention the mouth-watering 'foul brown sous' (probably a fowl in a brown sauce). One entry which puzzled the author for some time was 'cavetched albcho'. Hannah Glasse provided the answer: albecore tuna preserved (caveached) in vinegar after poking into it a mixture of pepper, nutmeg, mace and salt. A modern version of this, escabech, can still be bought in delicatessens in Spain and Portugal.

Entertainment value aside, the menu book shows that the food served at Admiral Digby's table, though generous and varied, was not haute cuisine. Vegetables seem to be served unadorned (although the 'grins' are sometimes served with 'beackon' and the cabbage as a ragout), the meat is either stewed or roasted, the fruit comes in pies or tarts and there is occasionally fried fish or bacon and eggs. Sometimes the meat is described as steaks, sometimes there is sea-pie or plum pudding (or plum dumplings) and on several consecutive days, a turtle, first appearing as 'turtil hid and fins'.

This book also indicates the precedence 'ratings' of the guests, a matter of great importance at all Georgian events. Although only a midshipman, Prince William Henry was the King's son, and so always the most important guest, to be seated on his host's right. Other guests, at admirals' and captains' tables, would then proceed through a mixture of personal social rank and seniority of service, with some nice dilemmas to be resolved. For instance, should a midshipman who is the son of a duke be seated 'higher' than an untitled but long-serving captain? And would that titled midshipman be wise to demur and seat himself at the foot of the table, thus gaining the approbation of a senior officer who might be inclined to help his career? (On the other hand, if his father was really influential, it might be he who could help the career of the senior officer.) In the wardroom the first lieutenant was the head of the table and host when they had guests. On guestless days, each officer may have had a precedent-dictated place and kept to it, but as always such things depended on the individual ship.

There were topics of conversation which were frowned upon: religion, politics and the fairer sex, or rather specific members of the fairer sex except in the most general terms. Whether or not the tone of conversation tended to the bawdy would depend on the ship, as would other topics – a 'reading' ship would discuss literature and classical history, a 'sporting' mess would discuss prize-fighting, cricket, fox-hunting and shooting. But the most common topics would be professional: technical aspects of seamanship, gunnery and tactics, ships sailed in and places seen, and sea-battles major and minor. Any newcomer or guest who had taken part in any of the famous actions would be avidly questioned for details (as would have been the same below decks). This last topic might be postponed until the cloth was cleared and the table could be used to map out the progress of the battle using glasses, decanters and biscuits to show the movements of the individual ships.

Once the loyal toast had been drunk (traditionally while seated, as the low beams would preclude standing properly erect[44]), the conversation, which up to that point would have tended to the formal and been led by the host, would become more general and, as the fortified wines and spirits took over from the weaker table wines, more boisterous. Other toasts would be drunk, guests toasting each other, and there were other toasts, traditional to each day of the week: on Sunday it was 'Absent friends', on Monday 'Our ships at sea' or 'Our native land', on Tuesday 'Our men' or 'Our mothers', on Wednesday 'Ourselves, as no-one else is concerned with our welfare', on Thursday 'A bloody war or a sickly season' (both good routes to rapid promotion), on Friday 'A willing foe and sea room' and on Saturday 'Sweethearts and wives' – to which the proper response was 'May they never meet!'

Nautical poems, many written by sea officers and describing battles or shipwrecks, would be declaimed and the gathering would often break into song. Wybourn reports of his New Year's dinner 'conviviality and harmony subsisted until 1 o'clock with songs, glees etc', and on many of the larger ships there were bands which would play on the quarterdeck. *Victory* had a band; Leonard Gillespie, the physician to the Mediterranean fleet describes it as playing from 2pm 'until a quarter to three, when the drum beats "The Roast Beef of Old England" to announce the admiral's dinner', after dinner ('a sumptuous repast at which the best wines and most exquisite viands were served up, ending with coffee and liqueurs at about 5pm…'; then the band played for another hour while the diners walked the deck before returning to the cabin for tea and conversation until about 8pm when a rummer of punch was served with cake and biscuits. This all sounds rather decorous, and was soon followed by Nelson retiring to bed, usually before 9pm.[45]

Eating and Drinking

Until the fashion of dining 'a la Russe' (where food was served to each diner by servants in a standardised set of courses, much as we know them today) came in at the beginning of the nineteenth century, formal dinners of the day consisted of mixed courses where the diners helped themselves and each other. There were usually two main courses, followed by a dessert course at the most formal dinners, each course consisting of a mixture of dishes which were arranged symmetrically on the table according to a plan devised by the cook, the table ideally being covered but not crowded. Some dishes were designated 'corner' dishes in recipe books, to describe their preferred position on the table; others, such as soup, were called 'removes' as they were intended to be taken away after a set time to be replaced by other dishes. The first course, which would consist of soup (to be removed and replaced by fish), meat, game, sauces and vegetables and perhaps one sweet dish, was arranged before the diners came to table. After a decent interval, the table was cleared of dishes and another course was brought while the guests waited. The second course was generally lighter but included some meat and fish as well as a variety of puddings, pastries, jellies and creams. The dessert course, when it was served, was preceded by a general clearance of the table, including the cloth, before re-laying it with plates, cutlery and glasses, and a collection of fruits, jellies and sweetmeats. At sea, this course was probably curtailed or omitted but in port would be retained for the most formal dinners with important guests or ladies; the ladies took themselves away after a while, to powder their noses, while the gentlemen remained to drink their port and discuss the important matters of the day before joining the ladies to drink tea.

Chapter 6

WHAT OTHER NAVIES ATE

TWO OF THE QUESTIONS which senior academics in the fields of military and naval history ask their students are 'How did the other side do it'? and 'Did the difference in the way we did it and the way they did it have an effect on the outcome?' On the subject of victualling it has proved extremely difficult to obtain information in any depth for any of the navies the British faced at sea. A combination of bureaucratic tidiness, an inclination to dispose of documentation relating to loss of face, enemy action during various wars and other accidental losses seems to have conspired to hide the detail one would hope to find. We are extremely fortunate in Britain to have so much naval documentation going back so far and in so much detail. One of the fortuities relating to victualling documentation is that the Victualling Office was in a different building to the Admiralty, the Navy Board and the Sick and Hurt Board, which meant that instead of popping down the corridor to obtain agreement and a signature, they had to write a letter to the other body, who had to write a reply. If only someone had thought to write a detailed report on the food supplied on enemy ships; we can only hope, as with the missing details on British naval victualling, that some contemporary documentation will turn up, or that a modern student of those countries will turn their attention to delving in what archives remain. In the meantime, here is what has been found.

THE AMERICAN NAVY

The US Navy did not come into being until the mid-1790s and remained quite small during the Napoleonic Wars and the War of 1812. A slim set of naval regulations was issued in 1802, which appears to have been modelled on (but is much less detailed than) the 1790 British *Regulations*.[1]

As far as victualling is concerned, under the duties of the captain or commander these regulations merely state that no-one is to sell liquor to the ship's company; under the duties of the master they state only that he is to inspect the provisions when they come on board and report to the captain any items which 'appear not good'. For the cook, the same three clauses appear as in the British *Regulations*: he is responsible for the steep tubs and the meat in them, is to see it duly watered, to see that the provisions are properly cleanly and cooked and delivered to the men 'according to the practices of the navy'. For the purser there are a total of twelve clauses, some of which appear in other sections in the British *Regulations*. Several deal with the purser's responsibility for ordering and issuing food, the expenditure on fresh food purchased in port, how to report losses and prepare his accounts. Damaged or spoiled provisions are to be surveyed and condemned by a committee of three officers, one of whom must be the commanding officer. If food has to be rationed by the commanding officer's order, the men are to be paid for the balance, but if there is a shortage of one type of meat, the other should be substituted. Officers are not to receive full rations when the men are on short rations. The two differences between American and British regulations are the sizes of meat pieces (ten pounds for beef, eight pounds for pork), and the statement that each man is to have at least half a gallon of water a day unless the captain decides to ration it (British *Regulations* make no statement about water quantities). Finally, each ship is to carry a seine net and use it to fish whenever convenient.

There is no printed table of the daily food and drink allowances, but we can construct one from the diet laid down by the Secretary of War in 1798:

	Beef (lbs)	*Pork (lbs)*	*Potatoes (lbs)*	*Salt fish (lbs)*	*Bread (oz)*	*Cheese (oz)*	*Butter (oz)*	*Peas or beans (pts)*	*Rice (pts)*	*Spirits (pts)*
Sun	1½				16				½	½
Mon		1			16	4		½		½
Tue	1½		1		16					½
Wed					16	4	2		½	½
Thur		1			16			½		½
Fri			1	1	16		2			½
Sat		1			16	4		½		½
Total	3	3	2	1	112	12	4	1½	1	3½

Potatoes may be replaced by an equal weight of turnips, butter may be replaced by two ounces of molasses or six ounces of oil, and half a pint of spirits may be replaced by two quarts of beer. The liquid measures are the American version, so half a pint of spirits is 240ml, a little less than the British wine measure of 250ml. The average daily calorific value of this ration is about 4340;

however, if the spirits are changed for beer, it becomes 4030.

There were several minor changes both to the ration and to its component items in 1801, 1805 and 1806, until in 1813 it looked like this:

	Beef (lbs)	*Pork (lbs)*	*Flour (lbs)*	*Suet (lbs)*	*Bread (oz)*	*Cheese (oz)*	*Butter (oz)*	*Peas (pts)*	*Rice (pts)*	*Molasses (pts)*	*Vinegar (pts)*	*Spirits (pts)*
Sun	1¼		½	¼	14							½
Mon		1			14			½				½
Tue	1				14	2						½
Wed		1			14				½			½
Thur	1¼		½	¼	14							½
Fri					14	4	2		½	½		½
Sat		1			14			½			½	½
Total	3½	3	1	½	98	6	2	1	1	½	½	3½

No substitutes for peas or spirits are shown.[2]

To summarise these changes, the beef ration had increased by half a pound per week, the bread ration had reduced by two ounces per day, the peas to one pound a week, the cheese and butter rations had halved and the potatoes or turnips, salt fish and beer had disappeared, and a standard ration of molasses, vinegar, and flour and suet for pudding had arrived. The average daily calorific value had reduced a little, at 4240 with spirits, or 3930 with beer replacing the spirits.

The US Navy's spirit ration was originally rum, served watered as grog, but the new Secretary of the Navy, Robert Smith, changed this to the American sour-mash corn (maize) whisky called bourbon. It was served in two parts, after dinner and after supper; any man who tried to get an extra serving was likely to find himself on the flogging list the following day.

Soon after 1798, during the quasi-war with France, American ships began to find themselves far from friendly ports where they could replenish their provisions from the local Navy Agent. When operating off Hispaniola in 1799, *Constitution* had to replenish her stocks at sea from merchant ships. She did this at approximately monthly intervals, taking two days each time to transfer everything from one ship to another by the boats. When she finally returned to Boston in August 1800, she had been at sea continuously for 349 days. The norm for ships leaving port for a long cruise was to stock them with provisions for six months and water for three months.

Like the British, the US Navy employed older or disabled men as cooks in their warships. They dealt with steeping the salt meat and had charge of the boilers in which the men's food was cooked. It is suggested that the meat and vegetables were all cooked together, but as discussed previously, this would create some difficulties of serving and allocation. It is more likely – especially considering that quite a lot of the men serving on US ships had previously served on British ships and could have pointed out the advantages – that a 'mess net' system was used. The men ate in messes of eight to ten members, with one member serving by rotation as mess cook and everyone having the option of changing messes at the beginning of the month if they wished. They ate picnic-style on the deck, each mess having its own space and using a piece of old canvas as a 'table' cloth. They ate and drank from metal dishes and cups, both probably tin or pewter. There were three meals a day: breakfast at 8am, dinner at noon and supper at 4pm, one hour being allowed for each meal. As always, the men were free to buy extra food from shops in port or from bumboats.

Officers ate in their own messes, either eating ration food or buying their own through an elected mess caterer. The captain was entitled to six rations (or the money for them), the wardroom officers two rations each and both captain and wardroom had their own cook and mess attendants. The midshipmen and other warrant officers only drew a single ration, and had only a boy to look after them.

The Dutch Navy

Strictly speaking, it is incorrect to refer to a 'Dutch navy' before 1815 and the beginning of the Kingdom of the Netherlands. Before that there was a Dutch republic made up of seven provinces (each a sovereign state) of which three in Holland, one in Zeeland and one in Friesland had an Admiralty, each of which might provide ships in wartime. Victualling arrangements and other logistical and command arrangements were decided (and subsequently decreed) at that point and applied to that war or campaign only. Once decreed at that level, the actual responsibility for provisioning each ship devolved to its captain, who often delegated the actual purchasing to his wife. The provisions themselves varied little over time, variations being more in the line of quantities of various items rather than changes in the items themselves, although there were certain items which were traditional substitutes, such as salt or fresh fish, soft bread or biscuit.

Dutch sailors ate in a group of six men called a 'bak'. Although this translates literally to 'tray' or 'trough', it can also be taken to mean 'mess', as in 'bak-mates' or 'mess-mates'. Some care was taken to ensure that each bak was made up of men who could get along with each other, putting trades and ranks together; one of these was known as the 'fodder' bak, consisting of the men who worked in the galley. They ate on a shift system, with the first shift being the essential watch-keepers, the third was for the fodder bak and the officers who had been on watch with the first shift, and the second was for everyone else. They were summoned to eat by a bell. Even now, the bak is used as a basic organisational unit in the Royal Netherlands Navy, with the morning roll call 'baksgewijs' meaning 'fall in by bak'.

The bak itself was a wooden or tin serving dish (and was sometimes used to eat from), with the food fetched by the 'zeuntje'. This word translates literally as 'sonny' but means the same as the British 'mess-cook': a member of the bak who serves on a rotating basis. The bak was rectangular, roughly four feet by one foot by one foot, and marked with an individual name or motto by which the bak was known. When the meat was distributed, it was this name which was called out in reply to the question 'Who shall have this?' Each man was issued with a wooden, bone or tin spoon, a small wooden butter saucer, and usually (but not always) two plates, one deep and one shallow; these plates were either wood or coarse earthenware. Each man would also have his own personal general-purpose knife.

The precise amount of food is not known with any accuracy, as the cooked food tended to be issued as a bakful rather than a specified amount. Breakfast every day was a bakful of groats per bak plus one pickled herring for each man. On Sundays and Thursdays one pound of meat was issued for each man at noon, but intended to serve for both dinner and supper. This meat could be either beef or pork, but because beef cost more (and the captain was paying) it was more likely to be pork. On every other day, one stockfish or hake was issued for each man at noon, with a spicy dip. The dip, made by the ship's cook, consisted of a butter and mustard base with other spices or herbs as available. In addition, every day, once at noon and once for the evening meal, a bakful of cooked pease was issued, and on Mondays (but intended to last for the whole week) each man received five pounds of bread or biscuit, eight ounces of salted butter and one pound of hard Dutch cheese. The modern equivalent to this cheese would be Gouda; now these cheeses are kept fresh by a thin layer of paraffin wax, but then it would have been tar. To drink there was beer, in unlimited quantities until it ran out. Some captains provided wine or brandy; many, especially those in the Mediterranean, also provided lime or orange juice and sometimes raisins. All of this gave about 4700 calories daily.

Some variations to the diet included pickled cabbage and onions, or sometimes there was a thick broth made of groats or peas and meat or fish. Outside the English Channel and North Sea there would be regional variations such as pasta or rice, seal meat, poultry and eggs, and whatever fish they could catch or buy from fishing boats. Plus, of course, whatever the men chose to buy for themselves; since the traditional way to eat a pickled herring is to dip it in chopped onions, they probably made sure they had a stock of onions.

Apart from eating in the grand cabin, there were no special arrangements for the officers. The captain was paid a fixed sum per head for food, and to him the officers were just heads. They could draw the official ration or lay in their own stocks of something better; most of them probably did. Admirals received a sum of table money for official dinners; de Ruyter, the famous admiral who blockaded the Thames and the Medway for two months in 1667, received 1000 guilders a month (at that time an able seaman's annual wage was 150 guilders).[3]

The French Navy

The French naval ration was set in 1689 and remained unchanged through several 'Ordonnances' in 1747, 1765 and 1786. The daily ration was laid down as one and a half pounds of biscuit, a midday dinner of bacon, salt beef, fish or cheese and a supper of dried pease or beans, cooked and dressed with oil and vinegar.[4] There was also a monthly issue of mustard seed; at the beginning of the eighteenth century, Shelvocke reported sailing on a French ship which had two cannons but only one cannon ball: '...this round could not be fired as it was used to crush the mustard seed we used with our cochon boucanné'.[5]

Jean Boudriot provides a little more detail, stating that the provisions were provided by contractors on a six-yearly contract; these contractors also provided the purser and his assistants, a cook, a butcher, a baker and a cooper.[6] Flour was provided and the baker made bread, mainly for the sick and the officers but also some for the men. The beef for the crew arrived in salted form and although some came from the west-coast ports of Nantes and Bordeaux, the best came from Ireland or Denmark. The salt fish included herrings and sardines as well as cod.

There were two cooked meals each day, dinner at around 11.30am and supper at 5pm in winter, 6pm in summer for the crew, 1pm and 9pm for the officers. The meat was tied to large skewers which bore the mess's number and were put in the copper at random, the number of each skewer being called out when they were removed.

Live sheep and chickens were carried for the sick, the numbers being calculated at five sheep per month for each 100 men (or six if from Brest, where the local sheep were small) and one chicken per month for each seven men, but no more than a four-months supply being carried in total. Boudriot points out that on his archetypical 74, some 350 chickens were carried for the men plus 200 other assorted poultry for the officers, necessitating 6000 pounds of grain to be carried to feed them; and 100 sheep for the crew and 50 for the officers required almost 7000 pounds of hay. Other items for the sick included soft bread, rice that was boiled in the meat broth, and stewed prunes.

To drink, there was wine (always red), two types being carried, one a light young wine intended to be drunk early in the commission, the other a mature red to keep for later months. The ration was one-third of a quart per day. Brandy (Cognac) was carried, but intended only for exceptional circumstances. Ships operating from the Channel ports might use beer or cider, issued at twice the rate of wine.

The officers were fed by the captain, for which he received an allowance of table money to pay for the food, the cooks who prepared it (the number of these would depend on the size of the ship, but would probably include a pastry cook), the waiters and the tableware. Boudriot provides an impressive list of the private food stocks carried by officers, although to those who know the French attitude to food, this is not surprising. In addition to the usual hams, tongues and pickles, this list includes beef, duck and goose 'confit', four types of cheese including Roquefort, dried mushrooms and truffles, five types of prunes and plums, fruit preserved in brandy, and vintage wines.

Boudriot's 74-gun ship is of the pre-Revolutionary French Royal Navy and one wonders to what extent the previously high-living officer would have felt obliged to modify such a lifestyle after the Revolution in the interests of keeping his head on his shoulders lest his newly-republican crew might denounce him as one of the hated 'aristos'. Many royalist officers left the navy soon after the outbreak of war; they were replaced by a different class of men who may not have chosen, or been able to afford, to buy luxurious foodstuffs.

As for the crew, although their official ration may not have changed, whether they actually got it, or what its quality was, is another matter. It was often very bad, due to dishonest supply officers whose practices included resupplying food which had been condemned and returned to stores. This is one of the reasons live animals and poultry were carried in such large numbers, and for an experiment in grinding flour on board ship with a windmill mounted on the stern. This mill had adjustable sails, but the whole thing was too fragile and was soon carried away in a gale.[7]

French crews who captured British ships during the wars of 1793 to 1815 were renowned for looting and one of the things they aimed for was the provisions, which indicates that the system which had been in operation previously had broken down. Proof of this comes from 1795, when the British squadron blockading Brest were landing French prisoners of war with scurvy, and even earlier, in the summer of 1793, after the French squadron from Brest had been sent to sea in the spring to dissuade the British from supplying the Vendée rebels, so many of them were suffering from food shortages and scurvy that they mutinied and demanded to return home, doing so in September.[8]

As the war progressed, the general food situation in France grew worse. As early as 1794 the convoy of grain ships which evaded Admiral Howe at the end of May was eagerly awaited to stave off bread shortages in Paris. At the end of 1800 an intelligence report received from Phillip d'Auvergne included a comment on the scarcity of provisions at Brest.[9] France, like Britain, had suffered a series of poor harvests due to bad weather and once Napoleon was in power, his empire-building campaigns took more and more men for the army. Many of them were farm-workers and this had an inevitable effect on food production. The prolonged and successful British blockades of French ports, first those of the West and Channel coasts and then the Mediterranean coasts as well, cut France off not only from overseas supplies also from internal supplies, which were generally moved by sea. This would have been bad enough for the Brest fleet, as Brittany was nowhere as well developed agriculturally as it is now, but it must have been worse for the French fleet in Toulon. The hinterland immediately behind Toulon is not conducive to arable farming or market gardening on a grand scale, and it should be remembered that a high proportion of the crops grown there today are courtesy of the irrigation supplied by the Durance canal, and, further west, from the Rhône. Cut off from supplies brought in by small coasters by sea, and given that the available road transport would have been both slow and restricted in bulk-carrying capacity, providing enough provisions for the fleet cannot have been easy.

One final thought on naval food in the French navy is that whatever the official Ordonnances said, there must have been the regional variations that can be seen today: butter, beef, leeks and apples in the north; olives and their oil, pork and dried fruit in the south.

The Spanish Navy

Information on Spanish naval food has proved to be very sparse. After 1768, there seems to have been a basic daily ration of wholemeal biscuit, vegetables and wine with salt meat or pork with 'animal fat' provided every day except Friday. On Friday, and Thursday and Saturday during Lent, salt cod, olive oil and vinegar were served. Sometimes, but on an irregular basis, there was cheese instead of the meat or fish. For the sick there was chicken and biscuit made with white flour.

Some further possibilities can be found from the rations supplied to the navies of the new South American republics of Chile and Argentina, which were probably based on those of Spain, and that of Portugal, which had the same sort of terrain and thus agriculture as Spain itself. Created in 1818, the Chilean Navy gave a daily issue of one pound of dried or salt beef, one pound of biscuit, one ounce of animal fat, half a pound of lentils, quarter of a pint of spirits and quarter of an ounce of red peppers. Given such a small quantity of peppers, these were almost certainly hot (*ie* chilli) peppers in dried form rather than the sweet red capsicum which we eat raw in salads. When in port, they had fresh bread instead of biscuit, and potatoes and vegetables instead of lentils and peppers, and a double ration of spirits, which was mainly rum. For the sick, there was half a chicken, six ounces of chick peas, one pound of fine biscuit, one ounce of animal fat and a quarter of a pint of rum.

The Argentinean Navy, when they prepared for their first war against Brazil in 1826, loaded food for 1300 men for thirty days consisting of almost 40,000 kilos of dried meat (this works out to just over two pounds of meat per man per day), 30,000 kilos of biscuit (one and a half pounds per man per day) and 7500 kilos of rice (just under half a pound per man per day), 1900 gallons of rum (just under half a pint per man per day) and a small amount of animal fat. This seems rather heavy on meat and completely lacks any element of vegetables, so perhaps it was intended to obtain other supplies in due course. It does however indicate the use of local methods of meat preservation: drying rather than salting, which would have the virtue of reducing the total weight carried.

A decree of 1797 set the basic ration for the Portuguese Navy at a daily ration of one pound of biscuit or one and a half pounds of flour, two-thirds of a pint of beans or onions, one pint of wine, one-thirtieth of a pint of oil, one-fifteenth of a pint of vinegar, coffee and sugar, and a meat ration of either one pound of salt beef or three-quarters of a pound of pork, or eight ounces of rice with two ounces of pork fat, or (on Fridays and fast days) half a pound of rice and salt fish.

Some general comments on these rations: 'animal fat' could be interpreted as beef or mutton suet or pork fat (*ie* lard). 'Meat' presumably does not mean pork, as this is listed separately but, although it could mean sheep or goat meat, was probably beef. Fish would have been served rather more frequently than once a week, given that all of these countries were Catholic; the actual frequency would have depended on the incidence of Saints' and fast days, the piety of the captain, and/or the influence of any priests on board.

Sheep, goats and poultry were carried, probably belonging to the officers. One can surmise that these officers would have provided themselves with better food than the men enjoyed.[10]

Conclusions

Thinking of those two academic questions, it seems that there really was very little difference in the way different navies fed their men. Like the British navy, all were restricted by what was currently available and would keep in good condition for a long time, and with some regional variations, this came down to biscuit, salt or dried meat or fish, cereals, dried pulses and a little cheese and butter or oil with fresh food when in port. Quantities must have been adequate most of the time or there would have been more mutinies, especially in the French Republican navy where the men were less respectful of their officers; on the other hand, they did suffer from scurvy rather more than did the British and in some cases this affected them strategically.

Taking that second academic question ('Did the difference in the way we did it and the way they did it have an effect on the outcome?'), although there was a general opinion among British seamen that foreigners were not as good in a fight as 'an Englishman', there is no evidence that this, even if true, was related to the quality or quantity of food, other than those reports of hungry men raiding the British provision stocks. The real reason for French and Spanish inadequacies during the Revolutionary and Napoleonic wars were more likely to have stemmed from the fact that British blockades deprived them of sea time and practice.

Chapter 7

DIET IN HEALTH AND SICKNESS

WE HAVE SEEN THAT THE Georgian seaman's food was, if not full of variety, at least plentiful and of reasonably good quality. In an age when a sequence of poor harvests might, and in some parts of Europe did, turn the fear of serious food shortages into actuality, those two certainties were not to be sniffed at. Looking at it with modern eyes, people might consider that the official ration was over-heavy in meat and fat but in the short term, given the work those men did, it would have done little harm as it would mostly have been burned off to provide energy and warmth. The problems that might follow from an excess of animal fats do not usually manifest themselves until late middle age and it must be remembered that most seamen were considerably younger than that. The next aspect of the ration which brings a frown to the modern brow is the high salt content; although the salt meat was steeped before cooking, it was probably still very salty. We fear salt-induced strokes, but as with arterial problems, that is an affliction of late middle age. Nobody appears to have kept any statistically-significant records of health problems in late middle-aged ex-seamen, so we cannot know if any of these problems did manifest themselves.

As far as we are concerned here, there are two sorts of health problem: those which were not reported in a form which allows us to identify them as relating to diet and those which were. By 1800 there was a standard printed form for the ships' surgeons to complete each week and where these forms were not available a hand-written version in the same format was used. A number of these forms have survived, the greatest number of them for the Mediterranean Fleet during the period 1800 to 1805, when the fleet was under the command of first Lord Keith and then Nelson.[1] For Keith's fleet there are forms for individual ships, while for Nelson's fleet there are consolidated forms prepared by the Physician of the Fleet, one per week, for whichever ships happened to be with the battle squadron at that time. In both cases, the purpose of these forms was obviously to keep the commander-in-chief informed and he, in turn, passed this information back to the Admiralty.

It should be stressed that the available report forms for the Mediterranean are merely those which have survived and also are only those for the ships which were actually in company with the commander-in-chief at the time they were submitted. We do not have a complete set of reports for the whole Mediterranean Fleet, and although there are some returns of numbers in hospital, these are also sporadic, do not necessarily report the specific conditions involved, and do not always distinguish between Royal Navy personnel and prisoners. So we cannot draw any comprehensive conclusions on the level of sickness throughout the station from these reports, but they do give an indication of the prevalence of certain medical conditions and of the numbers of men involved. We do have some commanders-in-chief's reports for the Channel Fleet for the period 1793 to 1801, and we will come back to these shortly.

Alcoholism

The most obvious of the diseases which were not reported as such is alcoholism. Five-sixths of a modern gallon of small beer per day does not do too much harm to a man whose life consists of extremely hard physical work in cold, damp conditions; he burns it off pretty quickly. Nor does a daily five-sixths of a pint of wine do much harm. Indeed, by current thinking, it would counteract the potentially harmful effects of all that fatty meat. Half a pint of very strong rum is another matter: although it would take some time before it irrevocably damaged the liver, it would have kept some men in an almost permanent state of intoxication.

Although there are no actual figures, it was often remarked that many shipboard accidents were caused by rum: falls from the rigging, falls down open hatchways, heavy items being dropped, heads meeting low beams, drunken fights, etc. Keith remarked on it: 'a large population of the men who are maimed and disabled are reduced to that situation by accidents that happen from [drunkenness]'; and the surgeon Blane pointed out that the incidence of insanity in the Royal Navy was seven times that of the general population (*ie* one in 1000 as opposed to one in 7000). Blane suggested that this was mostly due to head injuries from drunken accidents.[2] Quite a few men were invalided out as insane and there is a suggestion that many of these were in the advanced stages of alcoholism or showing the effects of blows to the head from those low beams. Quite a few officers were invalided out for what, in their case, tended to be called 'diseased liver'. However, it should be pointed out that as far as the lower-deck men were concerned, since many of them were 'quota men' who had been wished on the navy by local authorities who saw this as a way to clear their jails, many could have already been borderline, if not actually, insane from the outset, and this could be what skewed the figures.

Night Blindness

The next problem which was rarely reported unless it afflicted a high proportion of a ship's crew is night blindness. An outbreak was reported in the West Indies squadron in the early 1800s and Gilbert Blane reported having encountered it in soldiers during the siege of Gibraltar in 1779.[3] Night blindness is brought about by prolonged deficiency of Vitamin A in the diet – 'prolonged' meaning anything up to two years before the stores in the liver of normally-nourished people are diminished. Vitamin A comes in two forms: retinol or beta-carotene. Retinol is found only in animal or fish foods, the greatest amounts in liver and lesser amounts in dairy products and eggs. Beta-carotene is converted in the body to retinol and is found in yellow and green vegetables and some fruits. The deeper the colour, the more beta-carotene, so there is more in the outer leaves of a Savoy cabbage than the inner and even more in watercress, more in carrots than dried peas. The only fruit with appreciable quantities are mangoes, apricots and plums. For full details of amounts of Vitamin A in food, see Appendix 4.

Given that the recommended daily intake of Vitamin A for an adult man is 1000 μg, and that there is very little of it in the standard species of provisions except for butter and cheese, on those foreign stations where neither butter and cheese nor the alternative sources were available, it is likely that it occurred far more than anyone realised. Since night blindness is not a debilitating affliction, it may only have been noticed when lookouts or steersmen in restricted situations failed to see something at night or in other dim light. This is the most likely reason for so few reports, not, as has been asserted, because of the general introduction of portable soup. There are two problems with this assertion: the first is that portable soup was only given to the sick; the second is that it does not contain any Vitamin A. The belief that it does contain Vitamin A arises from the statement that portable soup was made with offal, the erroneous assumption here being that 'offal' in 1756, when Mrs Dubois started making portable soup for the Sick and Hurt Board in London, meant what it does now and thus would include the retinol-rich liver and kidneys.

Alas, the secondary source which reported the use of offal failed to read on down the original document, which defines offal as 'legs and shins' of beef, then adds that one-third of the meat could be mutton.[4] The following year, the appropriately-named Mrs Cookworthy was contracted to make portable soup at Plymouth, both she and Mrs Dubois using meat provided by the Victualling Board slaughterhouses. By 1804, a letter confirms that the only meat used since 1756 was leg and shin of beef with one-quarter of mutton. Shin of beef contains quite a lot of gelatinous connective tissue and it is this which makes the broth set like jelly, not the addition of calves feet suggested by yet another misguided modern writer. Anyone who is in the habit of cooking from basic ingredients will be aware of this property of shin of beef and will also know that liver and kidneys do not produce that result when boiled. Indeed, it was that knowledge which made the author, deeply sceptical, seek out the original documents, one of which fortuitously included the recipe. This showed that the meat was simmered for several hours, then drained and pressed to extract all the stock, which was then seasoned with celery seed, black pepper, garlic and essence of thyme. The end product, after reduction and drying, was a cake of solid jelly (stamped, of course, with the King's broad arrow mark), one ounce of which would make one quart of soup when dissolved in boiling water.[5] Contrary to some modern comments, this soup bears no resemblance to glue; it is extremely tasty (see Appendix 6 for the recipe).

Before moving on to the main dietary deficiency disease of sailors, scurvy, it is worth remarking that, while there are other vitamin deficiency diseases, we have no evidence that they afflicted sailors on a grand scale, which is not to suggest that they did not, merely that they were not reported in a form which makes them recognisable as such.

Scurvy

Scurvy was something you could not miss. It has easily recognisable symptoms: bruising and ulceration of the skin, haemorrhaging and joint pains, loosening of the teeth, loss of hair, opening-up of old wounds, lassitude and depression, hallucinations and blindness, and finally death. Now we know that it is due to a deficiency of Vitamin C which leads to the breakdown of the body's production of the connective tissue collagen; then all they knew was that it was a disease which wreaked havoc among sailors on long voyages.

Scurvy was reported in two forms: scurvy and ulcers. Sometimes there was a separate entry on the forms for 'scorbutic ulcers'; but it is probable that almost all, if not all, of these were of scorbutic origin, persistently ulcerated skin being one of the common symptoms of scurvy.[6] They would not have been peptic ulcers, as these were not identified until 1857;[7] this is not to say that seamen did not suffer from such ulcers, but that these would have been listed under different headings.[8] The ulcers reported would probably have been mainly on the lower legs and feet; Dr Snipe, the Physician of the Mediterranean Fleet, remarked on the high incidence of such ulcerated scratches and condemned the practice of going barefoot as the cause.[9]

The earliest record of scurvy is from Vasco da Gama's voyage to India in 1497, when he lost 100 of his 160 men; there have been many since. Perhaps the best known to British naval historians is Anson's circumnavigation in 1740. Of the more than 1900 men who sailed with Anson, some 1400 died, and although some died of dysentery and the crew of the *Wager* of starvation, it is thought that the majority died of scurvy, many possibly because they were already weakened from having been confined to their ships at Spithead during a series of Admiralty-induced delays.[10] Despite the good effects of citrus fruit having been known as an antiscorbutic since at least 1600, when the East India Company surgeon John Wooddall recommended it, the Anson expedition carried no citrus or other antiscorbutics.

It was the reports of this expedition which inspired the young Scottish naval surgeon James Lind to seek an effective cure for scurvy. He was not the first to think that scurvy could be cured by diet supplements, but he was the first to set about finding a cure by conducting logical experiments. This was, of itself, somewhat of a novelty at the time; previous attempts to find a cure having been on a rather hit-or-miss basis. It is when you consider some of the theories on the causes of scurvy and the 'obvious' cures that you begin to see the gulf between Georgian and modern medical theory.

The first thought, because some of the symptoms were similar, was that scurvy was a venereal disease. After all, sailors were known to be promiscuous and since no-one thought to question the sufferers on the matter and collate the answers, it was never disproved. Another theory, based on the doctrine of four humours, was that scurvy was a corruption of the blood, leading to putrefaction. This demonstrates another great gulf between modern and ancient medical thinking; now, when disease occurs on a grand scale, we believe it must have a specific cause rather than being a generalised imbalance of the whole body. The doctrine of four humours was originally promulgated around 400 BC by Hippocrates, who believed that the four humours were the principle seats of disease. Galen, some 500 years later, taught that as well as the four humours, there were four qualities, four elements and four complexions, all inter-related. His theory was that good health came from a good blend of all these; that specific diseases were linked to an excess or deficit of some, and that different foods had different qualities in different degrees. So, if you were suffering from an affliction which was hot and moist, you needed food or medicine which was cool and dry, and depending on the degree of the affliction, so you needed a balancing degree of the appropriate curative. At this point, a cynic might observe that such a complex doctrine could only be understood by a learned man, and that such a man would charge a large fee for his hard-learned knowledge and would also defend it vigorously against any alternative theories.

The 'putrefaction' theory, expanded upon by Sir John Pringle in a paper read at the Royal Society in 1750, was that disease came about from putrefaction which was best treated by alkalis. David MacBride took Pringle's theories a little further, deciding that carbon monoxide, which he called 'free air' and which came from fermentation, would prevent putrefaction. He proposed a cure based on the fermentative quality of fresh vegetables and malt. Lind also subscribed to the putrefaction theory but felt that both alkalis and acids were needed; he recommended oranges and lemons for their acid qualities.

Lind's experiment, carried out in 1747, consisted of dividing twelve sailors with scurvy into six groups, treating each with a different remedy. Their main diet was identical for all: fresh mutton broth, puddings (undefined), boiled biscuit with sugar, barley, raisins or currants, rice, sago and wine. Group one were given a quart of cider each day, group two had twenty-five drops of elixir of vitriol, group three had six spoonsful of vinegar, group four had half a pint of seawater, group five had two oranges and one lemon each day and group six had a paste made of garlic, mustard seed, horseradish, Balsam of Peru and gum myrrh and a drink of barley water acidulated with tamarinds and cream of tartar. Group five were reported as eating their fruit with greediness, and despite the treatment stopping after six days when Lind ran out of fruit, one of those men was by that time fit for duty and the other was well enough to help in nursing the others. Group one showed some recovery after two weeks, and the others showed no effect.

Shortly after conducting this experiment, Lind left the navy to concentrate on his doctoral thesis. This was not on scurvy but on an aspect of venereal disease; however, it won him his degree and licence to practice as a physician, first privately and then at Haslar naval hospital at Portsmouth. In 1753 he published his *Treatise of the Scurvy*; it was virtually ignored. There were louder voices crying their own theories, one of these being MacBride whose answer to the problem was wort, the thick concentrated form of beer produced by long simmering. This was one of the ideas originally tried as an answer to running out of beer at sea, the theory being that if mixed with water (one part wort, twelve parts water) it would quickly turn into beer. It actually did do this, but having got the reputation of being a medicine, this beer was rejected by the men.

Cook carried wort on his first voyage and reported on his return that he found it an effective antiscorbutic, but then contradicted himself by remarking that 'we have been a long time without any, without feeling the want of it…'. This statement was omitted when the report was presented at the Royal Society in Cook's absence. Cook also carried, and made his men eat, sauerkraut which is mildly antiscorbutic, as well as syrup of oranges and lemons, and went ashore for fresh food whenever he could. These latter aspects were also ignored. MacBride published two reports on sea trials of wort: these were, however, flawed, one having been carried out by his brother, the other involving a voyage which included a stay of several days on an island where the scorbutic men soon recovered.[11]

Meanwhile, various voices were crying about the effectiveness of fresh food and others about lemon juice. The fresh food believers tended to be those who thought scurvy was caused by salt; they thought it was fresh meat which principally effected the cure. At first only a few realised that the fresh vegetables which traditionally accompanied fresh meat had anything to do with the cure, but the idea that fresh vegetables were helpful gradually came to be accepted. There is, incidentally, a little Vitamin C in fresh meat, but only if you eat it soon after slaughter; when the meat is hung, the Vitamin C is gradually lost. This was the reason rats were an effective antiscorbutic: they were eaten soon after being killed. Nelson was of the 'fresh meat and vegetables' persuasion and he placed much faith in onions, arranging for them to be bought in large quantities whenever possible. Onions are anti-scorbutic, 100g of raw onions containing the minimum daily dose of 10mg of Vitamin C. Another of the prominent naval doctors of the time, Thomas Trotter, was also a fan of fresh vegetables. When serving as Physician to the Channel Fleet in 1795, he insisted on fresh vegetables for the fleet, going round the growers and markets to such effect that one greengrocer complained that Trotter had ruined his business by sending all the salad to Spithead.[12]

Lind, in his essay on preserving the health of seamen, recommended that ships' companies should grow their own salad (cress) on wet cloths and to put out blankets in rainy weather to soak them before sowing the seeds, so that 'the whole ship both above and below shall be replete with verdure'.[13] In 1775, Messrs Mure, Son & Atkinson, the contractors supplying the British army in America in the winter of 1775, sent out a supply of mustard and cress seeds, suggesting that they could be grown on wet blankets or shallow trays of earth.[14] Pasley had such trays with him on board *Jupiter* in 1781 and his could not have been shallow, as when some of his scurvy sufferers asked to be covered in earth to alleviate their sufferings, he said he buried them in the trays, so these must have been at least 12 inches deep. This odd treatment seemed to work, although its effect can only have been psychotherapeutic: 'the men who were carried and lifted in and out of it, incapable of moving a limb, walked of themselves today.'[15] Pasley's salad trays seem to have been for his own use, rather than intended for the crew, but in 1803 a letter to the *Naval Chronicle* from Sir W Young, who had lived in India for several years, recommended sprouting peas to provide a 'living vegetable'. His method reads exactly like the modern method for sprouting mung beans (as used in Chinese cooking): take some small tubs of about two-gallon capacity, three-quarter fill them with pease, add water to just cover and leave them to sprout. He suggests feeding them to the men twice a week, ideally raw.[16]

Lind, Trotter, Nelson and his surgeon Leonard Gillespie also advocated citrus fruit. Others were only semi-convinced that the fruit itself or its juice were necessary. Citrus fruit is acidic, they reasoned, the curative property was acid, so it would work just as well if they used cheaper acids, such as vinegar or 'oil of vitriol' (sulphuric acid!). The high cost of citrus fruit (or the sugar required to make it palatable) is a recurring theme in the ongoing history of treating or preventing scurvy. It is interesting to note that the French navy's answer to scurvy, sorrel (*Rumex acetosa*), also tastes acidic.

The person who had turned the tide in favour of citrus juice is generally believed to have been Dr Gilbert Blane, who had been personal physician to Sir George Rodney and Physician to the Fleet before he became one of the Commissioners for Sick and Wounded Seamen (commonly known as the 'Sick and Hurt Board'). Blane was a strong believer in citrus juice, but dubious of the efficacy of the 'rob' (syrup) which Lind had advocated, believing – correctly as it happens – that heat impaired the properties of the juice; however, it seems that although he publicised the idea, he was not responsible for the Sick and Hurt Board's enthusiasm, which came from an experiment conducted just before he joined the Board.[17] In 1794 an experiment was made using fresh lemon juice on *Suffolk*, on a non-stop twenty-three week voyage to India. Two-thirds of an ounce of lemon juice with two ounces of sugar was mixed with grog and given to every man in the ship. Only fifteen showed signs of scurvy, which disappeared when the lemon juice ration was increased. The dosage of two-thirds of an ounce of lemon juice gives just short of the modern recommended minimum daily allowance of Vitamin C. It should be mentioned, however, that the requirement for such things is not absolute; requirements differ between individuals. It is interesting to note when studying ships' sick returns that even on ships where there is not a serious outbreak of scurvy, there are always one or two cases each week. There are various possible reasons for this: perhaps these men were debilitated when they joined the ship, perhaps they did not like the taste of lemon juice and did not drink their ration, or perhaps they were heavy smokers or tobacco-chewers and thus needed more than the usual amount of Vitamin C.

The successful experiment on *Suffolk*, together with Blane's influence as a member of the Sick and Hurt Board, persuaded the Admiralty to arrange for an issue of lemon juice in the following year. This tends to be lauded as the end of scurvy in the navy. It might have been, if it was a regular, general issue to every man on every ship, but that is not what happened. In 1795, the Admiralty had agreed to send a supply of lemon juice and sugar to the two squadrons blockading Brest and Quiberon Bay, to be issued 'at the discretion of the ship's surgeon'.

This phrase 'at the discretion of the ship's surgeon', together with the influence of the Physician of the Channel Fleet, Trotter, meant that the lemon juice was not used as it should have been. The problem with Trotter was that while he advocated citrus juice as a cure for scurvy, he was very much against using it as a preventive. He believed that daily doses of lemon juice weakened the constitution. When St Vincent succeeded to the command of the Channel Fleet in 1800, having seen the efficacy of lemon juice in his previous command in the Mediterranean, he almost immediately clashed with Trotter on this, and other, health matters, and within a few weeks Trotter was ousted and replaced by Dr Andrew Baird, who did agree with St Vincent.[18] This led to supplies of lemon juice eventually being issued to all ships of the Channel Fleet and this, together with regular supplies of fresh vegetables and fruit, allowed the blockading ships to remain on station for longer periods.

By 1803, when Nelson took over the Mediterranean Fleet, most ships going on foreign service carried a supply of lemon juice, again to be issued 'at the discretion of the ship's surgeon'; it was not included in the list of standard rations or as a substitute for fresh food. This was because it was still regarded as a medicine and thus under the control of the Sick and Hurt Board, not the Victualling Board. In 1806, when a new edition of the *Regulations* was issued, the single mention of serving out lemon juice was in the chapters for surgeons, where it states that on long voyages, if there is insufficient lemon juice for the whole ship's company, they are to give the captain a list of those men most in need. The instructions for the Physician of the Fleet say 'he is to point out to the commander-in-chief whatever he may think necessary for the recovery of the health of the crew of a ship particularly sickly, or for the preservation of the health of the fleet in general'. Even as late as 1825, the *Instructions to Pursers* state that lemon juice is not to be issued while the ship's company are 'making use of beer, or are furnished with fresh beef, or enjoying a supply of fruit or vegetables; nor during the space of a fortnight after the issue of [the above listed items] unless for the state of health of the crew, the surgeon should think the same necessary….'[19]

The responsibility for dispensing lemon juice was divided. The Sick and Hurt Board wanted to keep control, but also wanted the Victualling Board to store and issue it. At the point at which it was agreed that it should be issued to all ships on foreign service or blockade duty, the Sick and Hurt Board wrote to the Admiralty to inform them that they were ready to start delivering packed lemon juice to the Victualling Board stores and asking for the Victualling Board to provide a list of ships it went to, so they could send instructions to the surgeons on how to use it. This request was passed on to the Victualling Board who promptly pointed out that it would be more sensible if they were given a supply of the instructions to deliver with the lemon juice, as otherwise ships might have sailed before the instructions reached them.[20]

This shuffling of responsibilities continued: in 1806 the Sick and Hurt Board was put under the control of the Transport Board (and in 1816 became a department of the Victualling Board). In 1812 the Transport Board suggested that as lemon juice had 'now become a class of victualling of the first necessity', the Victualling Board should take on its provision 'in the same manner as other articles of provisions, furnishing such quantities thereof as the Transport Board ... require for the use of the sick'. The Victualling Board did not want to do this and replied that they did not agree that lemon juice fell under the denomination of a 'regular article of diet'. Its use had been introduced by the medical department and they felt that the responsibility for it should stay there, adding rather waspishly that it was difficult enough to find enough space for 'indispensable articles of the first necessity' let alone anything else.[21] However, it seems they were obliged to take on this task, for in 1813 they were complaining about the cost of the sugar that was traditionally served with lemon juice, and managed to persuade the Admiralty that they should revert to serving it only as a cure, not a preventative.[22]

When the decision was made to supply lemon juice (and they did refer to it as juice, not rob) on a grand scale, in 1796, it was packed in cylindrical bottles in sectioned cases, each case containing eighteen half-gallon bottles. Earlier bottles had been much larger, some containing as much as eight and a half gallons.[23] It had originally been proposed that the bottles should be square, but these were found to break more easily than the round ones.[24] There had been some experimentation with the preparation of the juice, and it was finally decided that owing to the risk of adulteration at source if bought ready-squeezed, the lemons should be squeezed in Britain. There was some discussion about the extra cost of importing whole fruits but the conclusion was that the difference in freight cost between lemon juice and whole lemons was about the same as it would have cost to set up a reliable squeezing operation abroad and that they would prefer to have this done 'under the eye of the board'. One wonders what they did with the peels: were they just thrown away, or did some enterprising person see their possibilities for making lemon marmalade or drying them for lemon 'pepper'? By 1804, when Nelson's Physician of the Fleet, Dr Snipe, went to Sicily to supervise the Board's contract for lemons, the situation seemed to have changed, as he ordered juice rather than lemons: a total of 50,000 gallons, at least 10,000 gallons of which went to Nelson's fleet while the rest went back to England.[25]

What about actual scurvy cases? During the early stages of the Brest blockade, before fresh vegetables and lemon juice were provided, the commander-in-chief, Lord Bridport, sent back two reports of numbers of sick: on 16 August 1795 this consisted of some 475 cases in thirteen ships, most of these scorbutic, but during September this figure had risen to 861 cases in ten ships. While lemon juice was only used as a cure not a preventive, the situation changed little, but when St Vincent took command in 1801 there was a significant difference; we do not have specific figures on scurvy, but we do have those for numbers of sick men at Haslar hospital at Portsmouth: 15,141 in 1779, 1667 in 1804.[26] For the Mediterranean Fleet which he had previously commanded, and where he had used lemon juice as an antiscorbutic, the picture was very different. The number of cases reported on the available forms for 1800 to 1805 rarely reached even double figures – this in squadrons totalling between 3000 and 7000 (Keith's) or 4500 and 6000 men (Nelson's) – except on the occasions when there was an outbreak on specific ships. The figures for ulcers, although still representing only about 0.5 per cent of the men, is higher, running between 35 and 50 cases each week. Overall the level of sickness in these squadrons, judging by the returns which have survived, was very low, running at a level which rarely exceeded 5 per cent of the numbers borne.[27]

Nelson commented on various occasions on the remarkable healthiness of his fleet.[28] We do not know how he was judging this, other than the figures reported by the Physician of the Fleet, or what he was using as a comparison; if it was the recent experience of a similar squadrons in a similar location

(Keith's), as we have seen above there is little difference between them. It may have been his experience of serving in the West Indies in the 1780s, when yellow fever and other tropical diseases cut a swathe through British sailors.[29] Alternatively it may have been his experience at Corsica in 1794 when he reported 'we have upwards of one thousand sick out of two thousand, and the others not much better than so many phantoms'; at one point, the crew of *Agamemnon* became so weak that they were unable to raise the anchor and had to buoy it and cut the cable.[30]

In this context of remarkable health and scurvy cases it is interesting to study the logs of a couple of Nelson's ships in the Mediterranean, *Triumph* and *Gibraltar*. Between January and May 1803 *Triumph* was at Malta, where she took on considerable quantities of provisions; by the middle of June she had joined the main battle squadron off Toulon. Apart from a two-week period at the end of July when she was in Gibraltar having her bowsprit replaced and waiting for a convoy of transports, she remained with the group off Toulon during the next year. When she had been at Gibraltar she received daily supplies of fresh beef and substantial quantities of other provisions; off Toulon she received occasional small amounts of various items from other ships in the squadron, but otherwise, with the exception of live sheep and bullocks whilst at the Maddalena Islands, all her provisions were the basic ration items and these came from transports, either at sea or whilst moored at Palma Bay or the Maddalena Islands.

Her master's log gives frequent details of provisions received and it is noticeable that she reports receiving only three amounts of onions (fourteen bags on 19 December 1803, three bags on 16 March and 1000 pounds on 22 March 1804) and no citrus fruit or juice after September 1803. From this it appears that the only Vitamin C available after July 1803 was the small amount present in fresh meat and those few onions. Hardly surprisingly, by May 1804 she had thirty-seven men with scurvy; her captain reported this to Nelson, who ordered a special issue of lemon juice. It is possible that she had none on board, as during the course of the following month she received eight casks of lemons from *Royal Sovereign*, and a total of eleven cases of lime juice from transports.[31]

Gibraltar had been in the Mediterranean for some time when Nelson arrived in July 1803, and by this time she was an unhealthy ship. At the end of March 1803 she had discharged twenty-one sick men into a transport, and between then and the beginning of May she had sent eleven men to hospital, one of them the surgeon. Between 28 June and 21 July three men died on board the ship; no reason is given for their deaths, or for sending the other men to hospital, but one can speculate that the reason for at least some of this sickness was scurvy, as on 6 August she moored at the Maddalena Islands, built a tented hospital and sent 135 scurvy cases on shore. She remained there for ten days, where she reports receiving sixty-four bullocks (and killing eighteen of them) and 16,700 onions, 101 pumpkins and 100 pounds of grapes 'for the sick'. One man died in the hospital, but by 16 August the rest were back on board and they went back to rejoin the squadron with the commander-in-chief. She was then sent to Naples, arriving on 20 September, and there she stayed for the next eight months, apart from making a two-week round trip to Sardinia to collect the Duke of Genevois and his retinue. While she was at Naples, she received deliveries on most days of fresh beef, cabbages, pumpkins and onions or leeks, as well as other provisions and wine. During the whole of her time at Naples she reported no further deaths or outbreaks of scurvy.[32]

Even more telling is the fact that there were several serious outbreaks of scurvy in the fleet during 1803 and 1804 and several more after Spain declared war against Britain in December 1804, thereby cutting off a major source of fresh food.[33] There would have been no difficulty in obtaining a plentiful supply of lemon juice for the fleet, as lemons were grown extensively in Sicily; Nelson was fully aware of this, having sent his physician, Dr Snipe, to buy large stocks of lemons both for his own fleet and to send back to England. The fact that scurvy continued to be a problem indicates that this supply was not fully utilised.

This demonstrates that the general thinking of many modern writers that everyone, from the Board of Admiralty all the way down to individual ships' captains and surgeons, was convinced that citrus fruit or its juice was a sure preventative of scurvy is incorrect; if they were convinced, captains and surgeons would not have needed to be told to buy lemons or issue the juice. There is other evidence of this lack of conviction: as commander-in-chief, Nelson could have issued a general order on the subject of issuing lemon juice, but his order book does not include such an order; only one on the format in which the remaining stocks of lemon juice should be reported.[34] In addition, the large batch of ships' logs which were examined during the author's research did not show regular receipts of lemon juice or lemons in the quantities which would have been required for a standard regular issue.

This fleet in the Mediterranean was not the only one which continued to suffer from scurvy. In 1811 the commander-in-chief of the East India station, Rear-Admiral William Drury wrote of the 'ravages of scurvy and dysentery' in his fleet. It was probably the dysentery which caused, or at any rate worsened, the scurvy: dysentery raises the pH of the contents of the gut and in the process destroys the ascorbic acid. In a vicious circle, sailors with lowered resistance due to scurvy were also easy victims to dysentery. The term dysentery does not appear frequently in the ships' medical reports; 'flux' does and whether this flux was full-blown amoebic dysentery or just diarrhoea caused by bad water or failure to wash food or hands, the effect would be much the same. Drury found it difficult to obtain lemons or limes, although one wonders why supplies could not have been taken out to him by the East India Company ships. Equally, it is strange that he did not know about the coconut, which should have been easily available on the East Indies station; it had been known as early as 1766, when Commodore John Byron reported using it on his circumnavigation. Although comparatively low in Vitamin C, at 2mg per 100g of the fresh flesh or milk, if sufficient was available it would have done the trick.

However, Drury did know of another good cure: nopal (*Opuntia*) was believed on the East Indies station to be the best remedy for scurvy and hepatitis. Its alternative name at the time was 'Mexican cochineal plant', from the cochineal beetle which lives on it (*Dactylopius cocchus*), but we know it as the Prickly Pear. The varieties we know today are very spiny; however, there is a spineless variety (*O. ficus-indica*) which may have been what was available there. Alternatively, they may have used a variation of the technique used today in Mexico where the spines are burned off with a blow-torch; Georgian sailors could have used the 'bundle of brushwood on a stick' method to singe the spines before handling them. The recommended dose was 'one leaf per man per day' in the soup, or a pickled version which could be made on board. Nopal's properties were discovered by the Physician General to the Madras army, Dr Anderson, who got his first plant sent out from Kew Gardens by the good offices of Sir Joseph Banks.[35] He reported to Banks in 1808 that several East India Company ships were using it to good effect; unfortunately it is not one of the items listed in the standard works on food composition so we cannot know its vitamin levels.

Drury was a believer in nopal and grew large amounts in his garden at Madras, offering as much as was wanted to any ship's captain who cared to come and fetch it. He recommended its use in a pickle, with vinegar and various spices, including allspice. Even here, someone had to interfere and change the recipe on the grounds of cost. Drury had died and his pickle recipe was altered by the resident naval commissioner, Peter Puget, who decided because the price was too high, to omit the allspice. As it happens, it did not matter but how could he have known that? If they were prepared to accept that the bark of the cinchona tree could have such a valuable effect on fevers, why should the seed of allspice not have been effective with scurvy? But no, a few pennies were more important, as they were deemed to be later when limes were substituted for lemons. In fact, this view of the cheapness of limes proved to be faulty; they turned out to be more costly and less effective than lemons. It was not until the 1930s, when Casimir Funk and a sequence of other chemists identified the four main dietary deficiency diseases (scurvy, beriberi, pellagra and rickets) as such and went on to isolate and then commercially produce Vitamin C that there was a cheap and effective antiscorbutic available for those whose diet denied them the Vitamin C they needed.

Food for the Sick

So much for the food that might have prevented sickness. When they went on the sick list and were moved to the sickbay or to a hospital, the responsibility for feeding the men shifted to the surgeon. He decided whether they should be on full, half or low diet, liaised with the purser on how much of their official ration they should have, and with the captain when the need for mutton broth required a sheep to be killed, or when the sick needed wine at a time when the rest of the crew was on beer or spirits.

The general theory was that their consumption of 'salt provisions' should be, if not completely stopped, restricted to what was needed to make gruel or 'sowins', which is a type of very thin oatmeal porridge. The dictionary definition (which also offers the alternative spellings of sowens or sowans) suggests this was traditionally made with the floury residue left in the husks of oats after crushing, conjuring up the picture of extreme desperation, washing the inedible husks for what little nutriment they could yield. Another name for this dish was flummery, originally sweetened and with milk added, it gradually developed through the eighteenth century to a rich dessert with cream and Madeira, and eventually fruit. Hannah Glasse offers a 'French Flummery' with cream, rose water and orange-flower water; fit for the Admiral's table perhaps, but too rich for the sick bay. Since there would have been no oat husks on board, the sowins would have been made with the oatmeal that was part of the sick men's usual ration. The *Regulations* go on to say that the men's allowance of flour should be used to make soft bread or puddings and that 'these, together with their molasses or sugar, when allowed, and raisins, the necessaries in [the surgeon's] charge, and portable soup, will constitute a wholesome diet for the sick'.

The surgeons' 'necessaries' were provided ready-packed in boxes. There seem to have been three sizes of box: half-single for 25 men, single for 50 men and double for 100 men, each meant to be sufficient for three months. In each case, the amount of contents doubled up as did the number of men they were meant for; although it does not specifically say so in the *Regulations*, this must have meant the number of men in the complement, not those in the sick bay, so *Victory*, with her 850 men, would have eight double and one single box for each three months of her expected service. The double box contained, as well as linen and flannel, one saucepan, one canister each for tea and sago, 4½ pounds of tea, 4 pounds of sago, 8 pounds of rice, 16 pounds of barley, 32 pounds of soft sugar and 2 ounces of ginger (presumably this would have been the powdered sort), except in the Mediterranean where the barley was replaced by macaroni, and in the West Indies where it was replaced by arrowroot. Replacements of items used were provided by the local officer of the Sick and Hurt Board on production of certificates of what had been legitimately used; on stations where there was no such officer, the surgeon could purchase these necessaries to the tune of twopence per man per month. Portable soup and lemon juice were dealt with on a much longer list of drugs and equipment for the sickbay, including pillows, night caps, bed-pans and spitting pots.[36]

The list of dietary necessaries had changed over the years. The version quoted above was that for 1806; earlier versions had included cocoa or chocolate, garlic, shallots, almonds, tamarinds and the spices nutmeg and mace. Toward the end of the Napoleonic Wars, after the development of canning, tins of 'preserved' veal and soup joined the list. In naval hospitals on shore, milk, sometimes eggs, vegetables and, after about 1805, potatoes joined the list. Milk also featured on the diet on hospital ships; they must have carried goats or even milch cows. Goats were quite common on all ships, and although they usually belonged to the officers, it is unlikely that their milk would have been denied the sick. It was also common practice for delicacies from the officers' tables to be sent to the sickbay.

With the exception of these goodies from the wardroom, the general trend of the diet for the sick seems to have been soft and non-challenging food, rather like the diet in Victorian schoolrooms, with the addition of those spices to add some flavour. Men on full diet, probably those in the latter stages of recovery, did get some meat; the others only got meat broth or soup, with those soft puddings or gruels. To men used to large amounts of solid food, this diet would not have encouraged malingering. But, in northern Sardinia at least, there were those grapes, possibly a forerunner of that classic gift of hospital visitors.

CONCLUSIONS

WE HAVE ALREADY LOOKED at two of the standard academic questions that should be applied to any study of military history. There are two more which we should now ask: 'Did they do a good job?' and 'Would they have done a better job if they had done it differently?' In answering these questions, especially the second, it is necessary to remember that we are dealing with a very different world from our own and that what appears obvious with hindsight was not necessarily so obvious at the time. But first we must consider the two fundamental points: who 'they' were, and exactly what the job was.

It would be easy to define 'they' as the Victualling Board and its head-office employees; they were the people who gathered the ingredients of the seaman's diet and sent them off to arrive on his plate. But they were not the only people involved: there were many others along the way who were involved in getting the job done and getting it done properly. As we have seen, this included the manufacturing, packing and despatch personnel at the Victualling Board's depots at home and abroad, the individual commanders-in-chief who directed the intermediate stages of delivery, and the various people who dealt with delivery on board the ships – the captains, the pursers, the masters and lieutenants, the cooks and the stewards. Each of these, as we have seen, was concerned to get the food on the plate and then to leave the men in peace while they ate it, and each understood the importance of keeping the men well fed. There was a mechanism in place for complaints when things went wrong, but there seem to have been very few such complaints, certainly not enough dissatisfaction to cause a major mutiny such as affected the French Brest fleet in Quiberon Bay.

So just what was the job? To put it very broadly, you could say it was to provide the fuel that enabled the fighting machine to perform well in the face of the enemy. The key phrases here are 'to perform well' and 'in the face of the enemy'. There can be no doubt that the British naval fighting machine did perform well throughout the period we are considering. Ignoring the manpower losses caused by disease, which affected the enemy as badly if not worse than they did the British, such failures as did occur during the various wars from 1750 to 1815 were caused by political indecision, grand strategic failures and some poor senior appointments, not by the lack of enthusiasm of the fighting man on the spot (you might say that the enthusiasm was lacking at Spithead and the Nore in 1797, but the men involved in those mutinies made it clear that they were prepared to do their duty if the enemy threatened). There are numerous little stories that show that enthusiasm. Typical of these is Sir Sidney Smith's letter to Earl Spencer in 1795, describing his strategy of sending his ship's launch 'to seek adventure' whenever they were close to land. He commented that not only did he have difficulty in selecting a crew from amongst the many volunteers, but that even the petty officers attempted to 'slip in and secrete themselves in order to go'.[1] Whilst a man might fight on a badly- or inadequately-filled stomach, he will not do so with enthusiasm and consistent success. There is a vulgar modern military aphorism which neatly sums it up: 'You can't **** on cornflakes'. So let us put aside the two big myths about Georgian naval food: it was not skimpy and it was not foul.

'In the face of the enemy' implies that the fighting man is in that position and can stay there for as long as it takes to do the job; in order to stay on station, whether the task is blockading or actively seeking out the enemy and fighting him, that 'fuel' has to be delivered regularly and in a timely fashion. It has been argued, to good effect, that the failure to do this, due to the inexperience of the Treasury staff who were given the task of supplying the British army in North America during the War of Independence, was the primary cause of the British failure in that war.[2] The Victualling Board had many decades of experience to call on, and had set up systems to supply provisions wherever they were needed. With very few minor hiccups, they did so.

There were many subsidiary aspects to that broad task. Quality standards had to be established and maintained, and there had to be a system for dealing with sub-standard items. Opportunists and deliberate fraudsters had to be discouraged or caught and punished. Justice had to be seen to be done by discouraging the sort of favouritism that can lead to industrial unrest. And last, but by no means least, the public purse (or as they saw it, the King's purse) had to be protected from excessive spending. Whilst the commanders-in-chief and shipboard personnel had their part to play in these desired results, the drive to achieve them had to come from the responsible body at the top of the pyramid, the Board of Admiralty. Here, with a couple of reservations, we can accept that the public employees did a fair job. The reservations relate to their attitude to the peripheral personnel – the commissioned sea officers, the pursers, the suppliers and the contractors. Here they often displayed the sort of pig-headed righteousness that tends to infect all bureaucrats. They were more concerned to get their forms filled in correctly than to allow a little leeway to the form-fillers; they certainly did not see it as any part of their job to be kind to pursers.

They were perfectly prepared to experiment in the interest of improving quality, saving money or solving the age-old problem of vermin. The records are full of suggestions received, trials being organised and reported on. A few, such as iron water-tanks, were successful and wholesale changes were made. Others, and there were many more than the few recorded in these pages, were so weird that one has to wonder whether they really believed they might work, or were just paying lip-service to an influential idea-suggester. Contemplating such ideas as the lobsters as weevil-repellents, one realises the depth of the void between the Georgian world and our own; we are so bombarded by information on all possible topics that it would surely be difficult to find anyone today who would believe that a lobster could survive in a barrel of weevilly flour, let alone drive out the weevils.

So why, we might ask, if they were so happy to experiment and happy to adopt new things which had proved successful in trials, did they not immediately adopt the new technology of food canning? Mainly because the concept came too late. The inventor of the process, the Frenchman Nicolas Appert, had offered samples to the French navy for trial in 1803 and they had responded with enthusiasm, as did the government committee appointed to investigate. He was awarded 12,000 francs to publish details of his process, but these were not available until 1810. The process was then patented in Britain and the Dartford firm of Donkin & Hall developed the process. After sending samples to Sir Joseph Banks and Lord Wellesley, they persuaded the Victualling Board to give their canned food a sea trial. The three captains who performed the trial in 1813 were also enthusiastic but the Victualling Board was not happy about the high price of canned food (nor, it should be said, was the general public when cans were put on general sale). Although it was supplied to ships bound on polar and other voyages of exploration from 1814, tinned food did not become a standard part of the ordinary ship's provisions until 1847.[3] It might have gained a wider and faster use if the invention had come ten years earlier but by the time those trials were completed, it was becoming obvious that the long war was coming to an end. The Victualling Board's attention was increasingly focused on running down and then disposing of the food stocks they did have, and innovations were a long way down their priority list. So they cannot be blamed for not trying to fix something that showed no signs of being broken.

What about improving the seaman's diet? Should they not have been doing something about that? Actually, no: the Victualling Board's job was not to act as dietary consultants, even had the concept existed at the time. Their task was one of pure logistics – to obtain good-quality supplies and deliver them to the end user without delay, to get value for money and generally to see that the rules were complied with. When the rules were changed, for instance when it was decreed that fresh meat and vegetables should be supplied, they quickly set up systems to do so. It certainly was no fault of the Victualling Board that it took the medical profession so long to accept that citrus fruit was the answer to scurvy.

Could they have done a better job if they had done it differently? By the end of the Napoleonic War they were doing it differently from the way they had been doing it seventy years earlier. Although in some areas they had to be pushed by the Parliamentary Commissioners, in general they regularly refined and improved their systems and thus the effectiveness of what they achieved. They had gone from a situation where almost everything was supplied by outside contractors to a point where the greatest proportion was supplied by the Victualling Board itself. As the theatres of war expanded and shifted, so the Victualling Board organised local collection points for supplies and when those were not easily reachable, they provided the pursers with cash and a system which allowed them to buy supplies wherever they found themselves.

It is hard to see how they could have done anything else differently, allowing for the available technology and the administrative systems of the day. Reading about some modern examples of supplying fighting forces far from home, those of Vietnam, the Falklands campaign and the Gulf wars, one soon realises that modern technology does not make that much difference. The problem with modern technology is that it only works properly when a complex infrastructure exists: big aircraft need proper airports, big transport ships need proper unloading facilities, and both need proper storage facilities to put the goods in and road or rail transport systems to move the goods from the port to the user, all of which are vulnerable to enemy action.[4] At the end of the day, you can use computers, aircraft and container ships but you are still at the mercy of the sea and the weather, the co-operation of the locals, and above all, the competence and drive of your personnel. And in the set of wars we are discussing, while those last two factors may not have been perfect, they were well above the average and well above that of the competition, and that made all the difference.

So, allowing for the fact that sometimes the desire to get value for money moved higher up the priority list than was strictly necessary, and allowing also for the fact that any government trough will always attract a number of opportunist snouts, we have to come to the conclusion that the Victualling Board and everyone else involved in the supply and delivery chain did a pretty good job most of the time. By reliable and regular deliveries of food and drink to the British fleet, that fleet was enabled to remain at sea, to reach its destinations and to remain on station, month after month, year after year, throughout all the long years of struggles against the French and Spanish, the Dutch and Americans, and all the other nations which threatened British freedom.

Appendix 1

WEIGHTS AND MEASURES

Few of the forms of measurement used in Georgian times are in use today. The following will, I hope, clarify matters for those who are not familiar with the old forms of British weights, measures and money.

Weights and Measures

1 ton equals 2240 pounds (not to be confused with the metric measure of 1 tonne, which is 1000 kilograms).
1 hundredweight (cwt) equals 112 pounds.
1 pound (lb) avoirdupois equals 454 grams.
16 ounces equals 1 pound.
1 ounce equals 28.375g (but is generally converted as 25g in recipes).

An English pint is 20 fl oz (560ml), an American pint is 16 fl oz (448ml). In both cases, 8 pints equals 1 gallon.

'Wine measure' is slightly less than the usual English liquid measure 'Beer measure'. The wine measure, which is ⅚ of beer measure, equates to the modern American liquid measure. This difference dates from 1844, when the British dropped the old Queen Anne measure but the Americans retained it.[1]

Barrel Sizes

'Barrel' and 'Cask' are both general terms and both refer to the old wooden, roughly round, containers which were used for both liquids and dry stuffs.
A tun, also known as a leaguer, contains approximately 250 gallons.[2]
A pipe contains approximately 105 gallons, and is generally used only for wine.
A hogshead contains 52½ gallons; a half-hogshead, about 26 gallons.

A butt contains 108 or 126 gallons (depending on whether the content is wine or beer).

A firkin contains 56 pounds of butter or 9 gallons beer.

A puncheon could contain anything from 70 to 120 gallons, but was more likely to contain dry stuffs. Half-puncheons were also used.

A bushel is a dry measure of volume containing 8 gallons.

Money

It is almost impossible to calculate modern value equivalents of Georgian money; all one can do, therefore, is explain how the currency worked.

One pound sterling, written £1, or £1.0s.0d, consisted of 20 shillings, or 240 pennies. Thus 1 shilling consisted of 12 pennies, and was written as 1s, or 1/-. Its modern decimal equivalent is 5 pence.

Pennies could be divided into halfpence and farthings and were written as 1d, ½d or ¼d. The decimal equivalent, as such, does not exist, but to put it the other way round, 1 decimal penny is worth 2.4 old pennies.

Other coins included the crown, which was worth 5 shillings (25 decimal pence); half a crown, which was worth two shillings and sixpence (12½ decimal pence), the florin, which was worth two shillings (sometimes referred to as 'two bob' and now worth 10 decimal pence), the sixpence (a 'tizzy' or later, a 'tanner' and now worth 2½ decimal pence) and the threepenny piece or 'thruppenny bit'.

1 guinea was worth £1.1s.0d, or 21 shillings.

Appendix 2

OFFICIAL SUBSTITUTES FOR SPECIES OF PROVISIONS[1]

'When it may be found necessary to issue any other Species of Provisions or Substitutes for the above, it is to be observed that they are to be furnished in the following proportions, viz.

A pint of Wine, or half a pint of Spirits, is equal to a Gallon of Beer, and when Wine or Spirits are demanded, one fourth part only of the whole proportion is to be issued in Wine.

Four pounds of Flour, or three pounds thereof, with one pound of Raisins, are equal to a four-pound piece of Salt Beef. Half a pound of Currants, or half a pound of Beef Suet, is equal to one pound of Raisins. Four pounds of Fresh Beef, or three pounds of Mutton, are equal to four pounds of Salt Beef; and three pounds of Fresh Beef, or Mutton, to a two-pound piece of Salt Pork, with Pease.

One pint of Calavances, or Doll, is equal to a pint of Pease.

Whenever Rice is issued for Bread, Pease, Oatmeal, or Cheese, one pound of Rice is to be considered as equal to one pound of Bread, a pint of Pease, a quart of Oatmeal, or a pound of Cheese.

A pint of Wheat, or of Pot Barley, is equal to a pint of Oatmeal; five pounds and three-quarters of Molasses are equal to one gallon of Oatmeal.

When Sugar is substituted for Oatmeal, Butter, or Cheese, one pound of Sugar is equal to two quarts of Oatmeal, one pound of Butter, or one pound of Cheese.

A pint of Oil is equal to a pound of Butter, or two pounds of Cheese; and half a pound of Cocoa, or a quarter of a pound of Tea, is equal to one pound of Cheese.'

Appendix 3

CALORIFIC VALUES OF NAVAL FOODSTUFFS

The figure of 4500 calories usually quoted for the naval diet appears to be derived from a chart which is seriously flawed in several respects: first by reading 'bisket' as 'brisket' in the document from which the list of food was taken (the difference in calories per 100g between the two foodstuffs being 290 calories), secondly by faulty conversions from eighteenth-century weights to grams/millilitres, and thirdly for several inaccurate calorie-counts.[1]

A more accurate calculation is as follows:[2]

Item	*Weekly issue*	*g/ml*	*Cal per 100g/ml*	*Total cals*
Biscuit	7 lbs	3178	436[3]	13,856
Beer	7 galls (wine measure[4]) = 5.8 galls	26,250	25[5]	6562
Beef	4 lbs	1816	146[6]	2651
Pork	2 lbs	908	320[7]	2906
Pease	2 pints = 2 lbs	908[8]	328	2978
Oatmeal	3 pints = 1½ lbs	681[9]	375	2554
Butter	6 oz	170	740	1258
Cheese (Cheddar)	12 oz	340	406	1380
Vinegar	½ pint	283	25[10]	71
Weekly Total				34,216
Daily average				4888

As can be seen from the notes, it is difficult to be exact on some items, since the modern calorie counts are calculated on modern types of beer and specific cuts of meat; the Georgian sailor could not know which cut of meat he was going to get until it arrived on his plate.

However, even as calculated, the amounts of total calories issued is still subject to many possible variations, not least of these being the official recommendation that on one day each week, the issue of beef should be replaced with 1½ lbs of flour and ½ lb of raisins. This substitution alone would bring the weekly ration up to 35,560 calories, and thus a daily average of 5080. Substitute suet for the raisins and the daily average goes up to 5134. The following table gives the calorie counts of the other types of food and drink used as substitutes. Note that there is a considerable difference between beer, wine and spirits; a man on red wine receives 624 calories less per day, one on spirits 420 less per day than those on beer.

Item	*Recommended amount*	*g/ml*	*Cal per 100g/ml*	*Total cals*
Flour (wholemeal)	1½ lbs	681	310	2111
Raisins	½ lb	227	246	58
Suet	¼ lb	114	826	938
Tea			0	
Cocoa			312	
Sugar			394	
Rice (white)			138	
Olive oil			820	
Vegetables[11]			25	
Spirits			222	
White wine			75	
Red wine			68	

Appendix 4

VITAMIN CONTENT OF NAVAL FOOD

The table below gives the Vitamin A and C content of naval foodstuffs which contained them. Where an item is not listed, it is because it contained neither. Some other items which are now known to be high in those vitamins are also listed. However, it should be noted that the figures given are close approximations only and cannot be as accurate as those obtained from modern commercially-produced products; the amount of vitamin (or any other property) in foodstuffs varies according to the variety of the plant, the soil conditions on which it was grown, the weather conditions during its growth and, particularly with Vitamin C, how and for how long it has been stored since harvesting. The same applies to animal products: breed, age, feeding, as well as the cut and storage of meat all give varied readings to the end product.

Vitamin A is necessary for vision in dim light; prolonged deficiency causing night-blindness. It is present in liver (including fish liver), kidneys, dairy produce and eggs, and to a certain extent in carrots, dark green or yellow vegetables, the amount of vitamin increasing with the darkness of the colour of the vegetable. The Vitamin A in meat and dairy products is of a type called retinol, that in vegetables of a type called beta-carotene, which the body converts into retinol and which is usually presented (as here) in 'retinol-equivalent International Units', shown as μg. The recommended daily allowance for a man between 19 and 50 is 1000 μg per day. The only standard species of official provisions containing Vitamin A were butter and cheese which would deliver weekly amounts of 1507 μg (butter), 1234 μg (cheese). The substitute items delivered hardly any.

Vitamin C is necessary for the maintenance of healthy connective tissue. Humans are among the few animals which cannot form their own Vitamin C. Prolonged deficiency causes bleeding, especially from capillary blood vessels and the gums, and wounds heal more slowly. If uncorrected, scurvy follows and eventually death. There is some in fresh meat (best is kidney or liver) but most in fruit and vegetables. The recommended daily allowance for a man between 19 and 50 is 90mg per day. Note that although the amount of Vitamin C shown in the table is less in cooked vegetables than raw, this is because the vitamin has leached out into the cooking water; where the end product is soup, the vitamin is still available to the eater.[1]

	Vit.A (retinol equivalent units) µg per 100g	*Vit. C. mg per 100g*
Apples (eating)	0	2
Apricots	91	6
Bananas	0	11
Blackcurrants	0	200 raw, 150 cooked[2]
Butter	887	0
Cabbage (average)	35	49 raw, 20 boiled
Carrots	1260	6 raw, 2 boiled
Cheese (Cheddar)	363	0
Cocoa (powder)	7	0
Cod liver oil	18,000	0
Eggs (boiled)	190	0
Grapes	0	4
Kidney, pigs (raw)	160	14
Lemon juice	0	40-60
Lime juice	0	25-30
Liver, lambs, fried	20,600	12
Liver, ox, stewed	20,100	15
Mangoes	300	37
Milk (whole)	55	1
Onions	2	10 raw, 6 boiled
Orange juice	0	40-50
Plums	49	4
Potatoes[3]	0	9
Raisins	2	0
Rosehip syrup	0	200
Sauerkraut	0	10-15
Scurvy grass[4]	0	200
Suet	52	0
Watercress	420	662
Wort	0	0.1

Appendix 5

BILLS OF EXCHANGE

'Form of a Bill of Exchange'[1]

(Place & Date)

£	Sterling	Exchange at	per cent
	Premium at	per cent	
	Discount at	per cent	

Thirty days after sight of this my first (second, etc) Bill of Exchange pay to the order of (A. B.) the sum of *(expressed in words)* Sterling for value received by me, in the currency of this place, amounting to *(expressed in words)* and no more, according to the Rate of Exchange, Premium, or Discount above stated, and charge the same to my Account, for the services of His Majesty's Victualling Establishment as per Advice.

.... Agent

To the Commissioners for Victualling
His Majesty's Navy

We do hereby certify that the Rate of Exchange, Premium, or Discount upon Bills drawn on London, drawn for the Public Service, were precisely as stated, on the .... Day of ....18.... At this place

.... (*two principal merchants*)

I hereby certify the Truth of what is above stated, and that the two Merchants are Persons of Respectability, and considered capable of judging what they have certified.

.... (*Collector of the Customs*)

I approve of this Bill, and believe the Rate of Exchange, Premium, or Discount to be correctly stated.

.... (*Commissioner or Commander-in-chief*)'

How Bills of Exchange and Imprest Accounts Worked

Bills of Exchange are an ancient form of what are now known as 'negotiable instruments' which can be passed from hand to hand without the consent of the person or body on whom they are drawn. They are simply a promise to pay a stated sum of money at a stated time. Bank notes and cheques are types of Bills of Exchange.

So if a purser were to give a merchant a Bill drawn on the Victualling Board for £100, that merchant could expect to present it to the Victualling Board and exchange it for that £100. That scenario would require the Bill to say 'Pay on sight', or as modern bank notes do, 'Pay on demand'. More often they would say, as does the example on page 181, 'Pay thirty days after sight', which meant that the Victualling Board would not pay out until thirty days after the merchant presented it to them. Some Bills were 'ninety-day' Bills or, rarely, even longer periods. Merchants would not be very keen to accept such delayed payments unless there were a guarantee of some interest in compensation for the delay. On the other hand, they may have needed to get some money in their hands quickly, and thus would be prepared to sell the Bill to someone else at a discount. This was the common method of paying for all business transactions at the time, and the system worked very well. There were groups of British merchants all over the world who would buy such Bills at appropriate discounts, and many foreign merchants would happily accept them as well, unless their country was at war with Britain; even then they could cope with the situation by charging a bigger discount.

Strictly speaking, it should have been irrelevant to the validity of a Bill that it stated that it was to be used for a particular purpose and countersigned by a particular set of people. However, the person or organisation that is to pay is entitled to impose conditions if they wish, provided that the person accepting the Bill in payment is aware of these conditions. Apart from the fact that it would have been obvious the moment the Bill was proffered, merchants in ports frequented by the Royal Navy would have been aware of the Victualling Board's conditions; those who did not like them might be mollified by being shown the relevant part of the printed *Regulations*, or would just insist on being paid in cash, which is why pursers were issued with 'necessary' money.

Sooner or later someone would have to produce the Bill to the Victualling Board in London in order to receive their money, and for merchants abroad this would involve finding someone who was going to London, sending the Bill to an agent in London, or just selling it to someone else locally (a larger merchant or a bank) who had London correspondents. With small Bills, there was rarely any hesitation over payment, the Victualling Board dealing with any possible problems by charging the amount to the issuing person's imprest account.

The easiest way to describe the concept of imprest accounts is to liken them to modern overdraft accounts, secured, in the case of pursers, by their unpaid wages and the bonds lodged by their guarantors when the purser took the job. The imprest was not cleared (or the wages paid) until all the requisite paperwork was produced and checked to ensure that the money had been spent properly. The imprest system was applied to victualling contractors as well as pursers, the only difference being the magnitude of the sums involved. Both purser and contractor were effectively in the same line of business, one as what we might call a retailer and the other as a wholesaler, and both, by drawing Bills, were doing what the modern business person does when they write a cheque for stock purchases. And just like the modern wholesaler does when they can see the necessity of writing a large cheque which will take them over their overdraft limit, these contractors wrote to ask the Victualling Board if they might increase their imprest limit.[2] If the amount was large and they had no forewarning of it, the Victualling Board might write to the Admiralty and ask permission to accept the Bill, just as the branch manager of a bank might write to his head office today. The reason for this was that the Admiralty could not just spend money as it pleased; it had to stick to the limits agreed for each year by Parliament and if it was likely to exceed those limits it would have to go back to Parliament and ask for more. Given that this would cause serious unpopularity in politically fragile times, it is perhaps not surprising that on some occasions, when presented with an unexpected large Bill, the Admiralty might decide to refuse payment, or in modern terms, 'bounce the cheque'.[3]

However, accepting a Bill did not necessarily mean it was paid out at the specified interval. There were long periods when the Admiralty's subordinate boards just did not have the money available to pay their Bills, and in this case they would apply interest to the amount they would eventually pay and advise the owner of the Bill to watch 'the course of the exchange'. This was an official statement as to when certain tranches of Bills would be paid. For instance, in January 1795 the Treasury stated that Bills from April to September 1791 were 'in course of payment' and that those from that period to March 1793 were 'funded in five per cent' interest.[4]

Appendix 6

EAT LIKE A SAILOR – RECIPES

Ships Biscuit

The original method

The biscuit-making process at Deptford victualling yard was on a grand scale, producing almost 25,000 pounds of biscuit a day from twelve ovens, each baking twenty batches a day, and being fed with raw biscuits by a team of seven men. To knead the dough they used a device called a horse; this consisted of a circular platform on which a big lump of flour and water dough was placed, and a wide lever mounted on a central pole which a man 'rode' like a hobby horse, jumping it up and down to knead the dough, working his way round the circle as many times as it took to bring the dough to the desired state. It was then passed, in sequence, to a series of men who cut the dough, moulded it into shape, stamped it, split it into two biscuits, arranged it on a peel and 'shot' it into the oven to bake.

A modern version

Ships biscuit is easy to make by hand if you do not mind spending the time to knead the flour sufficiently. If you lack the time or the enthusiasm, you can either put the dough through a pasta machine as many times as it takes to achieve the desired silky texture, or put the ingredients into a bread-making machine and run the dough cycle, then roll the resultant dough by hand. Use white flour for the captain's table, wholemeal for the mess decks. If intending to keep the biscuits for any length of time, it is best to omit the salt as this will attract moisture from the atmosphere.

1 lb (454 g) (5 cups) plain (all-purpose) white or wholemeal flour
1 teaspoon salt
approx ¾ pint (15 ml) (1½ cups) water

Put the flour and salt into a large bowl (or mixing machine), add the water, a little at a time (you may need more than given above) and mix until you can pull the whole together into a ball of dough. (Alternatively, put the flour, salt and most of the water into a bread machine and start the dough cycle with the lid open, adding water a little at a time if the dough appears too stiff, then close the lid and leave the machine to do the rest. Keep neck-ties and hair well away from the machine.) Sprinkle a little flour on a level work surface, turn the dough out and allow it to rest for 10 minutes. Flour your hands and knead the dough for as long as it takes to make it smooth and silky: about 30 minutes.

Turn on the oven to heat to 160°C/325°F/Mark 3. Roll the dough out until approximately ¼ inch (6 mm) thick. Cut it into 3-inch (7.5 cm) squares or rounds, prick the surface with a fork. Lay the biscuits out on a lightly greased baking sheet, not quite touching, and bake for about 60 minutes. They should not be too dark. Put them on a wire tray to cool completely before storing in an airtight container.

Salt Beef

The Georgian recipes for salting beef included saltpetre, in a proportion of 2 oz saltpetre to 6 lbs of salt. The reason for adding saltpetre is mainly to give the meat an attractive deep pink colour, but it does tend to make the meat hard. It contributes nothing to the taste, and so can be happily omitted. Saltpetre is now virtually unobtainable in the UK, possibly because its cheaper version, 'Chilean' saltpetre (or sodium nitrate) is thought to create carcinogenic nitrosamines, but more probably because true saltpetre is one of the ingredients of gunpowder.

Beef for the Royal Navy was preserved with no more than salt (and salt-petre). For home use, sugar was often added (this helps prevent toughness) and there are many recipes for spiced salt beef. All use the same methods; try whichever takes your fancy.

2-3 lbs (1-1.5 kg) beef (rolled and tied silverside or brisket)
1 lb (450 g) sea salt (not 'free-running' table salt which contains additives to make it run) plus another 2-3 lbs (1-1.5 kg) sea salt for the brine
4 oz (100 g) brown sugar
1 teaspoon freshly ground black pepper
your choice of ground spices: ginger, coriander seeds, cloves, nutmeg

If using the sugar and/or spices, mix these into the first lot of salt. Rub some of the mixture (or plain salt) into one side of the beef, place it salt-side down in a large bowl or plastic bag and rub more mixture into the top surface of the beef. Close the container and leave it for a day. Next day, rub more of the mixture into both sides of the beef and put it back into the container with the liquid that it has generated. Continue to do this for two more days. Now drain off and throw away the liquid, put the beef back into the container and shake more salt over it, both sides. Leave it another day then drain it again.

Prepare a strong brine of water and sea salt. You will need about 2¼ lbs (1 kg) salt to 1 gallon (4.5 litres) water, but the real test is that when the brine is strong enough, the meat will float, so mix your brine in the tub you intend to store it in, stirring until all the salt has dissolved, then put the meat in and if it does not float, just add more salt until it does.

However, the meat must stay below the surface of the brine, so once the brine is strong enough, put a weight (in a plastic bag so it does not contaminate the brine) on the meat. Seal the tub and leave it in a cool place for as long as you feel inclined. The author has left some for 15 months and found it perfectly tender and edible (if a little on the salty side). But you should leave it for at least a couple of months for the authentic salt beef taste. Check it every week; if it has thrown a white deposit on to the surface of the brine, just skim this off and top up the brine mixture. Your nose will tell you if all is well.

When you are ready to eat the beef, take it out of the brine, rinse it off under a running tap and put it to steep in plain cold water. The longer it has been in the brine, the longer it should steep (say 1 hour steeping time for each month it has been kept) and the more times you should change the steeping water. Finally, put the beef and fresh water to cover it into a cooking pot (with a bay leaf if you wish, but no salt) bring it to the boil, skim if necessary, and simmer for 4-5 hours until tender. You could add some onions and carrots for the last half hour, or some dumplings (or both). Eat it hot with its gravy and accompaniments, or cold with a salad or in a sandwich (or with a ships biscuit).

Salt Pork

The Royal Navy way of salting pork was exactly the same as for beef. The modern French way of curing *petit salé* is dry cure, although with keeping, the dry salt runs to brine anyway. This is an easier method for home use.

For the classic *petit salé*, start by making flavoured salt:

2¼ lbs (1 kg) sea salt
12 peppercorns
4 cloves
4 bay leaves
1 teaspoon juniper berries
1 oz (25 g) white sugar
the leaves from 2 sprigs of thyme

Crush the pepper, cloves, bay leaves and juniper berries and mix well into the salt with the sugar and thyme leaves. This gives sufficient for up to 12 lbs (6 kg) of pork. The classic French pork meat is belly, but if you think this will be too fatty for you, use chops.

Put several handfuls of the salt mix into the bottom of a large container. Rub more into the pork and layer it into the container with plenty of salt between the layers. Cover it and leave it in a cool place for at least a week, but for anything up to two months.

When you want to eat the pork, take out as much as you want, rinse it off and boil it in plenty of unsalted water for 40-60 minutes, depending on the thickness of the meat. Taste the water after 10 minutes; if it is over-salty, throw it away and refill the pan with fresh. If the pork has been in the salt for more than two months, steep it for a couple of hours in fresh water before changing the water and cooking it. Serve it hot with *choucroute* (*ie* sauerkraut) or cold with salad.

Sauerkraut

Sauerkraut is, quite simply, cabbage which has been preserved in salt. Start with a tight cabbage (the white or pale green sort), cut it into quarters and remove the thick centre core and any damaged outer leaves. Shred the cabbage thinly and pack it into a large container with plenty of sea salt between the layers, pressing each layer down well. Find a plate that fits the inside of the container, sterilise it by pouring boiling water over it and place it over the cabbage, adding a weight on top to keep the cabbage compressed. Cover the container but check it daily, skimming off any scum from the brine, then re-sterilising the plate and replacing it. The cabbage will ferment and the brine will bubble; when this stops (after about three weeks), the fermentation process has ended and you could eat the sauerkraut then. Most aficionados think it tastes better after another three to four weeks. Expect it to smell while fermenting and when you open the container to take some out.

When you want to eat some, remove sufficient from the container with a ladle or pasta straining-fork and rinse it well before boiling it in unsalted water. You might like to add a chopped apple and/or some caraway seeds.

Pease

You can cook dried pease in plain water, but the flavour will be better if the water has started its career by being used to cook a ham, as long as it is not too salty. The trick of cooking any of the dried pulses is not to add salt until they are tender, as early salting may prevent their ever becoming tender. Use split pease (green or yellow), which will be without their skins, rather than whole dried green pease, which have their skins. If you buy a packet of dried green pease which includes a soaking tablet, change the water after soaking and before cooking or ignore the soaking tablet all together.

One pound of dried pease will be more than enough for four people. Start by soaking the pease overnight (which term actually means 'for seven or eight hours'; there is nothing magical about night time in this context) in about three times their volume of water. Use a very large pot, as otherwise the swelling pease can end up spilling over the top of the pot. Rinse them, return them to the pot, add lots of water, bring this to the boil, then cover them and turn them down to simmer for a couple of hours or until tender. Once they are tender, drain them, add salt and pepper, plus butter, if desired, and eat as an accompaniment to pork or ham, with boiled potatoes and a white or parsley sauce.

Pease Pudding

1 lb (450 g) (2 good cups) dried split pease (preferably yellow)
2 oz (50 g) butter
1 large egg
salt and pepper

Start as above, soaking and then cooking the pease until just tender. Mash them with the butter, egg and seasoning and place the result in a muslin or fine sail-cloth bag with your mess number attached. Tie one end of the bag to the handle of a saucepan, either containing ham or salt pork, or plain water. Bring the liquid to the boil and cook for at least an hour. (You can also make pease pudding in a pudding basin – butter the basin, mash the ingredients and put them in the basin, cover it with foil, tie this down and steam for an hour.) Turn the pudding out onto a serving plate and serve in slices with the meat; alternatively, allow it to cool completely before slicing, when you can eat it from the hand, accompanied by a biscuit, while standing watch on a cold night.

Pea Soup

Start as though making plain cooked pease, ideally in ham water, but use a larger saucepan. When the pease are tender, mash them and stir in a lot more water, bring them back to the boil and continue cooking until they have turned into a thick soup. Add some morsels of cooked ham or pork (or some crisply fried bacon crumbs) before serving. Expect any uneaten soup to set solid when cold. Reheat it carefully, adding a little more water to prevent it sticking and burning.

Duff – The Basic Recipe

Duff, or suet pudding, in its simplest form consists of a mixture of flour and suet, boiled in a pudding bag (or basin) and eaten with meat. By adding various things and treating it in a slightly different way, it can be transformed into a jam roly-poly, spotted dog, plum duff or sea pie.

Best results come from the simple 'half fat to flour' proportion, but making this by volume rather than weight; use American cup measures if you have them, otherwise use English tea cups. Use self-raising (self-rising) flour and prepared suet, which comes in little pieces, like grains of rice. To make duff for four people:

2 cups of self-raising flour
1 cup suet
pinch salt
enough water to make a soft dough

Sift the flour into a mixing bowl, add the salt and suet and mix together with a fork. Add the water, a little at a time, mixing with a fork until it comes together in a sticky dough. Flour your hands, turn the dough out onto a floured surface and knead it very gently, sprinkling on a little more flour if necessary, until it can be formed into a ball or sausage shape. Pop this into a pudding cloth (it has been suggested that the nightcap of one of your fellow midshipmen will serve if the pudding bag has disappeared), tie the bag and boil the duff for about an hour. You could also pinch off little pieces of dough, form them into balls, and let them boil for fifteen minutes in with the beef.

To make Plum Duff, add half a pound (200 g) of raisins or currants to the mixture and proceed as before.

To make Spotted Dog, add half a pound (200 g) of raisins and 2 ounces (50 g) of sugar to the mixture.

To make Jam Roly-Poly, instead of forming the pudding into a ball or sausage, roll out to a rectangle, spread it thickly with jam (raspberry, strawberry or plum) and roll it up into a sausage before proceeding as before. Beware when eating – the jam will be very hot!

To make a savoury Roly-Poly, substitute a mixture of chopped bacon, fried onions and mushrooms, or onions and mussels, for the jam and proceed as above.

Sea Pie

This can be made in a saucepan to cook on top of the stove, or in a casserole for the oven. It consists, quite simply, of a good rich stew with a suet pastry crust, so make your stew, and when it is almost cooked, make some suet pastry (*ie* basic duff mix) and roll it out to fit the inside of the saucepan/casserole. It should be about ½ inch (1 cm) thick. Fit it in on top of the stew, cover tightly and put it back on the heat for twenty to thirty minutes.

For a multi-decked sea pie, layer the stew and suet pastry as many times as you have room for, alternate the stew with fried onions, vegetables, or whatever you happen to have handy. The more layers, the longer the lower layers of pastry will take to cook, so check at intervals to make sure all is going well.

Lobscouse

Lobscouse is an ancient dish known under various similar names throughout the northern world. In Lapland it is called *lapskuis* and the recipe includes walrus, in Germany it includes both meat and herrings, in Sweden it is called *lapskijs* and is still made with salt meat, in the USA it appears as 'corned beef hash', using the type of salt meat which they call 'corned beef' (as opposed to the tins of pink boiled beef which is known in Britain as corned beef). So lobscouse is simply a dish made by mixing small pieces of meat or fish with broken-up ships biscuit, onions or leeks and/or potatoes.

1 lb (450 g) salt beef or pork or fish or walrus (or a mixture of all or any of these), cut into similar sized pieces, say about ½ inch (1 cm) cubes, raw or pre-cooked. (Or a large tin of corned beef.)
2 large potatoes, peeled and cut into pieces the same size as the meat
1 large onion or 2 large leeks, roughly chopped
2 tablespoons slush, or beef dripping, or lard, or even olive oil
3-4 ships biscuits, crushed in a bag with a belaying pin (optional)
salt and freshly ground black pepper
your choice of spices – cloves, nutmeg, mace, ginger (optional)

If using raw ingredients, start by boiling the meat or fish and the potatoes until almost done, then strain them. Slice the onions and fry them until golden brown. Put everything except the onions into a large frying pan (or casserole if you have an oven handy), pour the onions and their fat over the top and stir well. If frying, do so for 10-15 minutes, stirring regularly. If baking, add some hot water or some of the original cooking water, or beer, put a lid on the casserole and put in a hot oven for 30-45 minutes, or a medium cool oven for anything up to two hours. In either case, a fried egg is a good addition when serving.

Another variation on lobscouse is 'crackerhash', made by layering salt beef, cooked pease and crushed biscuit in a casserole, dotting the top with plenty of beef dripping or slush and baking it in the oven.

Burgoo

Burgoo is nothing other than oatmeal porridge. As with suet pastry, the mixture is two to one: two cupfuls of water to one cupful of porridge oats. This amount will serve four people. Start with the cold water in a saucepan and stir the oats into this gradually. Bring the mixture slowly to the boil, then turn it down to simmer for about fifteen minutes, stirring all the time. When the oats have changed into a smooth mass, serve it with sugar and cream, or butter and salt.

Portable Soup

The Original Recipe[1]

The original recipe is long, repetitive and rather cumbersome, so here it is paraphrased to give the essence (if readers will forgive the pun). Unfortunately it does not state quantities of meat nor the size of the boilers.

Fill eight boilers with flesh – three parts shanks and shins of beef, one part mutton, cover them with water and bring to the boil, then simmer for thirteen hours, skimming the fat as it rises and putting this into a barrel. As it settles, pour off the fat into another barrel and return the watery liquid to the meat boilers.

When the flesh is sufficiently cooked, remove it from the boilers, remove the bones, extract the marrow and return this to the boilers. Tear the flesh apart with forks, lay it on a sieve to drain, then put it into a press to extract the last of the broth. Prepare some tin buckets with hair sieves on top and pour the broth from the boilers through these into the buckets. Press the solid residue as above. Pour the liquid into evaporators and simmer, skimming as necessary, for about eight hours, until the soup becomes 'like a thick syrup and when cool is as stiff as tripe'. Add the seasoning, leave it until the next day to cool, then cut it out of the evaporators, take it to the drying room, melt it into flat tin frames about ¼ inch thick. Leave to cool, cut it out of the frames and cut it into pieces just a little larger than the broad arrow and dry these on canvas frames at 70 – 80 degrees 'of the thermometer' [one assumes this means Fahrenheit].

The seasoning: take 6 lbs celery seed, 3 lbs black pepper, beaten fine, leave these to stand for two days in three gallons of spirits of wine with a very gentle heat in a tin balneum (*bain marie*) then sieve and press this through a hair bag. Wash out the press, retain the liquid, add 20 lbs well bruised garlic to the pressed celery and pepper and put it all back in the *bain marie* for three to four hours then let the fire go out. Press out the solids and add the liquid to the first lot of celery water. To this, add up to 6 teaspoonfuls of tincture of thyme, made by adding 2 oz fresh oil of thyme to 1½ pts spirit of wine.

NB. The original recipe does not state what happened to the pressed meat – perhaps it went to a pie-maker?

Portable Soup, a modern version.

This is the author's version of the original recipe, tested and approved by her official taster (*ie* husband). The quantities given will produce sufficient to reconstitute into four generous bowls of soup. Note that you should not add any salt during the preparation stage, as this will make it difficult to dry the concentrate properly and thus invite deterioration. Salt should not be added until the soup has been reconstituted for immediate eating. Do not be tempted to use a different cut of beef, as shin has generous quantities of the connective tissue which breaks down into jelly.

3 lbs (1.5 kg) of beef shin meat, cut into chunks about 1 inch (2-3 cm) square
1 lb (500 g) stewing lamb, say neck, chopped into chunks
8-10 sprigs of fresh thyme (or 1 tablespoon of dried)
8 garlic cloves, crushed (or a generous squirt of garlic paste)
16-20 black peppercorns, crushed (or several good grindings from a peppermill)
1 teaspoon celery seed (or 6-8 stalks of fresh celery, chopped)

At the beginning, you will need two separate saucepans, as cooking the lamb separately will allow easier removal of the fat and also give you the two meats separately to do something else with after straining. The beef will produce virtually no fat.

Put the meat into the saucepans, add cold water until the meat is well covered and bring it to the boil, skimming off the scum as it rises. Then turn the heat down, cover the pans and simmer the meat for twelve hours. Check it at intervals to make sure the meat is still covered with liquid, adding more if necessary. When the meat is done, strain it, keeping the two types of broth separate. You can use this meat to make pies or whatever. Leave the liquid to cool completely, when you can remove the fat, which will now have set.

Put the two liquids together in a large saucepan and bring back to the boil. Add the seasonings and simmer for an hour, take the soup off the heat and let it cool a little before putting it through a fine sieve or jelly bag. Press well to get all the juice out and discard the solids. Now put the soup back into the cooking pot, having first wiped out any solid residue, and bring it back to simmering temperature, stirring to prevent it sticking, then leave it to simmer, uncovered, for as long as it takes to reduce by three-quarters, checking it at intervals to make sure it has not gone too far. Take it off the heat, let it cool for about half an hour before pouring it into a square or rectangular cake tin lined with baking parchment (fold this at the corners rather than cut it, so there are no holes). Leave it to cool completely, cut it into squares, and put these in a very cool oven for several hours to finish drying out. Once dry, wrap each square in parchment and store in a tin until needed. Alternatively, freeze it.

When you need soup, put one or more squares into half a pint of hot water, melt over gentle heat, and add more boiling water to adjust the thickness. Now you can add salt.

Punches

Many punch recipes call for the juice and zest of a lemon. Always use unwaxed and preferably organically-grown (*ie* unsprayed) lemons. Do not be tempted to squeeze the lemon and drop the remains in the punch if intending to leave it for any length of time, as the lemon rind will impart a bitter taste. If adding lemon slices, do so at the last minute for the same reason. An easy way to get the zest from a lemon when making punch is to use lump sugar and rub the lumps over the fruit hard enough to break the zest capsules on the skin. Calculate 5-6 lumps to a tablespoonful of sugar.

Negus (punch)

Negus was one of the most popular punches of the Georgian era. It was usually served hot, but can be chilled and served with ice cubes.

juice and grated zest of 1 lemon
2 tablespoons sugar
1 pint (600 ml) (2 cups) boiling water
1 pint (600 ml) (2 cups) medium-dry sherry
nutmeg

Put the sugar, lemon juice and zest into a large jug and pour in the boiling water. Stir until the sugar has dissolved, then add the sherry and stir again. Grate some nutmeg on top of the mixture just before serving.

Rum punch

You will need a large saucepan with a tightly-fitting lid and a calm sea for this recipe.

2 tablespoons sugar
1 lemon
½ pint (300 ml) (1 cup) rum
⅛ pint (75ml) (¼ cup) brandy
1 pint (600 ml) (2 cups) boiling water

Put the sugar and lemon zest into the saucepan with the rum and brandy. Warm the mixture over medium heat until the sugar has melted, turn off the heat and set light to the mixture. Let it burn for 2 minutes, then cover the saucepan to extinguish the flame. Squeeze the juice from the lemon and add it to the mixture with the boiling water. Stir well, cover and leave to stand for 5-10 minutes. Taste and add more sugar if deemed necessary before serving.

Lemon or Orange shrub

juice and grated zest of 1 lemon or 1 orange
2 tablespoons sugar
1 pint (600 ml) (2 cups) rum

Mix all together and bottle. Leave it for at least a week before serving with boiling water in the proportion three parts water to one part shrub.

Claret cup

1 unwaxed lemon
6 lumps of sugar
1 × 75 cl bottle of claret
2 fl oz (50 ml) (⅓ cup) brandy
10 fl oz (280 ml) (1¼ cups) soda water
1 orange, sliced
a handful of borage (*Borago officinalis*) leaves, crushed ice, if available

Rub the sugar lumps over the lemon to extract the oil and drop them into your punch bowl. Halve and squeeze the lemon juice over the sugar. Add the claret, brandy and soda water, stir to dissolve the sugar. Lightly crush the borage leaves and drop them in, float the orange slices on top and add ice if available.

Lemon 'pepper'

Lemon pepper is not pepper at all, but the zest of lemons dried in the oven and ground to powder. Use a sharp knife or sharp vegetable peeler to remove the zest, avoiding the bitter pith underneath. Spread the pieces out on kitchen paper on a baking tray and bake in a very cool oven (*ie* 100°C/200°F/Mark ¼) until brittle but not discoloured. This could take a couple of hours, but check it at regular intervals so it does not scorch. Let it cool completely, break it into small pieces with your fingers and grind it to coarse powder in a coffee grinder. Transfer it to an airtight container for storage.

Use the 'pepper' to sprinkle over cooked chicken or fish, or on top of a syllabub.

Syllabub

If, like Admiral de Saumarez, you have a Guernsey cow on board, you can give your guests syllabub for dessert. This is one of the quickest and easiest of all desserts to make. All the classic version requires is good cream – either double (heavy) or the sort labelled 'whipping' cream – white wine or cider, sugar and nutmeg, and perhaps crystallised violets or rose petals for decoration. Modern variations include substituting yoghurt for up to half the cream, using orange or lemon juice with orange or lemon liqueur such as Grand Marnier for the wine, or substituting elderflower syrup for the sugar.

The trick, whether making the classic or new versions, is to start by whipping the cream until it starts to thicken, then adding the other ingredients in small increments, whipping in between additions, tasting until it seems right, then continuing to whip it to the 'soft peaks' stage. Then pour it into the serving dish, decorate it and serve it with sponge finger biscuits.

For three to four people, you will need:

½ pint (300 ml) (1¼ cups) double or whipping cream
1 wine glass white wine or cider
2-4 tablespoons caster sugar (depending on the sweetness of the wine)
a generous grating of nutmeg
some crystallised violets or rose petals for decoration (optional). Place these at the last minute, or they will bleed colour into the syllabub

If using the variation ingredients, halve the quantity of wine for liqueur and use the juice of 1 large lemon or 1 small orange.

The diet-conscious can substitute yoghurt for up to half the cream, but whip the cream first, then add the yoghurt in small increments.

Macaroons

These little almond biscuits (cookies) are ideal to nibble with a glass of Madeira or sherry when fellow officers pay a call.

This recipe will make 20-24 macaroons.

the whites of 4 eggs
1lb (450g) (4½ cups) caster sugar
1lb (450g) (4½ cups) of ground almonds
1-2 tablespoons orange flower water
4-5 sheets of 'rice' paper (edible paper)
20-24 blanched almonds

Preheat the oven to 180°C/350°F/Mark 4. Beat the egg whites to the 'stiff peak' stage, adding the sugar in small increments as you go. Fold this gently into the ground almond, using the orange flower water to moisten the mixture if it becomes too stiff to work. Lay the rice paper in single sheets on baking trays and drop dessertspoons of the mixture onto it, leaving room for the macaroons to expand. Lightly push a whole almond into the centre of each macaroon. Bake for 20-30 minutes, until the macaroons are crisp and light brown. Allow them to cool completely on the baking tray, tear or cut the paper from round their edges, leaving a layer under the macaroon, and store them in an airtight tin until needed.

NOTES

Introduction

[1] J R Tanner (ed), *Catalogue of the Pepysian Manuscripts,* Vol I (London 1903), pp167–9.

[2] *Regulations and Instructions Relating to His Majesty's Service at Sea* (hereafter *R&I*).

[3] *R&I,* 13th edition, p61.

[4] In 1806 the oatmeal ration was halved and six ounces of sugar was substituted.

[5] R Arthur Bowler, *Logistics and the Failure of the British Army in America, 1775-1783* (New Jersey 1975), p8.

[6] D Marshall, *English People in the Eighteenth Century* (London 1956), p169, quoted in Stephen F Gradish, *The Manning of the British Navy during the Seven Years' War* (London 1980), p140.

[7] Simon P Ville, *English Shipowning in the Industrial Revolution: Michael Henley & Son* (London 1987), p97.

[8] Conrad Gill, *The Naval Mutinies of 1797* (Manchester 1913), p98; C Northcote Parkinson, *Edward Pellew – Viscount Exmouth 1757-1833* (London 1934), p189.

[9] Norman Baker, *Government and Contractors: the British Treasury and War Supplies 1775-1783* (London 1971), p99.

[10] Greg Dening, *Mr Bligh's Bad Language: Passion, Power and Theatre on the Bounty* (Cambridge 1992), pp74–6, 84.

[11] I am indebted to Jennie Wraight and Peter Berry of the Admiralty Library for this story.

***Chapter 1*: Basic Rations**

[1] Public Record Office [hereafter PRO] ADM 52/3616: Master's log, *Gibraltar.*

[2] National Maritime Museum [hereafter NMM] ADM DP/29a, 27 February 1809; DP29b, 4 September 1809.

[3] Despite the meaning of the word 'biscuit' ('bis' = twice, 'cuit' = cooked), this biscuit was only cooked once.

[4] Louis Pasteur worked on yeasts between 1857 and 1863. Compressed yeast was first manufactured around 1868.

[5] Deptford is on the south bank of the Thames, about four miles east of the Tower of London.

[6] Basil Hall, *Fragments of Voyages and Travels* (London 1832-1846).

[7] *R&I,* 13th edition, p61.

[8] Rodney M S Pasley (ed), *Private Sea Journals 1778-1782 kept by Admiral Sir Thomas Pasley Bt. When in command of His Majesty's Ships Glasgow (20), Sybil (28) and Jupiter (50)* (London 1931), p67.

9 *R&I*, 14th edition, p288.

10 Norman Baker, *Government and Contractors: The British Treasury and War Supplies* (London 1971), pp72–3.

11 J C Drummond & Anne Wilbraham, *The Englishman's Food: Five Centuries of English Diet* (London 1939, revised 1957), p190.

12 Daniel A Baugh (ed), *Naval Administration 1715-1750* (London 1977).

13 *R&I*, 13th edition, pp62–3. Readers wondering about the arithmetic of this can be assured that the author also wondered and has double-checked. Those totals are as stated, not a typographical error!

14 *Instructions and Regulations for the Guidance of the Officers of the Several Victualling Establishments at Home* [hereafter '*I&R Home*'] (London 1808), p136.

15 *I&R Home*, p67.

16 Sir Nicholas Harris Nicolas, *The Dispatches and Letters of Lord Nelson*, 7 vols (London 1844-6, reprinted 1997-8) [hereafter Nicolas], Vol V, p470; Vol VI, pp280, 313; NMM ADM DP/24 (separately bound packet of papers); DP/26, 8 August 1806; DP/30a, 26 April 1810; WAR/73, various.

17 PRO ADM 52/3616: Master's log, *Gibraltar*.

18 Sir William Henry Dillon, *A Narrative of My Professional Adventures 1790-1839*, 2 vols (London 1953), pp110–1.

19 Peter Padfield, *Maritime Power and the Struggle for Freedom: Naval campaigns that shaped the modern world 1788-1851* (London 2003), p213.

20 Baker, *Government and Contractors*, p3.

21 Although often referred to as a blockade, this was not a true blockade, for which there are rules and conventions to be observed. Nelson's intention was to tempt the French fleet to come out so he could engage it in a decisive battle rather than to keep it bottled up in port.

22 PRO ADM 106/2350, folio 72, 14 May 1799, letter book, Navy Board to Victualling Board.

23 PRO ADM 110/14, 28 June 1745; ADM 111/33, 10 November 1746.

24 2 Geo 1, C.16 (Ir) s i.

25 Sir R Vesey Hamilton & John Knox Laughton (eds), *Above and Under Hatches: Recollections of James Anthony Gardner* (London 1906, reprint 2000), p167, referring to 1794.

26 PRO ADM 7/890, Admiralty circular no 21, 3 May 1856.

27 NMM ADM D/47, 29 November 1804.

28 Jeffrey de Raigersfeld, *Life of a Sea Officer* (London 1830), p161.

29 C Northcote Parkinson, *War in the Eastern Seas* (London 1954), and *Trade in the Eastern Seas* (London 1937).

30 *R&I*, 13th edition, pp202–3.

31 Nicolas, V, p438

32 Janet Macdonald, *Pumpkins and Squashes* (London 1998), p1.

33 *R&I*, 14th edition, p272.

34 The trawl is mentioned in letter 20 of a sequence of letters from Captain Duff, which

can be found at www.kittybrewster.com/ancestry/George_Duff_letter_[number].htm.

[35] William Mark, *At Sea with Nelson, being the life of William Mark – a purser who served with Admiral Lord Nelson* (London 1929), p81.

[36] Hall, *Fragments*, p375.

[37] Raigersfeld, *Life of a Sea Officer*, pp163–4.

[38] M D Hay (ed), *Landsman Hay: The Memoirs of Robert Hay 1789-1847* (London 1953), pp88–9.

[39] *Ibid*, p170. Since this refers to an incident in 1809, and since he says 'water tank' in the singular, this is more likely to have been the scuttle tank than the larger water tanks in the hold, which were not introduced until later (see page 85).

[40] NMM WAR/18, 6 August 1813.

[41] *R&I*, 14th edition, p302.

[42] Wellcome Western MSS 3677, 4 September 1803, 20 September 1803.

[43] *R&I*, 13th edition, p205.

[44] PRO ADM 1/232, 21 August 1740.

[45] NMM ADM G/794, 22 October 1806.

[46] Dudley Pope, *Life in Nelson's Navy* (London 1981, reprint 1997), p154.

[47] NMM GRE/15, folio 117, 21 June 1797.

[48] Pasley, *Private Sea Journals*, p229.

[49] ADM 1/4833, 12 January 1810.

[50] *R&I*, 14th edition, p288.

[51] NMM ADM DP/45, 13 October 1803.

[52] William Robinson, *Jack Nastyface: memoirs of an English seaman*, (London 1836 as *Nautical Economy*, reprint 2002).

[53] Pope, *Life in Nelson's Navy*, p158.

Chapter 2: How It Got There – the Work of the Victualling Board

[1] Strictly speaking this organisation was called the Board of Commissioners for Sick and Wounded Seamen, but it was commonly known as the Sick and Hurt Board.

[2] Figures taken from Victualling Board pay books, PRO ADM 7/869.

[3] NMM ADM DP/17, 17 October 1797; ADM G/793, 5 September 1803; PRO ADM 110/48, 20 November 1802.

[4] Sometimes this was a lump sum and sometimes, when the post-holder wanted to retire and was not entitled to a pension, an agreed annual payment until death. Roger Morriss, *Naval Power and British Culture, 1710-1850* (London 2004), pp71-7.

[5] Mark, *At Sea With Nelson*, pp125-8.

[6] *The Eighth [and Ninth] Report of the Commissioners appointed by an Act of Parliament to enquire into the fees, gratuities, perquisites and emoluments which are or have been lately received in the several public offices therein mentioned, to examine into any abuses which may exist in the same: and to report such observations as shall occur to them, for the better conducting and managing the business transacted in the Victualling Office* (London 1788).

[7] NMM ADM DP/24, 6 June, 12 July, 24 August, 10 October and 19 October 1804 DP/31a, DP/31b.

[8] NMM ADM DP/31a, 26 April 1811.

[9] Matthew Sheldon, 'From "Fraudulent Brewers" to "Scandalous Abuses"; a century of progress at the Portsmouth Victualling Office', paper presented to the Society of Nautical Research (South), 12 October 2002; David Syrett, 'Christopher Atkinson and the Victualling Board, 1775-1782', in *Historical Research* (1996), pp129–42; Baker, *Government and Contractors...*, pp173, 216–20.

[10] PRO ADM 114/26 (most of this 'piece' is a bundle of documents relating to this fraud).

[11] Parkinson, *War in the Eastern Seas*, pp338-9.

[12] Alexander Cochrane, *The Fighting Cochranes* (London 1983), pp174–5; Donald Thomas, *Cochrane, Britannia's Sea-King* (London 1978), pp20–1; PRO ADM 112/118; Basil Cochrane, *A narrative of the transactions of the Hon. Basil Cochrane* (London 1818); The Hon Basil Cochrane, *A statement of the conduct of the Victualling Board to the Hon. Basil Cochrane during his transactions with them in India* (London 1820).

[13] PRO ADM 112/160, Tenders for Contracts; ADM 111/166, 30 March 1803.

[14] NMM ADM D/46, 30 April 1804; PRO ADM 111/169, 21 November 1803.

[15] NMM ADM D/45, 13 October 1803; ADM C/700, 25 November 1803; ADM D/46, 2 August 1804.

[16] NMM ADM D/45, 13 October 1803.

[17] NMM ADM G/792, 4 and 31 August 1801, 8 September 1801.

[18] Even if each man is only eating his two pounds of beef once a week (and suet pudding on the other beef day, as explained on page 18) this works out to a grand total of 11,451,544 pounds, which at an average of 500 pounds per beast gives 23,000 bullocks; the same amount of pork, when a good-sized pig might produce 100 pounds of meat gives us 115,000 pigs.

[19] These instructions were dated 22 December 1807 and issued, in printed form, in 1808.

[20] Bowler, *Logistics...*

[21] Wellcome Trust Library, Western MS 3679; NMM ADM G/793, 24 October 1803, Admiralty to Victualling Board, instructing them to send out coal and buy wine and lemon juice to freight the vessels home.

[22] Master's log of *Belleisle*, PRO ADM 52/3573; Wellcome MSS 3678, Richard Bromley's account of purchases, 2 November to 9 December 1803.

[23] NMM ADM DP/21, 20 October 1801.

[24] NMM ADM DP/25, 3 May 1805.

[25] Brown's accounts, PRO ADM 112/41; Wills' accounts, ADM 112/42.

[26] Nicolas, Vol II, p202.

[27] NMM ADM DP/16, 20 December 1796 (covering letter) and 14 November 1796.

[28] NMM ADM DP/21, 7 May 1801.

[29] Ford was not strictly correct here: two of the nine were frigates.

[30] Ford appears in many parts of the Victualling Board records, the most important of which are his accounts at PRO ADM 112/46 and his letter book at ADM 114/55. His

appointment letter and many letters from him to Nelson are in the Nelson papers at the Wellcome Trust Library, Western MSS 3677-8; see also Nicolas, Volumes V & VI.

Chapter 3: **Administration On Board Ship**

1 Nelson's General Order book for 1803-1805 is at the British Library, Add MSS 34970.

2 NMM ADM/DP 27, 29 November 1807.

3 Nicolas, VI, p126.

4 For example, 'Additional Orders and Regulations for the Government of His Majesty's Ship *Superb*, K.G. Keats Esq., Captain', manuscript book kept by John L Coppin, midshipman, NMM RUSI/110.

5 Excerpts from Prince William Henry's order book can be seen in Brian Lavery's *Shipboard Life and Organisation 1731-1815* (London 1998), pp93-101.

6 Master's log, *Triumph*, PRO ADM 52/3507.

7 BL Add MSS 34970, folio 15, 23 December 1803.

8 Pope, *Life in Nelson's Navy*, p154.

9 *R&I*, 13th edition, p203-5

10 See Brian Lavery's *The Arming and Fitting of English Ships of War 1600-1815* (London 1987), pp209–10 for some drawings of how boats were stowed.

11 It is difficult to give exact weights for any given set of provisions, as they could be in varied sizes of cask. However, a list of provisions for the *Thetis* frigate's lading in 1777 shows, amongst other items, 903 lbs of butter in 14 firkins as weighing 9 cwt (1008 lbs), 3560 lbs of flour in a hogshead and 9 barrels as 1 ton 15 cwt (3920 lbs), and 1207 lbs of cheese in 8 half-hogsheads as 12 cwt (1344 lbs). Figures taken from PRO ADM 95/64.

12 Brian Vale, *A Frigate of King George: Life and Duty on a British Man of War* (London 2001), p412.

13 Captain's log, *Victory*, PRO ADM 51/1467, 10 to 14 September 1803.

14 NMM WAR/12, 1 May 1808.

15 Using the muster books in PRO ADM 36 and pay books in PRO ADM 35, the survey involved 60 different ships (10 line-of-battle ships and 10 frigates) at each of three periods: 1794, 1803 and 1812.

16 *R&I*, 14th edition, p186.

17 Anne Petrides (ed), *Sea Soldier: The letters and journals of Major T Marmaduke Wybourn RM, 1797-1813* (Tunbridge Wells 2000), p73.

18 NMM ADM DP/29, 9 March 1809. (This is the Trevithick of steam engine fame.)

19 Robert Gardiner, *Frigates of the Napoleonic Wars* (London 2002), pp104–5.

20 Nicolas, VI, p57.

21 Brian Lavery, *Arming and Fitting…*, p192; Anselm John Griffiths, *Observations on some points of Seamanship; with practical hints on naval oeconomy, etc* (London 1824), pp261–2.

22 A-M E Hills, 'Health in the Royal Navy During the age of Nelson', in *Journal of the Royal Naval Medical Service* 86, No 2 (2000), p72.

[23] BL Add MSS 34790, 21 December 1803; Nicolas, V, pp110–11.
[24] *R&I*, 13th edition, pp202–3.
[25] NMM POR/A/51, 24 October 1808.
[26] PRO ADM 106/3574, 'Revision of Sea Stores, Regulations for the Officers of the Dockyards no 53', dated 1815 (no other date). The same order required sheep pens to be fitted in the waist.
[27] Francis Liardet, *Professional Recollections on Seamanship* (London 1849), p306.
[28] The fire on the *Boyne* is cited as an illustration of this by Peter Goodwin, but he must have confused her with another ship: *Boyne* was destroyed by fire, but it was started when a burning wad from marine practice firing fell onto the stern gallery, from where the fire spread through the quarter gallery and admiral's cabin. There was no hay involved. Peter Goodwin, *Men O'War: The Illustrated Story of Life in Nelson's Navy* (London 2003), p108; Court Martial on the loss of the *Boyne*, PRO ADM 1/5332, 1 May 1795.
[29] Court Martial on the loss of the *Queen Charlotte*, PRO ADM 1/5352, 11 April 1800. Augustus Phillimore (ed), *Life of Sir Wm. Parker*, Vol I (London 1876), p256; Master's log, *Amazon*, PRO ADM 52/3560; W N Glascock, *Naval Sketch Book* (London 1826), Vol I, p22.
[30] Robinson, *Jack Nastyface*, p132; NMM GRE/15, 16 June 1797.
[31] N A M Rodger, *The Insatiable Earl: A Life of John Montague, 4th Earl of Sandwich* (London 1993), pp190–1.
[32] *Additional Instructions relating to Books and Accounts*, 1813, p7.
[33] *R&I*, 13th edition, p148; 14th edition, p442.
[34] NMM GRT/10-23.
[35] Master's log, *Bittern*, 24 June 1803, PRO ADM 52/3575; Captain's log, *William*, 25 January 1804, ADM 51/1457.
[36] I am indebted to Mr E J Revell for bringing this story to my attention.
[37] Figures taken from the Nelson papers at the Wellcome Trust Library. It should not be assumed that these documents are a complete set, but they do indicate the comparatively minor problem.
[38] NMM G/738, 17 June 1813; NMM ADM DP/33a, 24 June and 8 July 1813.
[39] Lavery, in *Shipboard Life...* gives two versions of this figure (pp546 and 589): 165 messes is the correct figure, taken from RNM 83/1051 & 53/4.
[40] Dillon, *Narrative*, p373.

Chapter 4: How the Men Ate

[1] NMM JOD/45 *Amazon*; RUSI/110 *Superb*.
[2] *R&I*, 13th edition, pp63–4. One ell = 1¼ yards, or 45 inches. Canvas, as supplied for sailmaking, was 24 inches wide.
[3] *R&I*, 14th edition, p290.
[4] NMM WAR/18, 31 October 1813.
[5] *R&I*, 14th edition, p378.
[6] Pope, *Life in Nelson's Navy*, p89.

[7] Robinson, *Jack Nastyface*, p132.
[8] J Watt, E J Freeman & W F Bynum (eds), *Starving Sailors: the Influence of Nutrition upon Naval and Maritime History* (London 1984), p201.
[9] PRO ADM 95/17, 1 May 1757.
[10] Patent No 1271 of 1780.
[11] Lavery, *Arming and Fitting*, p293; PRO ADM 106/2508, 7 September 1779.
[12] NMM JOD/45.
[13] NMM GRE 15, folio 42, 6 July 1796.
[14] PRO ADM 1/1457, 11 December 1809; ADM 1/4833, 12 January 1810; C/66/4055, 6.
[15] Lavery, *Shipboard Life...*, pp356–7.
[16] NMM RUSI/110, order no 55.
[17] Parkinson, *War in the Eastern Seas*, p439; BL Add Mss 34970.
[18] Nicolas, V, p419.
[19] NMM GRE 15, folio 42, 6 July 1796.
[20] David Cordingly, *Billy Ruffian: The Bellerophon and the Downfall of Napoleon* (London 2003), p213.
[21] *Ibid*, p189.
[22] Lavery, *Shipboard Life...*, pp528–9.
[23] Wybourn, *Sea Soldier*, p73; Piers Mackesy, *Victory in Egypt 1801* (London 1995), p149.
[24] NMM JOD/45.
[25] BL Add Mss 34970.
[26] Dening, *Mr Bligh's Bad Language*, pp73–4.

***Chapter 5*: How the Officers Ate**

[1] Una A Robertson, *Mariners' Mealtimes and other Daily Details of Life on Board a Sailing Warship* (Edinburgh 1981), p110.
[2] Watt, Freeman & Bynum (eds), *Starving Sailors*, p41; In the 13th edition of the *R&I* this was set at 20 shillings a day and restricted to commanders-in-chief; in the 14th edition it was increased to 30 shillings a day and extended to all flag officers, including commodores having captains under them.
[3] *Five Naval Journals*, Navy Records Society (London 1951) pp7, 13.
[4] In 1793 the highest-paid lieutenant received £7.0.0. per lunar month, the lowest £5.12.0; by 1815 this had risen to £9.2.0 and £8.8.0 respectively. Details from Michael Lewis, *Social History of the Navy* (London 1960), pp294–8.
[5] RNM Portsmouth, Admiralty Library Manuscript Collection, MSS 1997/65, 17 July 1812.
[6] Lieutenant Alexander Dingwall Fordyce, *Outlines of Naval Routine* (London 1837), p26.
[7] Sotheby's sale catalogue *Nelson: the Alexander Davison Collection* (London 2002), pp62, 79–81.
[8] Some of these items can be seen at the Royal Naval Museum at Portsmouth. I am indebted to Richard Noyce, Curator of Artefacts at that museum, for this information.

[9] Christian Murray, Dolores Elkin and Damián Vainstub, 'The sloop of war HMS *Swift*, an archaeological approach', in *The Age of Sail*, Vol I (London 2002), pp109–11.

[10] Michael Duffy (ed), *The Naval Miscellany VI*, Navy Records Society (London 2003), p199.

[11] Dillon, *Narrative*... pp21–2.

[12] Raigersfeld, *Life of a Sea Officer*, pp11–12.

[13] Dillon, *Narrative*..., pp21–2.

[14] *Ibid*, p18.

[15] Frederic Chamier, *Life of A Sailor* (London 1832), pp27, 278.

[16] Captain A Crawford, RN, *Reminiscences of a Naval Officer* (London 1851, reprint 1999), p38.

[17] Nicolas, VI, p320.

[18] Pope, *Life in Nelson's Navy*, p93.

[19] *R&I* 13th edition, p151; quite why the tradesmen warrant officers had two servants when the commissioned officers only had one is not explained in the *Regulations*; this might be explained by one of these being more of a trade assistant than a personal servant, or it might have been a way of allowing for the wives whom some of these warrant officers took to sea with them.

[20] Gardner, *Above and Under Hatches*, p204.

[21] Peter Earle, *The Making of the English Middle Class: Business, society and family life in London 1660-1730* (London 1989), p47–8. It should be mentioned that the idea that spices were used to preserve food is a fallacy; they were used to add interest to the otherwise monotonous taste of salt meat.

[22] I am indebted to Dave Balderstone of the Compuserve History forum for this information. Further details can be found on http://www.kal69.dial.pipex.com/glossd.htm and http://tradisjoner.no/text16.html

[23] The Nelson Museum, Monmouth, E390 series; RNM Portsmouth, Admiralty Library Manuscript Collection, MSS 259/5 & 6 (readers who would like to see more detail without visiting Portsmouth can find it in *The Mariner's Mirror* 87 (2001), pp479–82).

[24] Quoted in Christopher Hibbert, *Nelson, a Personal History* (London 1994), p330.

[25] Wellcome MSS 3676.

[26] *Naval Chronicle* XXXVII, pp445–52.

[27] I am grateful to Lord de Saumarez for allowing me to use these items from the Saumarez papers, and to Tim Voelcker for bringing them to my attention.

[28] Michael Steer, 'The blockade of Brest and victualling of the Western squadron, 1793-1805', *The Mariner's Mirror* 76 (1990), pp307–15.

[29] Raigersfeld, *Life of a Sea Officer* pp163–4

[30] *Personal Narrative of Events from 1799 to 1815, with anecdotes, by the late Vice-Admiral Wm. Stanhope Lovell, Royal Navy* (second edition, London 1879), p33

[31] Hall, *Fragments*... p61.

[32] Using the modern definition of offal here – see p154.

[33] Hall, *Fragments*... pp151–66.
[34] Robertson, *Mariners' Mealtimes*, pp42–3.
[35] John Knox Laughton (ed), *Journal of Rear-admiral Bartholomew James 1752-1828*, Navy Records Society (London 1896), pp37–8.
[36] Pasley, *Private Sea Journals*.
[37] Gardner, *Above and Under Hatches*, p204.
[38] A Edlin, *A Treatise on the Art of Bread Making* (London 1805), pp33, 31.
[39] Crawford, *Reminiscences*, p33.
[40] Lovell, *Personal Narrative*, p30.
[41] Parkinson, *War in the Eastern Seas*, p350.
[42] Wybourn, *Sea Soldier*, p163.
[43] NMM JOD/10; for readers who would like to see more, some extensive sections are to be found in Lavery, *Shipboard Life...*, pp616–21.
[44] There are many myths about the origins of this tradition: one of which is that a particularly tall admiral decreed it after banging his head one time too many, but like all the other suggestions there is no truth in this one. It was just one of those things which was done for practical reasons in difficult circumstances, which has continued to this day, even though the reason is long gone. I am indebted to Jennie Wraight of the Admiralty Library for this information.
[45] Wybourn, *Sea Soldier*, p163; Christopher Lloyd, and L S Coulter, (General Editor J J Keevil), *Medicine and the Navy*, Vol III: 1714-1815 (London 1961), p152.

Chapter 6: What Other Navies Ate

[1] *Naval Regulations issued by command of the President of the United States of America January 25th 1802* (reprinted Annapolis, Maryland 1970).
[2] The information for this section has come from Tyrone Martin, and the website of USS *Constitution* at www3.teleplex.net/timonier/speaks/book12.html.
[3] I am indebted to Roel Mulder for this information. His sources were: J C de Jonge, *Geschiedenis van het Nederlands Zeewezen* [History of the Dutch Navy], 3rd edition (Zwolle 1869); J R Brujin, *Het gelag der zeelieden* [The Seaman's Diet] (Leiden 1978); *Maritieme Geschiedenis der Neerlanden* [Maritime History of the Netherlands] (Busum 1977).
[4] Adrien Carré, 'Eighteenth Century French Voyages of Exploration', in Watt, Freeman & Bynum (eds), *Starving Sailors*, p74.
[5] G Shelvocke, *A Voyage Round the World* (London 1726, reprinted 1928), p29.
[6] Jean Boudriot, *The 74 Gun Ship* (Paris 1977, trans 1988), Vol IV, pp158–81.
[7] Carré, 'Eighteenth Century French Voyages of Exploration', pp75, 83.
[8] Peter Padfield, *Maritime Power and the Struggle for Freedom* (London 2003), p78.
[9] Roger Morriss (ed), *The Channel Fleet and the Blockade of Brest, 1793-1801*, Navy Records Society (London 2001), p597.
[10] I am indebted to Brian Vale for this information.

Chapter 7: Diet in Health and Sickness

1 Wellcome, MSS 3680-1; NMM KEI 23/32-3.

2 M Lewis, *Social History of the Navy* (London 1961), pp396–7.

3 Drummond & Wilbraham, *The Englishmen's Food*, pp251–2.

4 The recipe refers to 'flesh', which means skeletal muscle and not the internal organs now known as offal.

5 NMM ADM F13, 14 September 1756; ADM F14, 5 February 1757; ADM D46, 16 January 1804.

6 Elizabeth M Bardolph, 'Power, prejudice, and putrefaction: The elimination of scurvy from the Royal Navy, 1747-1796', paper read at the New Researchers conference, 1997, p49.

7 Anton Sebastian, *A Dictionary of the History of Medicine* (London 1999), p575.

8 A survey dated 4 October 1803 on Lieutenant Edmund Waller describes him as suffering from 'impaired function of stomach' which might have been a peptic ulcer. Wellcome MSS 3669.

9 Lloyd & Coulter, *Medicine and the Navy*, Vol III, p150.

10 I am indebted to Professor Glynn Williams for his comments on this topic.

11 J Lind, A *Treatise of the Scurvy* (Edinburgh 1753), pp145–6; Bardolph, 'Power, prejudice and putrefaction'.

12 Lloyd & Coulter, *Medicine and the Navy*, Vol III, p324

13 James Lind, *An essay on the most effectual means of preserving the health of seamen*, quoted in Watt, Freeman & Bynum (eds), *Starving Sailors*, p28.

14 Bowler, *Logistics…* p82.

15 Pasley, *Sea Journals…*, p217.

16 *Naval Chronicle* X (1803), pp110–13.

17 Morriss, *The Channel Fleet and the Blockade of Brest*, p65.

18 *Ibid*, p14.

19 *Regulations and Instructions for the Pursers of His Majesty's Ships and Vessels*, 2nd edition (1825), p212.

20 *Ibid*, p151–4.

21 NMM ADM DP 32b, 14 August 1812.

22 *R&I*, 14th edition, pp274, 252; PRO ADM 7/793, *Regulations and Instructions for the Pursers of His Majesty's Ships and Vessels*, 1825, second edition, p212.

23 Morriss, T*he Channel Fleet and the Blockade of Brest*, p37.

24 *Ibid*, p145.

25 Nicolas, VI, pp334–5.

26 Lloyd & Coulter, *Medicine and the Navy*, Vol III, p170.

27 Calculated from the muster books of this fleet in PRO ADM 36 and the weekly sick returns in Wellcome MSS 3680. It should be pointed out, however, that these returns were not for the same ships every week, only those which happened to be with the commander-in-chief at that time, but they do give an indication of scale.

28 Nicolas, V, pp215-6, 420.

29 Lloyd & Coulter, *Medicine and the Navy*, Vol IV, pp140–1.

[30] Nicolas, I, p476; PRO ADM 51/1104, Captain's log, *Agamemnon*, 1 to 12 August 1794.

[31] PRO ADM 52/3507, 3701, Master's logs, *Triumph*; Nicolas, VI, p19.

[32] PRO ADM 52/3616, Master's log, *Gibraltar*.

[33] These are reported as follows: 29 August 1803, 12 in *Renown*, 10 in *Triumph*, 73 in *Gibraltar*; on 19 September 1803, 64 in *Gibraltar*; in 23 April 1804, 11 in *Triumph*; on 7 May 1804, 9 in *Donegal*. (Wellcome MSS 3680). However, it should be noted that the logs for *Gibraltar* show 135 scurvy cases on 8 August.; P K Crimmin, 'Letters and Documents relating to the Service of Nelson's Ships, 1780-1805: a Critical Report', *Historical Research* 70, No 171 (February 1997).

[34] BL Add MSS 34970, 24 September 1803.

[35] I am indebted to Mark Nesbitt at the Royal Botanic Gardens, Kew, for additional information on *Opuntia*.

[36] *R&I*, 14th edition, pp271–2.

Conclusions

[1] Morriss, *The Channel Fleet and the Blockade of Brest*, p126.

[2] Bowler, *Logistics....*

[3] Lloyd & Coulter, *Medicine and the Navy*, Vol IV, p99.

[4] Joseph Sinclair, *Arteries of War: a History of Military Transportation* (Shrewsbury 1992), pp40–5, 168; quoted in Martin Middlesbrook, *Task Force: the Falklands War 1982* (London 1987), p67.

Appendices

Appendix 1: Weights and Measures

[1] For more conversions see the web site: www.gourmetsleuth.com/conversions.htm

[2] According to the Chambers Dictionary: Leaguer: an old Dutch liquid measure, a large cask, from Dutch 'ligger' – a tun. *Tun*: an obsolete liquid measurement – 216 gallons of ale, 252 of wine.

Appendix 2: Official Substitutes for Species of Provisions

[1] Quoted from *R&I*, 14th edition, p288.

Appendix 3: Calorific Values of Naval Foodstuffs

[1] Stuart Thorne, *The History of Food Preservation* (Cumbria 1986); NMM ADP D/46, 9 July 1804.

[2] McCance & Widdowson's *The Composition of Foods* (London 2002) and MAFF Reference Book No 342, 'Manual of Nutrition' (London 1995). Other sources of these figures are the US Government website www.nal.usda.gov/fnic/foodcomp/Data/Other/ada2002_hg72.pdf

[3] Figure taken from a packet of Carr's Water Biscuits, as being the closest modern equivalent to ships' biscuit.

[4] 'Wine measure' is 5/6 of the normal English liquid measure.
[5] The type given in the reference is for bitter at 31 Cal per 100ml; the precise figure for small beer is not known, but taken here at 25 Cal per 100ml.
[6] This is the figure given in the reference for stewing steak, fat and lean mixed, and used here as being the closest equivalent to naval beef.
[7] The figure given in the reference for raw bacon is 428 and for leg of pork is 213. The figure used here is an average of the two, used as being the closest equivalent to navy pork.
[8] Calculated by weighing 1 pint of split pease (16 oz).
[9] Calculated by weighing 1 pint of oatmeal (8 oz).
[10] It is not known whether the vinegar would be wine vinegar or malt vinegar. The figure used is the same as for beer, on the assumption that malt vinegar would be more likely in a country where wine was not made.
[11] The figures for individual vegetables are as follows (all per 100mg): cabbage 26, carrots 24, turnips 12, onions 36. This gives an average of 25, as shown.

Appendix 4: Vitamin Content of Naval Food

[1] Vitamin counts are from McCance & Widdowson, Recommended Daily Allowances are from the American Government's Department of Agriculture website: www.nal.usda.gov/fnic/foodcomp/Data/Other/ada2002_hg72.pdf. Note that American recommended daily allowances are higher than British.
[2] Cooked without sugar.
[3] Note that the Vitamin C content of potatoes is especially variable, according to storage time and whether or not they are peeled. Boiled new potatoes have about 18mg of Vitamin C per 100g. Raw old (or 'maincrop') potatoes have 30mg per 100g when freshly dug, diminishing to 8 after 8 months storage; when boiled only 50–70 per cent of this Vitamin C is retained. McCance & Widdowson, p180–5.
[4] *Cochlearia officinalis.*

Appendix 5: Bills of Exchange

[1] *Instructions...Abroad,* p113 (Appendix 40). This is a direct copy of the wording and layout of the original document.
[2] For example, NMM ADM DP 32b, 31 December 1812, Victualling Board to Admiralty relating to the increase in prices of provisions at the Leeward Islands.
[3] For example, NMM ADM DP/35a, 11 January 1815, Victualling Board writing to Admiralty about a Bill written by Mr G Wood Bins.
[4] PRO ADM 114/96, Course of the Exchange.

Appendix 6: Eat Like a Sailor – Recipes

[1] Taken from the recipe used at the Ratcliffe Soup House, as given in NMM ADM D/46.

GLOSSARY

Banyan days – the days when no meat was eaten, so-called after a strictly vegetarian Hindu merchant sect who preferred to eat their meals under a banyan tree.

Bargemen – sailors slang for biscuit 'weevils', so-called because they were found in the container for the mess's biscuit, known as a bread-barge.

Becket – a loop of rope with a knot at one end and an eye at the other.

Bumboat – a boat bringing fruit, vegetables etc for sale to ships.

Britanniaware – a non-rusting alloy of antimony, bismuth, copper and tin, which polishes up to a deep silvery lustre.

Chest at Greenwich – a naval charity which provided pensions for disabled seamen, originally the 'Chatham Chest'.

Commissioned officers – those who were attached to the ship while she was 'in commission' (*ie* on sea service), or fighting officers. *See also* warrant officers.

Fiddle – a type of rail used to prevent dishes sliding from the table.

Frumenty – a dish made by simmering whole wheat grains, sometimes sweetened with honey or raisins.

Godown – Far Eastern name for a warehouse.

Head – the toilets on a ship – in the sailing navy days, these were at the very front of the ship, exposed to the open air.

Imprest account – rather like an overdraft, a type of account used by the Victualling Board to control pursers' and victualling contractors' expenditure.

Lanthorn – a closed lantern containing a candle.

Lemon pepper – a condiment made by grinding dried lemon peel.

Machine – as used at the time, this meant any form of device or implement.

Mess-kids – wooden containers for collecting messes' food.

Ordinary – ships 'mothballed' in reserve, *ie* those not in commission.

Orlop – the lowest deck in a ship.

Outports – the British naval ports outside London (*eg* Portsmouth, Plymouth).

Over-plus – food over and above what the men wanted to eat.

the People – naval term meaning the crew.

Purser (sometimes pronounced 'pusser') – the man who had charge of the food on board Royal Navy ships.

Rakes and peels – the rakes, in this context, would be for raking out the ashes, a peel is a long-handled flat paddle for moving bread in and out of the oven.

Roundhouse – a small cabin at the rear of a ship, often used as a toilet for officers.

Scuttlebutt – a cask for drinking water, kept on deck.

Sheathed or *coppered* – two methods of protecting a ship's hull from destructive worms and accretions of seaweed. Sheathing is an outer covering of wood, coppering is a cover of copper plates over the hull. Seaweed built up more slowly on a coppered hull, so the ship would sail faster when coppered.

Slops – ready-made clothes for seamen, bought in bulk; they tended to be made large and the men usually made their own adjustments. The word slops is derived from the Old English 'oferslop', meaning a loose outer garment.

Species of provisions – types of food items, for instance salt beef is one species, salt pork is another, biscuit is a third.

Starting the water – a method of quickly lightening ship (and thus allowing more speed) by spilling the fresh water in the hold and then pumping it out.

Steelyard – a weighing device consisting of a lever, from one end of which the item to be weighed is suspended, and on the other, longer end, a weight can be slid along.

Supernumeraries – people carried on board ship who were not part of her regular crew. An admiral was a supernumerary, as were his personal suite of servants and advisors, and so were naval personnel being given passage to their own ships.

Table money – an amount, additional to the salary of a highly placed official or officer who had to entertain as part of his job, or who frequently had to eat away from home.

Tops – the fighting platforms situated high on the masts.

Tracklements – a generic term for pickles, chutneys and other wet condiments used to give savour to food.

Victuals, victualling (pronounced 'vittles', 'vittling') – food and drinks, the supply of these.

Warrant officers – those non-fighting officers who were attached to the ship on a permanent basis, even when she was laid up in 'ordinary'. (But many of them did fight when necessary.)

BIBLIOGRAPHY

Primary Sources

Details of specific documents consulted are listed in the notes to each chapter, but the generality of sources consulted is as follows:

Official Publications

Regulations and Instructions relating to His Majesty's Service at Sea, 13th & 14th editions, 1790 & 1806.

Regulations and Instructions for the Pursers of His Majesty's Ships and Vessels, 2nd edition, 1825.

Instructions and Regulations for the Guidance of the Officers of the Several Victualling Establishments at Home, Proposed by the Commissioners for Revising the Civil Affairs of His Majesty's Navy, in their Twelfth Report, dated 22nd December 1807, and ordered to be carried into execution, by His Majesty's Order In Council of the 14th September 1808.

Instructions for the Agents of the Victualling Establishments Abroad, Proposed by the Commissioners for Revising the Civil Affairs of His Majesty's Navy, in their Twelfth Report, dated 22nd December 1807, and ordered to be carried into execution, by His Majesty's Order In Council of the 14th September 1808.

The Eighth [and Ninth] Report of the Commissioners appointed by an Act of Parliament to enquire into the fees, gratuities, perquisites and emoluments which are or have been lately received in the several public offices therein mentioned, to examine into any abuses which may exist in the same: and to report such observations as shall occur to them, for the better conducting and managing the business transacted in the Victualling Office (London 1788).

Naval Regulations issued by command of the President of the United States of America January 25th 1802 (reprinted Annapolis, Maryland 1970).

Public Record Office

ADM 1 – Secretariat in-letters
ADM 2 – Secretariat out-letters
ADM 7 – Miscellaneous Admiralty papers, including Admiralty Board Room journals.
ADM 8 – List books showing disposition of ships
ADM 36 – Muster books
ADM 51 – Captains' logs
ADM 52 – Masters' logs

ADM 106 – Navy Board letters and orders
ADM 109 – Victualling Board in-letters
ADM 110 – Victualling Board out-letters
ADM 111 – Victualling Board minutes
ADM 112 – Victualling Board accounts and Tenders for Contracts
ADM 113 – Pay lists for victualling yards
ADM 114 – Victualling depts miscellanea

National Maritime Museum
Admiralty documents:
ADM C series – Victualling Board, in-letters and orders from Admiralty
ADM D series – Board of Admiralty, in-letters from Victualling Board
ADM DP series – Board of Admiralty, in-letters from Victualling Board
ADM F series – Board of Admiralty, in-letters from Sick and Hurt Board
ADM G series – Victualling Board, abstract of in-letters and orders from Admiralty
ADM/L/ series – Lieutenants' logs

Miscellaneous documents:

GRT/10-23	Grant papers
GRE/15	Book of orders received by Captain Grey
KEI/23/32-3	Lord Keith's papers, sick returns for ships and hospitals in the Mediterranean 1800 to 1801
JOD/45	Manuscript copy of the order book for HMS *Amazon*, kept by John Skynner and Fairfax Moresby, midshipmen
MAL/101	Letter book of Captain Pulteney Malcolm
PAR/174	Letter and order book of Captain William Parker for HMS *Amazon*
RUSI/110	*Additional Orders and Regulations for the Government of His Majesty's Ship Superb, K.G. Keats Esq., Captain*, manuscript book kept by John L. Copperd, midshipman
WAR/12,18	Sir John Borlase Warren's papers

British Library

Add Mss 34935-6	Instructions from Admiralty and Secretary of State, 1803 to 1805
Add Mss 34964	Nelson's letter book, 20 May 1803 to 6 October 1804
Add Mss 34970	Nelson's orders to commanders of vessels, May 1803 to March 1804
Add Mss 36611-12	Commissions, Warrants and appointments granted by Lord Nelson, July 1803 to January 1805
Add MSS 34978-86	Logs of ships under Nelson as commander-in-chief Mediterranean

Wellcome Trust Library

Western MSS 3667-3681	Miscellaneous documents and letters relating to ships under Nelson's command 1780 to 1805

Nelson Museum, Monmouth

E900 series	Letter Books of Nelson's correspondence

Secondary Sources

Except where they are personally written and unedited memoirs of life at sea, or volumes of the Navy Records Society, I must caution readers against accepting at face value comments on victualling found in secondary sources. Many are naively misguided, others are, to be polite, unreliable, and many come at various places in the chain of repetition which starts with the unreliable and changes subtly to the seriously misguided as the chain advances. For this reason, I have made a practice of following these chains backwards until I come to the original document and wherever possible have used these original documents in preference to all others.

Articles and papers

Bardolph, Elizabeth M, 'Power, Prejudice, and Putrefaction: The elimination of scurvy from the Royal Navy, 1747-1796', paper read at the New Researchers conference, 1997.

Carré, Adrien, 'Eighteenth Century French Voyages of Exploration', in Watt J, Freeman E J & Bynum W F (eds), *Starving Sailors: the Influence of Nutrition upon Naval and Maritime History* (London 1984).

Condon, Mary Ellen, 'The Establishment of the Transport Board – a subdivision of the Admiralty, 4 July 1794', in *The Mariner's Mirror* 58, No 1 (1972), pp69-84.

Crimmin, P K, 'Letters and Documents relating to the Service of Nelson's Ships, 1780-1805: a Critical Report', in *Historical Research* 70, No 171 (February 1997).

____________, 'The Sick and Hurt Board and the health of seamen c.1700-1806, Did the health of seamen improve over time?', in *Journal for Maritime Research* (December 1999).

Dixon, Conrad, 'Pound and Pint: Diet in the Merchant Service, 1750-1980', in Palmer, S and Williams, G (eds), *Charted and Uncharted Waters* (London 1981).

Gillespie, T P, 'The diet and health of seamen in the West Indies at the end of the eighteenth century – some remarks on the work of Leonard Gillespie, M.D.', in *Journal of the Royal Naval Medical Service* 37, No 4 (1951).

MacDougall, Phillip, 'The Formative Years: Malta Dockyard, 1800-1815', in *The Mariner's Mirror* 76, No 3 (1990).

Mathias, Peter, 'Agriculture and the Brewing and Distilling Industries in the Eighteenth Century', in Jones, E C (ed), *Agriculture and Economic Growth in England 1650-1815* (London 1967).

Press, Richard, 'Markets and Marketing', in Mingay, G E (ed), *The Agrarian History of England and Wales,* Vol VI: 1750-1850 (Cambridge 1989).

Sheldon, Matthew, 'From "Fraudulent Brewers" to "Scandalous Abuses"; a century of progress at the Portsmouth Victualling Office', paper presented to the Society of Nautical Research (South), 12 October 2002.

Stead, Jennifer, 'Navy Blues: the Sailor's Diet 1530 – 1830', paper given at the 6th Leeds Symposium on Food History, April 1991.

Steer, Michael, 'The blockade of Brest and victualling of the Western squadron, 1793-1805' in *The Mariner's Mirror* 76, No 4 (1990), pp307–16.

Syrett, David, 'The Victualling Board Charters Shipping, 1775-1782' in *Historical Research* 68 (1995).

__________, 'Christopher Atkinson and the Victualling Board, 1775-1782', in *Historical Research* 69 (1996).

Ville, Simon P, 'The deployment of English Merchant Shipping: Michael & Joseph Henley of Wapping, ship owners, 1775-1830', in *Journal of Transport History*, 3rd series, 5 (1984).

Watt, Sir James, 'Health in the Royal Navy During the Age of Nelson: Nelsonian Medicine in Context', in *Journal of the Royal Naval Medical Service* 86, No 2 (2000).

Books

Baker, Norman, *Government and Contractors: The British Treasury and War Supplies* (London 1971).

Baugh, Daniel A, *British Naval Administration in the Age of Walpole* (Princeton, New Jersey 1965).

____________(ed), *Naval Administration 1715-1750* (London 1977).

Berckman, Evelyn, *The Hidden Navy* (London 1973).

Binney, J E D, *British Public Finance and Administration 1774-92* (Oxford 1958).

Boudriot, Jean, *The 74 Gun Ship*, Vol IV (Paris 1977, translation Rotherfield 1988).

Bowler, R Arthur, *Logistics and the Failure of the British Army in America, 1775-1783* (Princeton, New Jersey 1975).

Buchet, Christian, *Marine, économie et société. Un example d'interaction: l'avitaillement de la Royal Navy durant la guerre de sept ans* (Paris 1999).

Bugler, Arthur, *HMS Victory – Building, restoration and repair* (London 1966).

Burton, E, *The Georgians at Home, 1714-1830* (London 1967).

Chamier, Frederic, *Life of A Sailor* (London 1832).

Cochrane, Alexander, *The Fighting Cochranes* (London 1983).

Cochrane, The Hon. Basil, *A narrative of the transactions of the Hon. Basil Cochrane* (London 1818).

__________________, *A statement of the conduct of the Victualling Board to the Hon. Basil Cochrane during his transactions with them in India* (London 1820).

Colledge, J J, *Ships of the Royal Navy: an Historical Index* (London 1969).

Cordingly, David, *Billy Ruffian: The Bellerophon and the Downfall of Napoleon* (London 2003).

Crawford, Captain A, *Reminiscences of a Naval Officer* (London 1851, reprinted 1999).

Crowhurst, Patrick, *The French War on Trade: Privateering 1793-1815* (London 1989).

Currie, Ann, *Henleys of Wapping: A London shipowning family 1770-1830* (London 1988).

Davidson, Alan (ed), *The Oxford Companion to Food* (Oxford 1999).

Dening, Greg, *Mr Bligh's Bad Language: Passion, Power and Theatre on the Bounty* (Cambridge 1992).

Dillon, Sir William Henry, *A Narrative of My Professional Adventures 1790-1839* (London 1953).

Drummond, J C, & Wilbraham, Anne, *The Englishman's Food: Five Centuries of English Diet* (London, revised edition 1957).
Duffy, Michael (ed), *The Naval Miscellany VI*, Navy Records Society (London 2003).
Earle, Peter, *The Making of the English Middle Class: Business, society and family life in London 1660-1730* (London 1989).
Edlin, A, *A Treatise on the Art of Bread-Making: Wherein, the Mealing Trade, Assize Laws, and every curcumstance [sic] connected with the Art, is particularly examined* (London 1805).
Falconer, William, *A New Universal Dictionary of the Marine* (London 1815).
Farley, John, *The London Art of Cookery, 1783* (reprint edited by Ann Haly, Lewes 1988).
Fordyce, Lieutenant Alexander Dingwall, *Outlines of Naval Routine* (London 1837).
Gardiner, Robert, *Frigates of the Napoleonic Wars* (London 2002).
Gardner, James Anthony, *Above and Under Hatches* (London 1906, reprinted 2000).
Gill, Conrad, *The Naval Mutinies of 1797* (Manchester 1913).
Glascock, W N, *Naval Sketch Book* (London 1826).
Glasse, Hannah, *The Art of Cookery made plain and easy* (London 1747, reprinted 1997).
Glover, Richard, *Peninsular Preparation: the reform of the British Army 1795-1800* (Cambridge 1970).
Godden, Geoffrey A, *English China* (London 1985).
Goodwin, Peter, *Men O'War: The Illustrated Story of Life in Nelson's Navy* (London 2003).
Gradish, Stephen F, *The Manning of the British Navy during The Seven Years War* (London 1980).
Griffiths, Anselm John, *Observations on some Points of Seamanship* (London 1824).
Grigson, Jane, *Charcuterie and French Pork Cookery* (London 1967).
__________, *Good Things* (London 1971).
__________, *English Food* (London 1974).
__________, *Jane Grigson's Vegetable Book* (London 1978).
Grossman, Anne Chotzinoff & Thomas, Lisa Grossman, *Lobscouse and Spotted Dog: Which it's a Gastronomic Companion to the Aubrey/Maturin Novels* (New York 1997).
Hall, Basil, *Fragments of Voyages and Travels* (London 1832-1846).
Hamilton, Sir Richard Vesey (ed), *Letters and Journals of Sir Thos. Byam Martin* (3 vols, London 1898, 1900, 1902).
Harvie, David I, *Limeys: The True Story of One Man's War against Ignorance, the Establishment and the Deadly Scurvy* (Stroud 2002).
Hay, M D (ed), *Landsman Hay: The Memoir of Robert Hay 1789-1847* (London 1953).
Hibbert, Christopher, *Nelson, a Personal History* (London 1994).
Hill, J R (ed), *The Oxford Illustrated History of the Royal Navy* (Oxford 1995).
Hope, Ronald, *Poor Jack: The Perilous History of the Merchant Seaman* (London 2001).
Hughes, Quentin, *Britain in the Mediterranean and the Defence of her Naval Stations* (Liverpool 1981).
James, William, *The Naval History of Great Britain* (London 1837).
Lambert, Andrew, *Trincomalee: the Last of Nelson's Frigates* (London 2000).
Laughton, John Knox (ed), *Journal of Rear-admiral Bartholomew James 1752-1828* (London 1896).

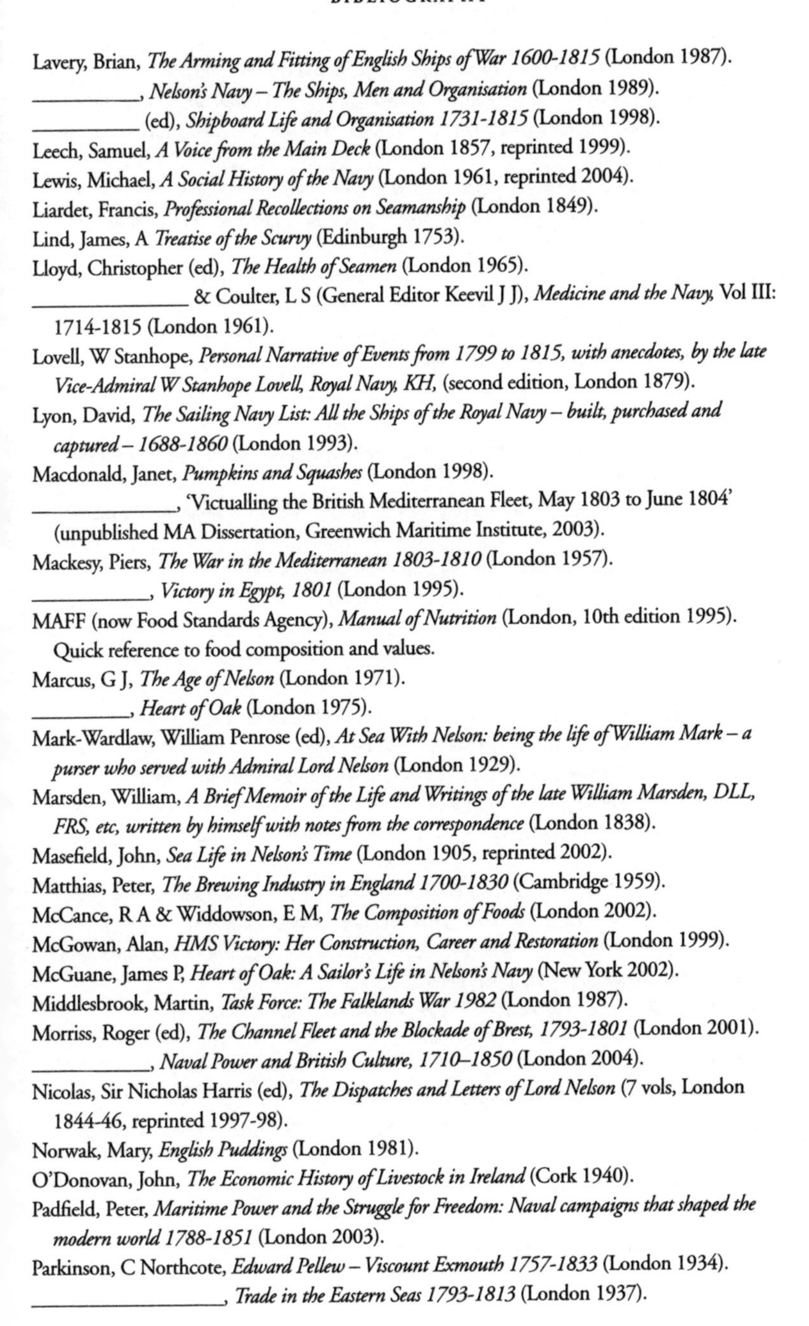

Lavery, Brian, *The Arming and Fitting of English Ships of War 1600-1815* (London 1987).

__________, *Nelson's Navy – The Ships, Men and Organisation* (London 1989).

__________ (ed), *Shipboard Life and Organisation 1731-1815* (London 1998).

Leech, Samuel, *A Voice from the Main Deck* (London 1857, reprinted 1999).

Lewis, Michael, *A Social History of the Navy* (London 1961, reprinted 2004).

Liardet, Francis, *Professional Recollections on Seamanship* (London 1849).

Lind, James, A *Treatise of the Scurvy* (Edinburgh 1753).

Lloyd, Christopher (ed), *The Health of Seamen* (London 1965).

______________ & Coulter, L S (General Editor Keevil J J), *Medicine and the Navy,* Vol III: 1714-1815 (London 1961).

Lovell, W Stanhope, *Personal Narrative of Events from 1799 to 1815, with anecdotes, by the late Vice-Admiral W Stanhope Lovell, Royal Navy, KH,* (second edition, London 1879).

Lyon, David, *The Sailing Navy List: All the Ships of the Royal Navy – built, purchased and captured – 1688-1860* (London 1993).

Macdonald, Janet, *Pumpkins and Squashes* (London 1998).

_____________, 'Victualling the British Mediterranean Fleet, May 1803 to June 1804' (unpublished MA Dissertation, Greenwich Maritime Institute, 2003).

Mackesy, Piers, *The War in the Mediterranean 1803-1810* (London 1957).

___________, *Victory in Egypt, 1801* (London 1995).

MAFF (now Food Standards Agency), *Manual of Nutrition* (London, 10th edition 1995). Quick reference to food composition and values.

Marcus, G J, *The Age of Nelson* (London 1971).

_________, *Heart of Oak* (London 1975).

Mark-Wardlaw, William Penrose (ed), *At Sea With Nelson: being the life of William Mark – a purser who served with Admiral Lord Nelson* (London 1929).

Marsden, William, *A Brief Memoir of the Life and Writings of the late William Marsden, DLL, FRS, etc, written by himself with notes from the correspondence* (London 1838).

Masefield, John, *Sea Life in Nelson's Time* (London 1905, reprinted 2002).

Matthias, Peter, *The Brewing Industry in England 1700-1830* (Cambridge 1959).

McCance, R A & Widdowson, E M, *The Composition of Foods* (London 2002).

McGowan, Alan, *HMS Victory: Her Construction, Career and Restoration* (London 1999).

McGuane, James P, *Heart of Oak: A Sailor's Life in Nelson's Navy* (New York 2002).

Middlesbrook, Martin, *Task Force: The Falklands War 1982* (London 1987).

Morriss, Roger (ed), *The Channel Fleet and the Blockade of Brest, 1793-1801* (London 2001).

___________, *Naval Power and British Culture, 1710–1850* (London 2004).

Nicolas, Sir Nicholas Harris (ed), *The Dispatches and Letters of Lord Nelson* (7 vols, London 1844-46, reprinted 1997-98).

Norwak, Mary, *English Puddings* (London 1981).

O'Donovan, John, *The Economic History of Livestock in Ireland* (Cork 1940).

Padfield, Peter, *Maritime Power and the Struggle for Freedom: Naval campaigns that shaped the modern world 1788-1851* (London 2003).

Parkinson, C Northcote, *Edward Pellew – Viscount Exmouth 1757-1833* (London 1934).

__________________, *Trade in the Eastern Seas 1793-1813* (London 1937).

____________________, *War in the Eastern Seas 1793-1813* (London 1954).

Pasley, Rodney M S (ed), *Private Sea Journals 1778-1782 kept by Admiral Sir Thomas Pasley Bt. When in command of His Majesty's Ships Glasgow (20), Sybil (28) and Jupiter (50)* (London 1931).

Petrides, Anne (ed), *Sea Soldier: An Officer of Marines with Duncan, Collingwood and Cockburn: the Letters and Journals of Major T Marmaduke Wybourn RM, 1797-1813* (Tunbridge Wells, 2000).

Phillimore, Augustus (ed), *The Life of Admiral of the Fleet Sir William Parker* (London 1876).

Pope, Dudley, *Life in Nelson's Navy* (London 1981, reprinted 1997).

Raffald, Elizabeth, *The Experienced English Housekeeper* (London 1782, reprinted 1980).

Raigersfeld, Jeffrey Baron de, *Life of a Sea Officer* (London 1830, reprinted 1929).

Robertson, Una A, *Mariners' Mealtimes and other Daily Details of Life on Board a Sailing Warship*, (Edinburgh 1981).

Robinson, William, *Jack Nastyface: Memoirs of an English seaman* (London 1836 as *Nautical Economy*; reprinted 2002).

Rodger, N A M, *The Insatiable Earl: A Life of John Montague, 4th Earl of Sandwich* (London 1993).

______________, *The Wooden World: An Anatomy of the Georgian Navy* (London 1996).

Sebastian, Anton, *A Dictionary of the History of Medicine* (London 1999).

Shelvocke, G, *A Voyage Round the World* (London 1726, reprinted 1928).

Shephard, Sue, *Pickled, Potted and Canned – The Story of Food Preserving* (London 2000).

Syrett, David, *Shipping and the American War 1775-1783* (London 1970).

Tanner, J R (ed), *Catalogue of the Pepysian Manuscripts*, Vol I (London 1903).

Thomas, Donald, *Cochrane, Britannia's Sea-King* (London 1978).

Thorne, Stuart, *The History of Food Preservation* (Kirkby Lonsdale, Cumbria 1986).

Vale, Brian, *A Frigate of King George: Life and Duty on a British man of war* (London 2001).

Ville, Simon P, *English Shipowning during the Industrial Revolution – Michael Henley & Sons, London Shipowners 1770-1830* (Manchester 1987).

Vilmorin-Andrieux, M M, *The Vegetable Garden: Illustrations, Descriptions and Culture of the Garden Vegetables of cold and temperate climates* (London 1885).

Watt, J, Freeman, E J, & Bynum, W F (eds), *Starving Sailors: The Influence of Nutrition upon Naval and Maritime History* (London 1984).

White, David, *The Anatomy of the Ship: The Frigate Diana* (London 1987).

Web Sites

http://www.jmr.nmm.ac.uk (downloaded 5 February 2003).

http://www.kittybrewster.com/ancestry/George_Duff_Letter_20.htm (downloaded 6 September 2003).

http://www3.teleplex.net/timonier/speaks/book12.html

www.gourmetsleuth.com/conversions.htm

http://www.nal.usda.gov/fnic/foodcomp/Data/Other/ada2002_hg72.pdf

INDEX

Warships are listed under the heading 'Warships': all are British Royal Navy unless otherwise indicated.